MYSTIC AT THE EDGE

About the Author

A native of Sydney, Australia, Maureen Chen has travelled, read and learned widely. She has studied and taught Raja Yoga Meditation with the Brahma Kumaris for over 40 years, establishing and sustaining Meditation Centres in Australia, Hong Kong, Cambodia, and the Philippines.

In Hong Kong, Maureen was the Moderator of the Hong Kong Network on Religion and Peace, Chairperson of Unity for Peace, Secretary of the Living Values Education and Secretary of the Asian Business Leadership Exchange, ABLE. She also helped to establish the Foodlink Foundation, an NGO linking hotels and restaurants with social welfare organisations.

Maureen went on to establish social enterprises for victims of landmines; the Khmer Independent Life Team (KILT), and the Peace Cafe; a vegetarian community cafe offering values and environmental training in Siem Reap, Cambodia.

In August 2010, she moved to India to devote her time and efforts exclusively to organising and facilitating over 50 programs for the *Future of Power* project, bringing leaders together to explore the use of personal power.

After returning to Sydney to coordinate activities at the national office of The Brahma Kumaris she was pulled back to Asia. Today she is based in Taiwan where she has opened a Meditation Centre in the southern city of Kaohsiung.

For further information about this book Maureen can be contacted at mysticattheedge@gmail.com.

MYSTIC AT THE EDGE

A Western Woman Coloured by Asia

MAUREEN CHEN

Subtle Lotus Publishers

Mystic at the Edge: A Western Woman Coloured by Asia
by Maureen Chen

Copyright © Maureen Chen 2020

The moral right of the author has been asserted.

All rights reserved. No part of this book may be reproduced by any mechanical, photographic or electronic process, or in the form of a photographic or audio recording, or stored in a retrievable system, transmitted or otherwise copied for public or private use without the written permission of the author.

ISBN Number: 978-0-6488621-0-9

First Edition 2020

Every effort has been made to fulfil requirements with regards to reproducing copyright material. The author will be glad to rectify any omissions at the earliest opportunity.

Edited by Rebecca Attwood
Cover Art by Peter Damo http://peterdamo.com/

Disclaimer: The tools and insights in this book are offered as suggestions which may help you. They are not intended as a substitute for psychiatric and/or medical help, counselling or other forms of treatment but as an additional support.

Contents

About the Author	iii
Introduction	ix
Acknowledgements	x
Reviews	xii
Preface	xiv

THE JOURNEY

1	Awakening the Heart	3
2	The Journey Begins	13
3	What Am I Looking For?	19
4	Stretching Our Beliefs	33
5	Hippie to Happy	43
6	Making Asia Home	51
7	The Long Haul!	57
8	More of Asia	77
9	The Happiest Time of My Life	85
10	Boomerang Back to Asia	89
11	A Big Project	105
12	Bhutan and Nepal	111

13	Home Soil	115
14	Chile	119
15	Taiwan	123

PRACTICAL SPIRITUALITY - MY THOUGHTS AND EXPERIMENTS

16	Relationships with Myself, Others and The World	129
17	More About Power	149
18	Love	155
19	The Power of The Other	173
20	Compassion	185
21	Universal Laws	195
22	Spirituality, Religion and Superstition	217

WIDER VIEWS

23	Raja Yoga	231
24	Meditation Practice	237
25	The Soul	249
26	The Source	263
27	Smrti, Vrtti, Drshti, Srshti, Prakrti, Krti	275
28	Where to From Here?	287

Bibliography — 299
About The Brahma Kumaris — 303
Other Resources — 305

Introduction

Living on the edge does not sound very comfortable. On the other hand, it is exciting and enables us to respond to the moment as we don't have to 'get up'. We are alert, ready to jump ... often into the unknown. A mystic living on the edge does not accept anything superficially ... they want to know the experience, to know it with their heart. They have an antenna for their personal 'truth' and gravitate towards that as if pulled by a magnet ... often needing all the courage they can muster. Their inner self is seeking to be whole, to unite with the Divine in which there is the experience of unity with the whole.

In Australian Aboriginal Wiradjuri language, *nirin*, is referred to as edge ... it invites us to cross over, to explore, to stretch our limited perceptions. One of the constants we live with is Change. Living on the edge enables us to not only respond to change but to create change. Otherwise we may settle into a position which does not serve us.

In India there is a festival called Holi, where people colour each other. On that day all are equal and everyone is free to colour whomever they please. I am privileged to have been coloured by many people, experiences and cultures throughout my life and I hope to share through this book, a picture of some of the multifarious colours I have been exposed to.

May your life too be richly coloured by all that you experience. The blacks and greys are just as impactful as the reds and greens. I am learning to welcome all the experiences. In hindsight I can now see how they have all added to the masterpiece that is me ... we are all one of a kind, a special combination!

Acknowledgements

"Life always begins with one step outside of your comfort zone."
Shannon L. Alder

I thank the Being beyond, The One who never comes into the cycle of birth and rebirth that we human souls journey through; untouched and unchanged, the Alchemist through whom I am slowly transforming from iron to gold.

Many have said that I am courageous for living outside my comfort zones for most of my life. I don't feel comfortable in comfort zones; I am too adventurous to stay there!

The search for Truth and to stay 'North' pushes us out of our comfort zones socially. In the 70's being a vegetarian was 'weird' and a challenge in social circumstances. Once a lady asked what I ate when lettuce and tomato were out of season - as if I had become a rabbit! We have come a long way since then. When I lived in Hong Kong, I was invited to speak to expatriate women and to college students just because I was 'different'. When I walk down the street in a white sari, many people are curious and approach, others cross the road!

I am grateful to my parents who, true to the Aussie saying, "Whatever makes you happy, Love", have given me the freedom to choose the way I live my life. I have lived with the security of knowing that I would always be welcome home, even though I did not realise until my later years that this was the very reason I could live on the edge so freely.

I am grateful for the wisdom and insights of the many great thinkers and writers who have inspired me, many of whom I have made reference to in this book. I have studied and applied their wisdom to the best of my ability. It has often been just one line from a book that has changed the direction of my thinking, and my life. I do hope you can explore their writings in depth.

Finally, I am grateful to Rebecca Attwood and the friends who have encouraged and supported me in bringing this book to fruition.

Some names have been changed to protect the identity of friends. Many I wish to acknowledge here for their contribution to my life.

Reviews

"She smiles and the world is at peace. That's Morni Chen, a 40-year veteran teacher of Brahma Kumaris Raja Yoga. "I'm too adventurous to stay in comfort zones," she writes. Her story, "Mystic At The Edge" spans Australia, Asia and South Asia, a true life experience that stokes the desires of all who seek peace and happiness through love, spirituality and meditation. Morni draws from great thinkers, how they've affected her life, to potentially help her readers' lives and to choose their meditation practices. Knowing and learning from Morni is joyful, unforgettable and infinitely rewarding. She exudes a positivity that's infectious, a rare commodity these days!"

Diana Lin, Former Presenter and Senior Executive Producer, TVB Pearl, Hong Kong

"It is rare these days for someone to commit to a particular path. Maureen has clearly chosen hers, and yet she is open and enjoys being challenged by conflicting beliefs. She reads widely and incorporates whatever she finds of benefit to her personal practice. Mystic at the Edge offers a rare insight into the life, and more interestingly, into the mind of a deep meditator. After all, don't you sometimes wonder what is going on when someone is sitting still in silence for hours?"

Paul Wilson, the 'Guru of Calm' (Times, UK), best selling author, columnist and meditation teacher

"Your journey is one of the most fascinating travelogues that I have come across in my life and I have read so many of them. In the process I have benefited a lot. Although I too now feel that I have developed a strong connection to my maker and 'maker and sustainer of the world', I have personally benefited from Mystic at the Edge."

(Retired) Major General Vinod Saigal, Delhi

"Competitive sport is like being on a roller coaster. Meditating, being vegetarian and developing a spiritual perspective has helped me to reign in my emotions and enjoy the ride. Maureen is inspiring and I am pleased that this wisdom is now in book form so that anyone can access what she has shared with me."

*Shikhar Dhavan, **Indian International Cricketer***

Preface

*"Once you have got the meaning, you can forget the words.
Where can I find a man who has forgotten words
so I can have a word with him."*

Chuang Tzu

I contemplated for a long time before attempting to write a book on meditation and the accompanying philosophy that has served me for so many years. Truth encompasses paradox; for every word said, the opposite is generally also true. This is why the tradition of meditation is basically an oral one, and perhaps this has contributed to making it appear rather mystical and elite. However, meditation can offer something for everyone, and is not half as difficult as it might seem.

The benefits can be subtle and not seen until we stop meditating, or there is a major crisis in our lives. Motivation is a key factor, and for that we have to clearly understand the many and varied benefits, including being able to maintain a calm mind, improved relationships, better health, and a philosophical approach to life that can act as a buffer to the many assaults we can encounter.

I have met very few people who have attained any experience or clarity about meditation from reading about it. The atmosphere, the consciousness of the teacher, an understanding that goes beyond logic - these are all essential ingredients in learning meditation. This may be the reason why the Taoist saying "Those who speak do not know", was coined.

Rather than sharing theory, I hope that sharing my experiences will enable you to see how we can practically apply meditation in our lives. My hope is that it will be of some benefit to those wishing to learn, or needing clarification about their own practice. Nearly all meditation practices are beneficial; it is up to the practitioner to find the one that works best for them.

The lotus has been a symbol for the spiritual path in the East for millennia. It represents the struggle to maintain pristine beauty, whilst taking sustenance from muddy water. I lived in Hong Kong from 1981 to 2002. While there, a colleague gave me the name *Mieu Leen* or, *Miao Lian* in Mandarin, meaning Subtle Lotus, a popular name for Buddhist nuns.

In India, my nickname is *Morni*, a female peacock. I once asked a senior meditation teacher how to live with my shortcomings; accept them whilst striving for such a high goal, and at the same time face criticism from those who were disappointed and even hurt by these shortcomings. The teacher reminded me of the ugly feet of the peacock saying, "Just keep dancing using your specialities, and no one will notice your feet, and nor will you."

I was brought up as a Catholic, married a would-be Buddhist monk, studied Buddhism for a few years, shopped for a teacher or path, and finally found Raja Yoga Meditation taught by the Brahma Kumaris World Spiritual University, which I have studied now for over forty years. The timeline starts in the 70's and so much has changed since then.

The Journey

I

Awakening the Heart

Can We Avoid Suffering?
"Wisdom is passion and tranquillity."

Helen Wambach

Can we avoid suffering? As far back as I can remember, this had been the question foremost in my mind.

When encouraging people to go into the depths of their being, they can often be reminded of spiritual experiences they had in their childhood. Many have had deep thoughts and experiences when they were children that weren't understood by adults. Because they were not listened to, given an opportunity to explore their experiences, nor received answers to philosophical questions, these experiences were eventually forgotten.

I grew up in a comfortable and safe environment with a loving family. I did not have any real suffering to speak of in my own life, but from a young age I was very aware of the suffering of others. At age eleven, horrified by the belief taught in my school that everything that was happening was 'God's will', I refused to attend a Catholic high school, and was clear about not believing in God. How could suffering be God's will? It was fortunate for both me and the school that I did not attend, as my good friend ended up hitting a nun. I sought fairness, truth, and integrity, and as a teenage rebel I feared that I too could have gotten nasty!

I questioned how God could create such disparity in the world. One nun explained, "Some people have to suffer so that others can realise how fortunate they are ..." to which I thought, "Really??!!!" She also explained that God had created a perfect world but had generously empowered us by giving us free will. Seeing what a mess we had made of it all, I concluded, If God did exist; this was **not** a smart plan. Bad design!

I wanted to understand the suffering of others. When I began working, I would buy *True Life* magazines to read about the challenges people were facing. I had a passion to help others, but I also became very emotional. I read Helen Wambach's book, *Life before Life*. Her words, "Wisdom is passion and tranquillity" were like an arrow, touching a part of me that I knew would be essential for my growth. I needed an understanding, a philosophy that would help me temper my compassion for others.

I grew up under the 'White Australia policy' and had no exposure to Eastern religions. It was an eye opener to learn about Hinduism, Buddhism and Islam whilst studying Indonesian in school. Religion seemed to inform the whole of the lives of these people, and connect them to nature as well. When I left school I supported two Indonesian children through World Vision. As well as helping them, my connection with a country I had come to love, was sustained. I could also practise the Indonesian language. My connection with World Vision opened my eyes to the many problems in the world that needed fixing – the poor, the disabled, the trees, the whales, anti-uranium mining – the list went on! But a dilemma arose within me; with so little time, money and energy, what could I do to make a difference?

What struck me most when I encountered the Eastern religions was a very basic understanding of the philosophy of Karma. I decided that as soon as I could, I would travel to Indonesia to learn more. Many search for God; I was looking for an understanding about suffering, and the Law of Karma was opening my mind.

Giving

"There are those who give with joy and that joy is their reward.
There are those who give with pain and that pain is their baptism.
And there are those who give and know not pain in giving,
nor do they seek joy, nor give with mindfulness of virtue;
They give as in yonder valley the myrtle breathes its fragrance into space.
Through the hand of such as these God speaks, and from behind their eyes
he smiles upon the earth."

Kahlil Gibran, The Prophet

I came across meditation and insights into the mind, and realised that in order for me to feel that I was making a difference in the world, the area where I should focus my attention was spirituality. In the opening sentence of the UNESCO Constitution it states "... since wars begin in the minds of men, it is in the minds of men that the defences of peace must be constructed." I had begun to realise this. Raising the consciousness of people was the only way to get to the root of all the problems. As noble and necessary as it is, feeding the poor and protesting to save the whales and the trees would not eliminate greed, the root. Working at developing qualities like generosity and benevolence would.

Engaging myself, not only in teaching meditation, but also in reaching out to world leaders and opening up opportunities to those who have tremendous influence could make a great difference. I deduced that reaching just one of these people, and opening their heart, would be more effective than me giving my meagre savings to a cause for the rest of my life. I have come to realise how people from all walks of life are looking for ways to effectively bring positive change. I have also experienced first-hand, the corruption in not-for-profit organisations that cause people to be wary and cynical.

The Law of Karma runs very deep. In India, it is said "The left hand shouldn't know what the right hand is doing." This means, if others come to know about our good deed or donation, then the return of that deed is reduced, especially if we accept praise for it. Accepting praise is said to be like "eating raw fruit." We gain a great deal more karmic credit by keeping any service we do incognito.

Another Indian saying is "Give what you need." If you need wealth, donate money; if you need respect, give respect; if you need health, use your body to serve. This can be a challenge when in a needy state, but living by this motto changes a 'scarcity mentality' into one of abundance, and opens the block. If you want happiness, give happiness.

Many avoid having full awareness of the huge polarisation of wealth – 'the haves and have not's' in our world. Consequently they do not want to acknowledge the bad in the world. It is denial for various reasons, and may include ideas like, "If it is happening to someone, it could happen to me", "If it is there, I should do something, but I do not want to part with my possessions, including my time and wealth" and, "It might bring up past memories which I have tried to leave behind, like a life of poverty or war." They have not tasted the sweet return of helping others, and may never do so. When someone is exposed beyond their personal, selective world, to what is happening around them, there can be a deep awakening in the heart.

After finding himself at a charity event with children living with disabilities, a new world opened up for Jackie Chan. He very quickly set up two foundations, the Jackie Chan Foundation and the Dragon Heart's Foundation. Both donate millions of dollars to charity. He now says, "Most of the time, I'm not even working; I'm just helping people, because I feel that I am too lucky." There are some aspects of Chan's life that I cannot relate to, however in terms of giving; he has become an inspiration to many.

So often when we become passionate about a cause or issue, we can also have feelings of sadness, anger, despair and frustration. We can become disillusioned with the politics and hypocrisy within the system and amongst NGOs whom people look to for support. If I didn't have a philosophy of life, I would be angry about the indifference on climate change and other environmental issues. In his book *The Conscious Activist*, James O'Dea says "As we recognize the root of our own being through reflective practices, we remember the common source of all beings. To be effective in conflict we need to move beyond polarised thinking of 'us and them', privileged and underprivileged, victims and perpetrators and good and evil. We must go beyond the projection of social problems onto other people rather than onto what needs to be changed. It is the heart that guides us to this higher vision. If we seek to change the world, we must learn the power of cooperation, of sharing ideas and to stay open."

The process of compassion being awakened is beautiful to witness. As hands and hearts open, I have seen people experience such joy from living a more connected and meaningful life. No doubt, the blessings from those they have given to have also lightened their minds, and their good karmas have brought them good outcomes.

Do We Really Ever Learn Anything 'New'?

"The true work of a teacher: not putting in but drawing out."

Robert John Meehan

We do not seek to learn. We seek to find something that resonates with the truth and wisdom that is latent within us. I do not believe we can ever teach anyone anything of the inner world. Our attempt is to simply remind them of what they already know.

The word 'educate' comes from the Latin, *educe*, meaning, to draw forth. The term "It doesn't fit in my intellect" comes to mind when I look back over my own spiritual search. I came across many teachers and organisations and saw that many practitioners were benefitting. Yet, it just didn't 'fit' for me, and I would move on.

In this life I began as a Catholic, and was very aware of what didn't fit. My questions were never answered satisfactorily, but perhaps the thing that drove me even further away was that the teachings in those days were based on fear. In my convent school, I did not encounter teachers who breathed the *joie de vivre*, exuding the peace and joy of the spirit. Childhood innocence and honesty heightened my expectations. Being told at seven years old that I must say my prayers at night in case I didn't wake up in the morning terrified me, and I tried to stay awake all night praying. Going to church in order to stay out of hell was another one. I often got in trouble with the nuns for giving my lunch to the stray dogs that were captured to be sent to the dog pound. I got into even more trouble for letting one go to save him from being sent to meet his death.

Since my school days, I have been fortunate to meet many wonderful Catholics, particularly nuns and priests in the Philippines, Hong Kong and Chile. I have encountered open mindedness, a very pure love for God, service, humility, and pure devotion. In contrast, I was left dumbfounded at an Active Nonviolence Meeting where I was told by a lay person that I would go to hell because I did not follow Christ. What an unfortunate attitude to have towards friends and relatives. It must be very worrying and stressful to live with this belief, and also to live with someone with this belief! Thankfully, the nuns and priests came to my rescue and decided to take this up at the next discussion on the topic of 'nonviolence'!

The Blind Date

"Friendship isn't about how long you know someone.
It's about who walks into your life, says I am here for you
and then proves it."

Nicholas Sparks

I met my husband Tom, on a blind date at a Chinese nightclub in Sydney at around 1am in the morning. When the nightclub closed we went for dinner ... at 4am! This was a very new world I was being exposed to. Tom was planning to be a Buddhist monk, and his good friend was trying to intercept those plans. Neither Tom nor I knew this at the time, and it was certainly strange for both of us to be there.

When Tom called me the next day I remember thinking that I would wear the clothes that looked the worst on me. If he was going to like me, it had to be for 'me', and not how I appeared; a most unusual thought for a nineteen-year-old! I hadn't had any experience with Asians, and I remember being surprised at how similar our thinking was. Somehow, I had thought he would be so different. Although Chinese people are generally quite fair skinned, we enjoyed the outdoor life, and when my seven year old niece met Tom she asked me on the quiet if he was wearing stockings because his legs were so brown.

We had only known each other for a few months before we decided to get married. My family and friends were not surprised because we connected so well. An interest in spirituality was what we shared most deeply, and even though we continued to go to the nightclub, we did not drink or smoke. We just enjoyed dancing and spending time with his friends. My brother had married a Polish woman and my Mum was happy to increase the little united nations that was building up in our family. At one time when I was living in Asia, someone asked me what I liked most about Australia, and the common Australian expression, "Whatever makes you happy, Love!" came to mind. This was indicative of my family; easy, light and open.

Living in Australia, had however, been a challenge for Tom up until then as it was so different culturally. He was a young innocent student from a traditionally Confucian family. His fellow Australian classmates were rather rowdy, and it wasn't common in Chinese culture to see such seeming disrespect for teachers. He told me that he once stood up in a class and asked everyone to be quiet. That was brave! Australians also have a habit of constantly making jokes. When English is not your first language, jokes are hard to navigate and he was never sure if they were making fun of him or not.

A Civil Wedding

*"Either God wants to abolish evil, and cannot; or he can,
but does not want to; Or he cannot and does not want to.
If he wants to, but cannot, he is impotent.
If he can, but does not want to, he is wicked. But, if God both can
and wants to abolish evil, Then how come evil in the world?"*

Epicurus

*Civil Wedding in Centennial Park: Dad,
Tom, Me and Mum*

It was interesting that our relationship went straight to the issue of God. Being Buddhist, Tom also did not believe in God. So, as we were both atheists, we felt it would be inauthentic to be married in a Catholic Church.

Before marrying, Tom made it clear ... "Please think about this... I do not intend to settle down. I do not want to bring children into this world. Children can be a bundle of joy but they are also a bundle of karma. I just want to understand what I am doing here." As is often the case, I thought, "Oh, he will change." In a state of being 'in love' we cannot imagine any future problems. Perhaps that is why it is said, "Love is blind". Or, does it mean that when we love someone, we connect to the essence of who they are and become blind to their shortcomings?

My father took us to meet several priests who did not win us over at all, quite the opposite! Finally he gave up and we settled for a civil celebrant marriage in Centennial Park in 1974. It was one of the first in Australia as the very first celebrant was only appointed in 1973. It has since become very popular with 79.7% of Australians being married by a civil celebrant in 2018.

Tom's legal name is Chen Mun Fook. Not realising that the Chinese write surnames before given names, the celebrant kept calling Tom "Mr Fook". Together with the ducks making so much noise in the background, it was hard to keep a straight face!

We kept it all easy. Tom happened to have a white suit and his friend, Szeto, our matchmaker, a red suit! We let my parents organise whatever they wanted for the reception and it was completely stress free.

* * * * *

2

The Journey Begins

Malaysia
*"If you want to walk fast, walk alone.
If you want to walk far, walk together."*

African proverb

Tom introduced me to Buddhism. I was comfortable with the practice as I did not have to believe in God, and I had already found a great deal of truth in the teachings about Karma. I felt that I finally understood something about suffering. I had accepted if Tom became a monk, I could become a nun. Our life was enjoyable. On weekends we would either go to the nightclub, drink orange juice and enjoy the music and dancing, or go camping and read spiritual books and meditate.

A few months after our marriage, we began a journey to India. We stopped in Bali, travelled overland to Sumatra and then took a cargo ship to Malaysia to meet Tom's family. Coincidentally, we both had the same book, *Across Asia on the Cheap*. This was before *Tripadvisor*, *Lonely Planet* and *Google*, and so it was our little 'bible' as we travelled overland from Bali to Lake Toba. In Lake Toba we lived an idyllic village life, joining the locals on their weekly visit to the market. As the book advised, we waited for someone to turn up and offer to do our visa extension and were relieved when they finally came!

Indonesia was my first experience of Asia and I was confronted by the disparity between the rich and poor. We were not rich, but I struggled with eating in a restaurant while I could see others around me starving. We started eating in the local market and gave the money that we saved to a beggar. However, I got sick and realised I needed to take care of myself as well. Having been brought up in Asia, and with his Buddhist perspective, Tom tried to help me reconcile it all.

Our 'bible' gave us guidance on how to live for AU$1 a day. We stayed in a *losmen*, a homestay, with a lovely Indonesian family. For just AU$0.30 each, we were given simple but pleasant accommodation, a meal and Indonesian coffee. I had not liked coffee up until then but this was sweeter in flavour and it was offered with great hospitality. I was fascinated with my first taste of Asia. It felt like being in another world, a very spiritual world.

Bali had just been discovered by backpackers. We checked out Nusa Dua and Kuta beach and could see the attraction, but preferred to be with the locals in Denpasar. It also gave me a chance to practise my Indonesian, although many of the locals were learning English from the tourists. Denpasar was so rich in culture with a temple on almost every corner and performances of *wayang kulit* puppetry and Balinese dancing with wonderful *gamelan* orchestras held throughout the town every evening.

We ventured into the hills to Ubud and on arrival were invited to view a dead body. Another first for me! Death was so accepted and the philosophy of reincarnation took away the feeling of loss and confusion. On our second day, I was cursed by a small girl for not buying her oranges. "You die!" she said. Fortunately she was not very powerful as nothing happened! Whilst most of the people throughout Indonesia were an absolute delight, I feel these types of experiences happen so that we do not let our guard down. There is still black magic in Bali but it seems to be kept amongst the locals, and the foreigners fortunately receive the white magic of friendliness and lightness.

From Bali we travelled to Sumatra taking in the wonder of the amazing Buddhist temples in Jogjakarta, and the hustle and bustle of Jakarta. We then took a cargo boat from Medan to Penang in Malaysia. Again, just as the guidebook suggested, we paid one of the crew to use his cabin rather than sit on the deck with only rice and fish heads to eat! Being vegetarians we would have just had plain rice. I was well out of my comfort zone on many levels, almost fainting in the rush to get on the boat, but it was adventurous and I enjoyed the surprises.

We ventured over to the east coast of Malaysia and again, following our guidebook, took a fishing boat to one of the islands. Perhaps we read the book incorrectly because there was no accommodation nor any shops on the island. We managed to get some stale peanuts to eat and had to sleep on the beach. However, it started to become cool in the evening. We knocked on a few doors and finally were able to sleep on someone's floor. The next day we sat on the dock for many hours, and finally to our relief, a fishing boat came by and we were able to return to the mainland.

The Chinese Wedding
"Love is not about possession, it is all about appreciation."

Chinese proverb

Offering Tea to Grandmother

Tom had been born in Malaysia to Chinese parents; his mother, Hokkien and his father, Hakka. Tom was educated in an English school and spoke Cantonese, the language spoken in Ipoh, where he had lived. His parents and siblings all spoke English but they communicated in Cantonese at home. Although his grandmother was Chinese, she was what they call a *nonya*, a woman culturally adapted to Malaysia in terms of food, language and dress. She wore a *sarong kabaya*, spoke Malay and cooked awesome Malay food. As I had studied Indonesian in school, I was able to communicate a little with her in Malay, which is very similar. She would say we were like "a duck and a hen" trying to communicate!

After finally reaching Tom's home, the arrangements for a traditional Chinese wedding were in full swing. This included me wearing a traditional Chinese dress, a *cheongsam*, (red for good luck), a gifting of jewellery to me, including diamonds, gold, jade and onyx, and in return, me offering tea to the elders. It was an amazing introduction into Chinese culture, and I was at the centre of it. The family accepted me, even though they had told Tom explicitly, not to marry an Australian!

The family home was behind a Chinese temple, where the three main Chinese religions of Buddhism, Taoism and Confucianism combined. These religions are all philosophically quite distinctly different, however Chinese temples often reflect the 'triple strands' or Three Religions, *san jiao*. Whenever I heard the drums of the lion dance, I would quickly pop over to the temple to see what was happening. The drums awakened my heart, and until today I still get excited when I hear them anywhere.

In this temple, there was a Taoist monk who would go into trance and give advice on every matter of the household. Tom's mother would consult the medium even if we wanted to go on a trip for a few days. There was a lot of trance, black magic and such things in Malaysia. Tom's uncle divorced and voodoo dolls were used to make him bleed. I saw it! I went to a Hindu temple with him to have the curse removed. He circled the Ganesh statue three times telling his situation and then queued up to see the very busy Hindu priest. Without speaking to the priest, the priest referred to his situation and told him what he needed to do.

I 'met' Tom's grandfather through a medium. He had passed away some time before our marriage. We travelled from Tom's hometown, to Penang carrying many items including chillies, limes, netting and a piece of clothing from each family member, including a piece of mine. We met with the medium, an elderly lady, and she channelled *Ah Gong*, Grandfather, into the room to meet the family. Tom experienced that she moved, spoke and behaved exactly as his grandfather did, even though this lady had never met Grandfather. We then moved on to the pagoda where Ah Gong's ashes had been enshrined after the cremation. There, the women knelt and wailed, and then just as the wailing started in an instant, it also ended instantly when they stood up. Wailers are often hired at Chinese funerals to express the love and respect for the deceased.

At home there were regular offerings and rituals going on, including the offering of sticky sweets to the Kitchen God *Chau Kun*, so he would not report on the wrong doings of the family. It was a lot of work for Tom's mother to keep up with all the rituals, and she was fearful of not fulfilling all her obligations. She often expressed how tiring it all was – marketing, cooking, offering and taking things to the temple.

Tom's brothers called me *Maureen Dai So*, eldest brother's wife. Robert and Andrew were still at school and Jimmy had a mental challenge. I enjoyed colouring-in with him, which included chasing the dog to match up the colour of her coat. The family found it strange that I said "please" and "thank you" for every little thing. This is not in Chinese culture, and is almost an insult to not expect their generosity.

In Malaysia, foreigners were called *ang mo kui*, meaning red-haired devil. I was a rare sight in the small town of Ipoh. When I went to the local swimming pool, I got quite a fright when I looked down and found many begoggled eyes looking up at me from under the water. We were charged more than the locals for everything. Because of his darker than usual skin, they did not realise Tom spoke Chinese. They would therefore talk about how much they could get from me for small items and say rude things about us being a mixed couple. On one occasion, Tom was hit from behind by a group of Chinese men in Penang. When they were reported, their defence was, "we did not realise they were married" - as if they would have been quite within their rights if we hadn't been married! However, generally Malaysians were light and friendly people, and for the most part it was a very positive experience.

We travelled quite often to Penang and enjoyed the holiday atmosphere and beaches there, and the fried bananas! When I came down with a cold, Tom's father said it was due to eating the fried bananas, which he said were "heaty". Most Chinese have a good knowledge of basic Chinese medicine and about foods that create heat or coolness in the body.

My parents, Tom and Valmai Harrison, came to visit Tom's parents, Chen Kim Foo and Yap Phaik Swat. It was rather amusing to see the two cultures collide in the funniest ways. "Do you eat rice?", my father-in-law asked my father. This is a common question expressing hospitality. "Love it with milk and sugar," was my Aussie dad's reply! They certainly livened the place up.

* * * * *

3

What Am I Looking For?

Finders, Keepers; Losers, Weepers
"One for you, one for me."
Afghani custom on finding lost property

The next part of our journey was a cheap flight to London on Aeroflot. We had to make an unexpected stop in Kiev, and as we were moved into the terminal, our passports were taken. It was rather worrying to have this experience in Soviet Russia as we could not understand what was happening, and had no translation. We were relieved to finally be allowed to board our flight. As we queued up, I realised I had left my handbag with our boarding passes, tickets, passports and travellers cheques at the Gate. I ran back ... and there it was, untouched, plain for all to see. What a relief, and what a credit to the people.

This was only one of many times I left my bag with all our valuables behind. I left it in restaurants and bathrooms in Bali, Greece, Holland, Italy and Afghanistan. Cool men did not carry bags in those days and although Tom panicked every time I left my bag behind, I still carried all the valuables. But it seemed there was an angel looking after us, because every time, I got my bag back. In Afghanisthan they have a special custom of giving half to the finder. In front of me, he, the finder, counted out the dollars … "One for me, one for you!" I was happy to get anything back!

Another challenge we faced in our relationship while travelling was arriving at places after a long bus or train journey and not knowing the language and where we could stay – cheaply! People were polite and keen to practise their English so it seemed that they would just say anything. Although their friendliness was greatly appreciated, it was very frustrating to be told, "Go left … go right … go ahead". Carrying our backpacks, tired, and often in need of a bath and food, Tom and I made a pact to 'zip it' at these times. Otherwise, we would react unnecessarily and create an uneasy tension between us.

The UK
"Not wholly good or wholly evil".

David Russell McAnally on the Leprechaun

Tom had friends in England who we stayed with, and who worked mostly in psychiatric hospitals. Although it was great to be with friends, and the hospital grounds were beautiful, it was strange to be in England and yet be surrounded by Chinese and eat Chinese food. Even our sightseeing was in China Town!

It was summer and people talked about the weather all the time. Thankfully the weather was agreeable as we could imagine being there in winter and the incessant conversations that we would have had about the bad weather! We went swimming in London, and although it was hot, the water was freezing! It was fun to walk the 'Monopoly Board' and see all those streets, familiar to me from my years of playing the game and buying up houses. The parks were beautiful, and it was insightful to see the land of those who colonised Australia.

After a few weeks we headed off to the beautiful Lake District to get a taste of local culture. We were not disappointed. The scenery was idyllic and local bands played in every pub. As tea-totalling meditators, in our fully coherent state, we perhaps enjoyed the music even more than the others!

Half of my heritage is Irish; the other Scottish. Unfortunately we did not venture into Ireland, but we travelled throughout most of England and up to Scotland. I'm not sure how I let Ireland slip away. I had learnt Irish dancing as a child and grew up listening to *Bonnie Boy* and other old Irish songs sung by my father, who was a wonderful singer; a semi-professional opera singer. Stories of mischievous leprechauns and their pots of gold at the end of rainbows fascinated me, and many lived in my desk in primary school! Perhaps it was the idea that none of us are wholly good, nor wholly evil, and we need to be discerning at every moment in life, that resonated with me.

Channelling Robbie Burns
"But pleasures are like poppies spread,
You seize the flower, it's bloom is shed;
Or, like the snow-fall in the river,
A moment white, then melts forever."

Robert Burns

Scotland was, as everyone had told us, cold and windy. We stayed in a youth hostel in Edinburgh. Robert Burns happens to be one of my ancestors, so I had to visit Scotland and take back a souvenir for my mum. Burns' talent has not rubbed off on me, but perhaps I did channel him on one occasion. When I lived in Hong Kong, many years after our travels, I was asked to preside over a Hindu child naming ceremony, and I wrote a poem about the birth of a child in preparation...

I am Precious
Before you invite me, please make sure that you have enough time to take care of me.
I need a lot of time. Not just to be fed. I need you to just "be" with me.
I will learn and grow from just being with you.

I also need to be played with - I do not see television as a substitute for your company.
I will not stop crying just because you put a dummy in my mouth.
Crying is my only way to communicate that I need something.
I hope that you will be sensitive to my needs and understand.
If you do not have time for me, please think again before inviting me into your world.
Before I come to you please be aware of how dependent I am on you.
I need to grow not only with the right nutrition but also with the right love and care.
Just as the body needs to be fed what it is made of, spirit too needs to be fed what it is made of - peace, love, happiness and truth ...
I know you think that you will love me but have you stopped to think about what love is?
It is not possessiveness. You will be my trustees but I am not yours.
You can never own anything or anyone so please look after me in trust.
In fact, I belong to the Eternal Father and will be coming from my Eternal Home.
I will be with you temporarily and cannot guarantee how long I will stay.
The simple introduction I can give of myself is this:
My nature is peace, my home is peace, and my Father is Peace,
Please try to preserve this peace for me.
If you speak to me reasonably, I will understand.
If you shout, I may just cut off or run away.
I cannot survive without peace.
Don't blame me if I use bad language, speak rudely or sulk.
I will be your mirror. I will copy you. You are my first teachers.
What I learn in the first seven years of my life will stay with me forever.
Please teach me to love, to share and to care.
I will also need to learn some lessons myself as I am growing up.
I will no doubt make mistakes.
I hope that you will be able to keep your trust in me at these times.
If you think you have the time, the patience and the love,
I am ready to come.

I may sound demanding and this may seem like a one sided deal
But I guarantee that if you can fulfil your side of the contract
I will return one thousand fold.
I am also your teacher. I am still tuned into the universe
And I can help you to reconnect with your own peace and love.
I will bring you boundless joy.
I will help you to see the world afresh if you take time to look
through my eyes.
I will remind you of your purity and innocence.
I will remind you of the lightness of laughter and play.
I will love you. Is it a deal?

Even before Tom told me of his wish not to have children, I had thought to myself as a teen, "I am sure all these parents think they know how to handle children, but as far as I can see no one does, so why would I be any different." I was aware of what a great responsibility it was. If you have flown a kite you would have practised the art of letting go and holding on. Hold on too tight and it just comes down, release too much and it will get tangled up somewhere. Managing our relationships with others is often like this, especially children. If we are too strict, their creativity and self-expression is deflated; too free, and they could find themselves entangled in compromising situations they do not have the experience to cope with.

Backpacking in Europe
"The traveller sees what he sees.
The tourist sees what he has come to see."
G.K. Chesterton

Tom and I took a boat from the UK to Oslo. After a few days of enjoying the freshness of Finland and its wonderful fruit soup, we tried to hitch a ride to Sweden. We had no luck, and after a few hours we simply crossed the road and went to Denmark instead! I loved being on the open road and letting life move us along. We had our tent and sleeping bags on our back and felt so free.

Europe was enjoyable, mainly because we were backpacking. In those days, people who tended to pick up backpackers were interested in the interchange and keen to meet travellers. It was a wonderful way to travel through Europe. We met many kind and generous people who opened their homes to us or let us camp on their property, sometimes just in their backyard. We stayed with people who owned a beautiful mansion in Switzerland with views overlooking their vineyards. From there we moved on to yet another youth hostel and trekked to the base of Mount Matterhorn.

Being members of the Youth Hostel Association, we had the chance to stay in amazing historic buildings, including an old castle in Scotland. It was a great way to meet people and save money, as we could buy local produce and cook at the hostels. On arriving in a city, we would first visit the supermarket to see what the local food was, buy what we liked, and prepare our own meals. Mostly however, we lived on bread and cheese. Every part of Europe had a different variety of bread and cheese so we never got bored with this staple. Meeting local people has always been the most interesting and enriching part of my travels. We were grateful that so many people showed us hospitality in Europe.

We enjoyed the Dutch culture of clogs and windmills, open mindedness and a feeling of freedom. In France we started the day with a bowl of coffee and a baguette; in Paris we enjoyed very good street theatre of mime and music, and we visited the Champs Elyse and the Eifel Tower. Germany was grand in many ways, stately and solid. Italy was 'good crazy'. However, after hearing about men touching up women in Rome, I talked Tom out of that adventure! Then it seemed that we were in and out of Belgium in the blink of an eye.

We felt we had arrived in Heaven when we landed on the highly recommended island of Crete, in Greece. We slept on the beach and reached the local bakery in time for the first warm batch of bread rolls to come out of the oven, enjoying them with grapes. Being vegetarians, we delighted in stuffed capsicum, yoghurt and spanakopita.

Then it was on to Yugoslavia, as it was known in the 1970's. They seemed not to have seen any Chinese people, or maybe it was because we were a mixed couple; whatever it was, they could not stop staring at us. I got so tired of it I once poked my tongue out at them!

Turkey prepared us for the Middle East. We marvelled at the grandness of the Blue Mosque and the spoils from India, beautiful jewelled canisters and lots of bling! The food was wonderful and it was not difficult to satisfy a vegetarian pallet there. We were once harassed to buy a carpet, which we could not imagine carrying on our backs anywhere.

Overland Through The Middle East
"Travel is fatal to prejudice, bigotry and narrow mindedness, and many of our people need it sorely on these accounts."

Mark Twain

It was still possible to travel through Iran and Iraq in those days, although it was not without its scary moments. This was mostly due to the misconception that travelling western women were 'fair game'. I was conscious of dressing appropriately and was even tempted to wear a *burkha* so as not to attract attention, and Tom had to keep his cool when the behaviour of some men stepped over the boundary. There was quite a dangerous moment in Iran when we were hitchhiking up to Afghanistan. A truck driver offered Tom money for me. Mixed race marriages were possibly confusing for these people, and they probably wondered about our relationship.

Being vegetarian on the road in the Middle East was a challenge. In Iran it was a plate of rice and a dollop of butter ... we passed on the skewer of meat! The melons were refreshing though, and we had picked up some dried bananas, so they saw us through to the cities. After our experience with the aforementioned truck driver, we gave up hitchhiking and travelled by bus instead. The landscape was surreal; mostly desert. As far as the eyes could see, it was all brown; barren land and mud brick houses. We arrived in Iran on the birthday of

Shah Mohammed Reza Pahlavi in October 1975, and were given sweets as we passed through immigration. It was still a very free country then, though change was in the air.

India – Home?

"To other countries, I may go as a tourist,
but to India, I come as a pilgrim."

Martin Luther King, Jr.

As we walked over the border from Pakistan into India Tom exclaimed, "It is good to be home." We looked at each other – "What did that mean?" Neither of us had been here before. I remember walking through the long pampas grass and feeling good.

Our first stop was Amritsar. Feeling 'at home', we let down our guard and were robbed by a smart young man who befriended us. Drinking *chai* together in the teashop downstairs from where we were staying, our new friend told us that all the people in the shop were his relatives. They did not understand English and smiled. He helped us change our money on the black market, and bang!, instant karma! As we sat with him in the restaurant following the exchange, he grabbed the bag with the money in it, and ran. Someone then offered to take us to the police station, but instead, he drove us to a deserted place and offered Tom money for me! Tom gave him the 'Kung Fu look' and he left us there, in the middle of nowhere, in the dark.

Feeling sorry for ourselves, we walked back to the town, to our hotel, and went to bed. When we woke up, the people from the chai shop had heard what had happened. None of them knew the young man. So much for his stories! They had brought *chai* and cakes, and a shawl for me. We were so touched by their generosity and felt we had easily received the equivalent of the $200 we had lost!

We reported the theft at the police station. Sadly all of the people in the *chai* shop were rounded up and detained, and money was extorted from their relatives to give to us. We had to sign a 'receipt'; one and a half pages of praise about the good work the police had done in getting our money back! We tried to return the money to the relatives, but they assured us that they would get it back from the thief, and would not accept our offer. As we really did need the money to get back to Malaysia we truly hoped that they would succeed in being repaid. In this one experience alone, we felt we had met the best and the worst in India.

It was hard to stay free of Delhi-belly, and by this time we were living on just bananas, peanuts and *chai*, which along with having the life boiled out of it, the main ingredient seemed to be sugar!

Exploring Buddhism
"Don't just do something, sit there."

A popular bumper sticker in the 70's

In our pursuit to study Buddhism, we visited Bodh Gaya to look into courses at the Buddhist monasteries there. Bodh Gaya was a rather dusty little place but we did get to sit under the Bodhi Tree where Buddha is said to have attained enlightenment. One of the last possessions that I relinquished, many years later, was a leaf from that tree!

We also visited Dharamshala where the Dalai Lama resides. We did not get to meet His Holiness, however it was lovely to join the Tibetan community one day as they lined the streets in anticipation of his arrival. I have not been back, but Dharamshala in those days was really very basic ... and cheap. There were very few hotels and none available for us, so we paid to stay in a room in someone's home. When we asked where the bathroom was, we were taken to the front door and the owner spread out his arms indicating, "The whole mountain is there for that." We bathed at a nearby well and washed our clothes there also. We enjoyed the experience, and these friendly people. We were not harassed at all, as we had been in other parts of India. There seemed to be a calm acceptance of all that is.

The Library was beautifully and colourfully ornate, Tibetan style. This is where most westerners hung out when they were not in their

Buddhist classes or trekking. There was an atmosphere of study and a yearning for enlightenment. We too, spent many hours a day in the library. I had been travelling with a heavy cold for some time. I felt a bit conspicuous in the silence of the library sneezing away. I consulted a Tibetan doctor and the herbs she gave me made me sneeze even more ... but, they did the trick!

We were also now on a tight budget to see us through the rest of our trip back to Australia. However we could not resist purchasing a Buddhist *thangka* depicting Buddha's life. Up until that point we had also been travelling with a wooden carving of the Buddha all the way from Bali!

Hoping to find a monastery where we could pursue our ideal to become a monk and a nun, and also to do some trekking, we visited Nepal. While in Agra, home of the beautiful Taj Mahal, we had seen a sign at the guesthouse asking if anyone wanted to share petrol costs to Kathmandhu. It had sounded like fun, so we took up the offer. Our travel friends were pleasant and good company, however they were quite heavily into dope. We were not that way inclined and denied their offers to share.

On arriving in Kathmandu, we went with our friends to a café. They had bought some hash cookies, and not taking it too seriously we tried them. Oh my! We could hardly walk back to the hotel and did not wake up until lunchtime the next day! We had paid to hire bicycles for the day, and decided to get out into the countryside. The only trouble was, my brain was so skewed, I could hardly coordinate to ride the bike and ended up wheeling it around most of the time. I can't say that drugs really suited us.

Our aim, when we planned our trip from Australia was to visit India and Nepal to explore Buddhism and to trek in Nepal. We had only gone to Europe because we were already half way there! By the time we got to Nepal however, we had seen so many mountains and lakes we felt too lazy to trek. Our resolve was also weakened by meeting people who were coming back from treks, jaundiced from contracting hepatitis. We decided to just walk to the Base Camp. It was by no means a tough trek, yet when someone offered us a lift part of the way, we even took that!

By this time, we had also lost our enthusiasm to take on Buddhism in this part of the world. We had adopted vegetarianism on the basis of Buddha's teachings on compassion, and we could not understand how the Buddhist practitioners in Asia were not following this. To justify consuming non-vegetarian food, some Buddhists say that Buddha died of food poisoning when eating pork. The word generally used in this context however, is *suukaramaddava*, which can translate literally as 'pig-soft', a soft food favoured by pigs, assumed to be truffle.

Another aspect that did not sit well with us was the worshipping of Buddha statues, and praying to the Buddha. We were pursuing a practice that would be based on study and meditation rather than worship. Having become Buddhists through our study of Buddhism, and not through association, we had quite a purist view, and had not read anywhere that Buddha had accepted worship. In fact, it was our understanding that he encouraged the pursuit of enlightenment through realisation, and strongly discouraged any form of worship of himself.

We also found the treatment of women challenging. At that time, many Buddhist congregations around the world did not accept requests from women to become nuns. When they did, the nuns were not given the same rights to study the scriptures and teach the Dharma as the monks. It was hard for me to accept any teachings that discriminated against women.

Burma
"Three things cannot hide for long:
the Moon, the Sun, and the Truth."
Buddha

During our visit to Burma in the 1970's, we encountered monks smoking cheroots and lepers in the market place. The strongest memory was of the beautiful temples scattered throughout the countryside and the broad smiles of the people, their faces powdered white to keep them cool and make them look fair. After so many months away from Asia, we delighted in the noodles and other Asian food. Even though many of the people were poor, they added gold leaf to Buddha statues whenever they could. We also saw a 'miracle' in one of the temples where a leaf hanging from a parasol kept moving constantly even though it was behind glass. The glass had a big circle and arrow painted on it so we did not miss it!

'Everyone' was bringing cigarettes and alcohol into Burma and selling them on the black market. We considered ourselves honest people, and yet we also followed suit. The money given was local and had to be spent in Burma, so we splurged and got the clothes that we had been wearing on the road for months, dry cleaned. We also bought some beautiful souvenirs, including of all things, a beautiful washing basket which we carried back to Malaysia and then on to Australia. What were we thinking!

After visiting the majestic Shwedagon Pagoda where we could donate money to have the lights come on in order to catch a brighter glimpse of the artefacts, we sailed from Mandalay on the Irrawaddy River to Bagan, the land of a 1,000 Temples. In the morning mist it looked like a dream.

Last leg ... Thailand

"Happiness cannot be travelled to, owned, earned, worn or consumed. Happiness is the spiritual experience of living every minute with love, grace, and gratitude."

Denis Waitley

Our last stop before returning to Malaysia on our way back to Australia, was Bangkok. We had one train ride left before we would reach Ipoh and used our last few dollars to purchase another beautiful etched painting of Buddha. I had never had a great appreciation for art, but the Buddha images were irresistible. We were now carrying three and were happy we were returning to Malaysia to offload.

In Bangkok we were surprised to find images of the four-faced Brahma everywhere, considering it was a Buddhist nation. Then we remembered we were in Indochina; the blend of influences was then understandable. Even people's names, *Krishna, Aroon, Kanya*, reflected the influence of Sanskrit.

The train ride was inexpensive and comfortable. We passed through lush vegetation all the way. It was relaxing, and a good way to end a very long journey 'on the road'. When we arrived in Ipoh, Tom's mother asked if we would be home for dinner. We were going out. There was no discussion about our travels. Tom's mum did not approve of us travelling - we were meant to be saving so that we could 'settle down'. "You are too young to be vegetarian and to meditate. Enjoy your life", she would say.

We had travelled from Australia, through Indonesia, Malaysia, England, Scotland, Norway, Finland, Denmark, Holland, Belgium, France, Germany, Switzerland, Italy, Yugoslavia, Greece, Iraq, Iran, Afghanistan, Pakistan, India, Nepal and Thailand, and were still searching!

* * * * *

4

Stretching Our Beliefs

Goat Farmer, Nun or Yogi?
"The best laid schemes o' mice an' men gang aft agley."
Robert Burns

We returned to Australia and thought, "Now what? How are we going to spend the next 50 years of our life? We had seen half the world - what was left?" We came up with three options. Plan A, was to stay in a Tibetan Buddhist monastery in Queensland. Tom left his job, I kept mine 'just in case', and we prepared to become a monk and a nun, ready to face the challenge of becoming detached from each other; the first lesson of Buddhism. We did have reservations about the ashram though. It was Tibetan Buddhist and still involved worship. We would also need to see if it was a vegetarian community, and if women were treated equally!

Plan B, if the monastery did not work out, was for Tom to go to India to find a guru. I would work to support him until he found something that might suit us. Plan C was to start a goat farm and sell goat milk, living in solitude in the country. At ages 20 and 25 respectively these were the only options we could think of!

Meanwhile, we were practising and studying Buddhism in all its variations, and also 'shopping' around for what might fulfil us, even though we were not sure what that was. We regularly visited the *Hare Krishna Feast* and were very touched by the energy in the food. However, we were not looking to worship anything or anyone. In 1976 we attended a program with Swami Satyananda in Sydney and even received a mantra. We spent a weekend at the retreat centre at Mangrove Mountain but we seemed to do more manual labour than learn anything.

Stepping into a community takes courage and we found this one to be quite cliquey. I say this not to criticise, but as a point of awareness for any community, including the one I am part of today. We need to welcome and embrace people who are brave enough to step into our home or community. Satyananda was just one of many organisations that just 'didn't fit'.

Wherever we visited, we met many good people and could see many were benefitting, but they were just not what we were looking for. In recent years, the Mangrove Mountain Ashram has come under the scrutiny of the Royal Commission into Institutional Responses to Child Sexual Abuse, and it has not fared well. Most institutions have needed major re-structuring in this regard.

We also visited the annual *Down to Earth Festival* where various organisations could be experienced in one place. People were telling us to visit the Brahma Kumaris Raja Yoga tent as they had had amazing experiences there. At the tent Tom got into a debate with the BK teacher about whether the soul was in the heart or the centre of the forehead. It was obviously not our time!

Later, one of my work colleagues was handed a pamphlet about Raja Yoga by a Brahma Kumari. I had interviewed this person for employment. Later, he told me he hadn't given me a pamphlet because he didn't think I would have been interested. According to him, I didn't look spiritual. Well, it seemed my Buddhist practise didn't show at all! Upon reading the pamphlet, I was put off by two words, 'God' and 'free'. I feared that they wanted me to have God more than I did, and that it would be pushed on me.

A week before leaving for the Buddhist monastery, Plan A, we were sorting through our meagre belongings and came across the BK pamphlet. We had become inured to words; by this time we had read and seen so much. We decided to check the Brahma Kumaris out, and were able to do the seven lesson introductory course in Raja Yoga meditation that week. The day after the course finished, we left for the monastery.

The Raja Yoga course had a very great impact on us. We just couldn't get the ideas we had learned, out of our minds. As we slowly travelled north to Queensland, it was as if we were piecing together a jigsaw puzzle and were seeing the wonder and meaning of the universe unfold before our eyes. Just 50 miles before arriving at the monastery we turned back to pursue Raja Yoga.

The Brahma Kumaris were vegetarian; that ticked the first box. It was not just for reasons of compassion, but also for the effect a vegetarian diet has on the mind. This wisdom derives from the ancient Indian medical system of Ayurveda, meaning 'the science of life'. Non-vegetarian food is referred to as *tamasic*, and is said to create inertia and drain life energy. Other negative effects include strong urges like greed, anger, and compromised reasoning skills.

Shakti power

"Women are like a teabag; you do not know how strong they are until you put them in hot water."

Margaret Thatcher

The second box also received a big tick! Not only are women treated equally in the Brahma Kumaris, they are encouraged to take up leadership roles. At the time I came across the BKs, the heads of the organisation were two elderly women, referred to as *Dadis*, meaning elder sisters. In India, feminine power is referred to as *Shakti*. The BKs feel that feminine power, that is the power that comes from qualities like tolerance, love and understanding, which are innate in women, offers the balance needed in the world at this time. It is not that they consider women to be more important than men, but they are considered to be **equally** important.

This was very appealing to me, and I was relieved. I did not want to take up the task of struggling for women's equality within the Buddhist world, something I would have had to address.

The BKs in fact, go beyond gender. 'Soul consciousness' is the basis of the practice of Raja Yoga meditation. The BKs teach that in 'body consciousness' we are under the illusion that we are a body. We develop tendencies like arrogance, greed, lust, anger and attachment, believing we need these to function as bodies. To become free of these, we need to transform our consciousness. We need to realise we are spiritual beings who use our bodies; we are actors on a world drama stage. To quote Shakespeare, "All the world's a stage, and all the men and women, merely players."

By remaining in the awareness of being a soul, we keep in touch with our true essence. The essence of our being is peace, happiness, love, wisdom, inner power and bliss. Everything we need is already within our own Self. We do not need love or peace from outside of us. We only need to turn within and get in touch with our own essence. We do not need to 'become' peaceful as we already are peace, we just need to let go of those things that we hold onto in our minds that stop us from being at peace.

The third box that received a tick was the Brahma Kumaris did not worship anyone or anything. There is no guru figure. It is a study; the meditation practice and lifestyle is a path to wisdom rather than worship and ritual.

Aim and Objective
*"If you do not know where you are going,
any path will take you there."*

Lewis Carroll

When I was asked by an incredulous Indian woman why I used to smoke and drink when I was a teenager, all I could say was, "Everyone else around me did it. I smoked and drank just because I did not have a reason not to." Unless we have an aim for our life, we waste a lot of time and energy and often move in a direction that is not our own. We become 'followers' who just want to fit in. The cause of so many of our bad habits lies in us not having a purpose. We need to do inner work to get on our 'line'. As far as we are 'off our line', that will be the amount of stress that we will experience in our life.

I've learnt that one of the greatest gifts we can bring to another is to help them see what's special about them. This will often enable them find their true destiny. For many years I taught in a Meditation Centre in Hong Kong. Noticing that one of the students was good at expressing herself clearly, I asked her to teach a Positive Thinking course. She hadn't been brought up in her native country, and perhaps held a belief that her communication was not good, so she could not believe that I was asking her. I offered to check if others agreed with me and she was amazed that they did.

In the Hindu epic, The Mahabharata, *Dronacharya*, the Guru of Archery, placed a wooden bird for five brothers to practise their archery skills. As they took aim, he asked each one, "What do you see?" Four of the brothers replied that they saw various parts of the bird. The fifth brother, *Arjan*, known for his excellent archery skills, replied "I only see the eye." This represents being clear about the goal and not being distracted by other things. It symbolises concentration and a clear aim.

With a little help, this student got 'on her line'. She realised her strengths and focused on a direction where they could take her. In order to build her confidence, she took a public speaking course, and today works in coaching and training.

Emotional Independence

"If I am I because thou art thou, and thou art thou because I am I, then I am not I and thou art not thou."

Rabbi Menachem Mendel Morgensztern of Kotzk

Raja is an Indian word meaning 'king'. The aim of Raja Yoga is to become a king, or master, of the self, and this is what attracted me to this particular path. I could see that I could attain emotional independence.

I used to get so affected by people's moods and emotions that I was seldom able to really be myself. Instead, I was a reaction to others. How can we ever know and be ourselves if we are being influenced and reacting to someone or something?

Having met only two years previously, Tom and I were still in our 'in love' stage, and the relationship was very alive. However, I would get so affected by his moods. If he was upset about someone or something and not speaking, I used to feel left out and unloved. It was painful. I would become demanding of his attention and sometimes even say something stupid like, "You don't love me."

Obviously when anger or another emotion is 'alive' we cannot feel love at that time. It does not mean the love has disappeared. There is a stronger emotion dominating and the mind has been diverted; we have let our feelings be hijacked because there is another need alive in us.

After beginning the practice of Raja Yoga, I became less demanding. I was able to keep myself happy and content, and was less needy. I was on the path to emotional independence and I felt a great sense of freedom and stability. This was one of my first real attainments, and yet being emotionally dependent is still the main weakness I need to work on.

Mike George, a fellow BK, had written about the difference between emotions and feelings in one of his early books. It didn't really grab me; I just saw it as semantics. But later on, in another of his books, he described how emotions cloud feelings and I could see this in myself. I understood then, that emotions always come from ego and are a reactive state. When we are emotionally disturbed, we cannot choose our feelings as we are not be able to be discerning and make decisions with clarity and accuracy. In his *Clear Thinking* articles, Mike says "Emotional intelligence is an oxymoron. The more emotional you are, the less intelligent you will be."

Magic
"Some say that the people here have magic in their eyes."
Eugene Romain

The group of yogis in Sydney were very young when I started. They ranged in age from 14-30 years old and were lots of fun. We did crazy things like dancing under the full moon, enjoying weekly ice cream parties, creating exhibitions and joining festivals to share meditation with others. Our meditation tent was well known for the experiences people had when they came to it. At one of the *Down to Earth* festivals organised near Canberra, it seemed that we were the only people there who were not naked. It was a unique opportunity to practise seeing the soul, and not the body, during our open-eye meditation sessions!

We were all having amazing experiences at the meditation Centre and would sit from 2 – 6am in the morning before a class, and then again in the evening from 5 -7pm. We would get high on meditation and the vibrations would attract people to the door. However, when the doorbell rang we were all so intoxicated that no one felt that they could talk to a 'straight' person. We would let them in but I do not know what they thought of us. They must have thought we were high on something... Yes, on high thinking!

Living in this state takes one away from desire; we experience an internal happiness that is far richer. In his book *The Way of the Wizard*, Deepak Chopra really speaks to my fascination for magic, "Without silence there is no room for the Wizard, no real appreciation of life. ... The Wizard doesn't think, he sees. ... A Wizard is empty so the universe can fill him with love ... Mortals are full of ego."

Staff at my work in Sydney used to enjoy a weekly 'happy hour' in the tea room. I disliked it immensely - I find small talk the hardest pastime. For the same reason, I could not manage teaching English in Hong Kong; I just could not do small talk. I was embarrassed when my young student complained, "That is the third time you have yawned." I realised then that I was just not cut out for it! My work colleagues in Sydney were happy that I was willing to look after the office while they had their happy hour, and I offered them a 'peaceful hour' where I got them all to meditate. They were blown out. Many had visions of light, and one colleague commented that I was a witch! There was a lot of mutual respect between us and they would come to me if something was bothering them.

Many of us have witnessed or heard of miraculous healing episodes. If Joe Dispenza were not so famous internationally, I would have found it hard to believe that he healed his broken back with visualisation and was able to live a normal life after twelve weeks, without an operation. How did he do it? In his book *Breaking the Habit of Being Yourself*, he explains, "The observer effect in quantum physics states that where you place your attention is where you direct your energy. An atom is 99.99999 per cent energy and .00001 physical. I am nothing more than I am something! The nothing consists of energy waves that carry information, and this force organises our physical structures and their functioning. It is personal and universal. This intelligence keeps our heart beating and the same consciousness prompts trees to grow fruit. It is mindful; it pays attention to us aware of our thoughts and dreams. It 'observes' everything into physical form. How can it be anything but love? In order to change we have to come to a new understanding of the Self and the world. Your thoughts have consequences so great that they can change your reality."

Anyone who has seriously understood and practised the science of the mind has his or her own stories. I have my own long list of 'magical' situations that really do seem hard to believe, and yet, thought has made them so! One such incident took place in 1993. I had the thought to go to Oxford in the UK, for the opening of our first Retreat Centre outside of India. I was a full time volunteer BK teacher, serving in Hong Kong at the time, and I felt that I was meant to attend. It was not so much a desire, more a 'knowing'. Although I had no idea how I would pay for it, I booked a ticket. Within two days, a student offered to pay my fare to London if I would accompany her as she was putting her daughter in Summer School; it just happened to be the same date that I had booked!

On another occasion in 2006, I was visiting South Korea conducting meditation programs and meeting a lot of amazing people. The sister looking after the Centre there asked if I could return a month later to help with a visit of one of our most senior teachers, Dadi Janki. There were no available funds for the ticket however. I returned to Phnom Penh where I was living at the time, and two days after I returned, I received an invitation to an interfaith conference in Seoul with all costs covered. The amazing thing was that the conference finished the day before Dadi Janki was to arrive.

In actual fact it is not magic. From research done in quantum physics, we can now understand it as being 'a science of the mind'. And, it makes life fun! Quantum physics describes the 'quantum field'. In this field, possibilities are infinite and we just have to pick up one of them. When we use our mind in the right way it certainly feels as easy as this. If we put out the thought, let go of the 'how', imagine ourselves having achieved the result, it comes to us as if by magic. This has worked for me on many occasions.

When I first visited the headquarters of the Brahma Kumaris in Mount Abu, a favourite pastime was to visit 'Baba's Rock'. Mount Abu is 1,300 metres above sea level and from Baba's Rock you can look down on farmlands and see for miles. Sunset is the most awesome time to visit. At that time even the monkeys used to sit with us peacefully. It was always magical. On one occasion, as we were settling into our sunset meditation, a young Australian girl began dancing in a trance like state. Upon sitting down, she was asked her name in English and did not answer. When asked in Hindi, she replied. Her name was Sukshum. I also once saw an elderly sister who was quite large in frame, dance over the rocks in a state of trance with her eyes closed. It was unimaginable that she could be so nimble and not fall, as the rocks were very uneven.

Our long meditation sittings in the evenings, called *bhattis*, meaning 'a furnace', were often concluded with a few meditators being drawn to dance in trance. The rest of us would get up and join them, and then after some time it would naturally come to an end and we would silently make our way to the dining hall for dinner.

Some of the female meditators (sisters) had the gift of trance and would bring 'back' messages that were full of symbolic meaning. They inspired the imagination and lifted the mind, and always left us thinking on another level.

* * * * *

5

Hippie to Happy

Give Peace A Chance
"All we are saying is give peace a chance."
John Lennon of the Beatles

I have loved the Beatles since I was eleven years old and in my travels I have come across people all over the world who know their songs - from an elderly Japanese professor to recently, a young Taiwanese interior designer, who could belt out a number of their songs even though he couldn't speak English. For me, the Beatles united people with a vision of peace and love in a way that nothing else had.

Like many people who grew up in the 1960's, Tom and I had embraced the hippie movement. In Asia the hippies had the reputation of being drugged out and enjoying a lot of sex. Perhaps whilst some did this, the aspect of the hippie movement that Tom, I, and many others were attracted to, was the call to peace. The Beatles were not just great musicians; many of their songs were filled with positive and clear messages about peace, love, freedom and non-violence.

In Australia, the heartland of the hippie movement was Nimbin, a small town in northern New South Wales. When Tom and I began practising Raja Yoga in Sydney, I envisaged I would transfer to our department's Murwillumbah office, a town near Nimbin, so I could share with my hippie friends all about the coming 'Golden Age'. I was sure they would all be interested! I applied for a transfer and when it finally came through we moved to the small township of Uki. Having rejected the culture of consumerism, our small apartment in Sydney only had a mattress on the floor, some cushions, a sound system and kitchen basics. The cardboard box for the sound system was our table! Therefore, we were able to fit all our possessions into our small Toyota Corolla. In Uki, we rented the old schoolhouse situated at the foothills of Mount Warning. We had a beautiful view of the mountain and sunflowers greeted us in the morning.

However, there was one problem. I worked for the Australian Department of Employment and Youth Affairs - the enemy organisation of the hippies. The people who had settled around Nimbin were young and had dropped out of 'the system'. They lived on the land, grew vegetables and built their own homes. There was very little employment in the area and the hippies did not fit well into the conventional '9 to 5' working day. Many received unemployment benefits from the government.

It seemed like my boss had been especially placed in our office. He hated hippies and called them "dole bludgers". My job was to interview people who were applying for the unemployment benefit (the dole). As soon as a hippie sat down at my desk, I would warn them about my boss because he would inevitably come along and rile them up. They needed to stay calm and not react to him; otherwise he would call the police and have them charged. My boss did have a point; tax payers financed the lifestyles of the hippies. However, I also felt this counter culture was needed in our society at that time.

Because of my job, I was treated with caution whenever Tom and I visited Nimbin. Although the clothes I wore did pass as 'hippie-like', I was judged for not being quite hippie enough. I realised that these people who were rejecting conservatism were actually just as body conscious as those who judged and rejected them. They too judged 'the book by the cover.'

The hippies were into meditation, and when we offered some meditation classes they showed a lot of enthusiasm. However, drugs tend to create a laid back feeling and it was hard to motivate this community; many were living in half-built houses! In the end there was really only one keen aspirant. We would visit him, his wife and child, and find them all completely naked. They were loving people, so we did not mind. It just went with the landscape!

However, we were unable to inspire our hippie friends with our vision and decided to move back to Sydney. I guess we were a little missionary-like in our enthusiasm, but we also missed the large yogi community in the city. There was also a strong pull to Asia. Before we left we helped set up a meditation Centre in Brisbane, and passed over all of our treasured Raja Yoga pictures that we had had in our little Centre in Uki.

Purity, The Mother of Peace and Happiness
"Purity is the mother of peace and happiness."

Indian saying

Everyone wants peace and happiness but they run a mile when the idea of living a pure life is brought up. I know I did! To me, it meant giving up all pleasures. It sounded very boring and wreaked of judgement.

We all want peace and happiness, so perhaps it is worth getting to know their mother! *Sat* is the prefix in Hindi for truth as well as purity. Many say that they value truth, but again, often only in small doses.

As with all words, there is so much baggage attached to the word purity. However, most can relate to pure air, water and food. Purity is when there is no mixture. It is healing, refreshing and empowering.

How pure are you? Let me give you a hint. It is related to those children! We can tell how pure we are by how peaceful and happy we are.

Many who think they are pure can be very disturbed by 'impure' people, i.e. people they consider are doing the wrong thing. This robs them of their peace and happiness.

Happiness

"Your attitude is far more important in determining your happiness than your money, appearance, social status or talent."

Stephanie Dowrick

Just as purity is totally misconstrued, the meaning and understanding of happiness is nebulous also. The happiest person I have ever met was paralysed up to the neck after a swimming pool accident. He would shiver with joy when I visited him in Mumbai. When I asked if I could send him anything from Hong Kong, his eyes teared up and his face filled with joy as he said, "I have everything I could possibly want."

Dadi Janki once said, "Happy people are lucky." When we are happy we do feel lucky … no matter what is happening. A friend and I once cooked for a group of people who were to join us on a picnic in Hong Kong. On our way to the picnic spot we took the wrong boat and ended up carrying the food around all day, finding ourselves in one situation after another with all kinds of unusual people. We spent more money that day than we had ever spent on an outing; we had no change for buses and at times had to take taxis, and so it went on. When something did go right, we would find ourselves exclaiming, "We are so lucky!", and laughing.

I have been fortunate to have happy parents, and perhaps I have taken my happy disposition for granted. Several times I have been asked by others how we can be happy, and for a long time I had not felt any inclination to explore this. I believe that teachers work on what they feel they need to develop in themselves, but perhaps this is why we can often come across as hypocrites! If the truth be known, I am not always happy; emotional maturity is still my challenge and where I tend to come undone, so this is what I work on. I cry very easily. My excuse is, "It keeps me healthy." It was pointed out to me that I still cry even after so many years of my practice. My response was, "At least I do not have any major illness!" I think there is some truth to this, as I cannot keep anything in. But it is rather confusing for others when I cry so easily as I generally come across as being happy and strong.

I have though, spent some time thinking about happiness, and realised how much I did know on the subject. The following are some of my thoughts …

- The first aspect is jealousy. We can often block another's happiness through jealousy. The root is laziness. When we find what is unique about ourselves and offer that in service, we begin to use our time in a worthwhile way, which brings inner joy.
- It is a well-known saying, "Company colours the soul." Seeking the company of, and learning from happy people, spending time with children and making sure we keep the left and right sides of our brain balanced, will all help us to maintain happiness.
- Some people don't feel they have a right to be happy, whilst others simply think it is unrealistic to be so positive. They believe they should suffer, perhaps because of a past wrongdoing or low self-worth, and so of course they do suffer.
- Fake it until you make it. Smile. Smiling stimulates an acupressure point that helps create happiness in the brain. It also takes only 7 muscles to smile, whilst it takes 40 to frown.
- Active appreciation. Develop an appreciative awareness of all that you have … and have had in the past. Write a list before sleeping of what you have to feel grateful for and this will grow each day. Also be grateful for what others have done or do for you, and appreciate their qualities.
- "The only effort we need to make is not to worry," says Dadi Janki. Remove the habit of worrying by increasing understanding. When there is wisdom we cannot worry, even if we try! We

have a deeper understanding of what is happening in our life. We need to learn to tolerate both happiness and sorrow. If we allow ourselves to get excited by happiness then we will also be affected by sorrow. One of the main qualities of a yogi is equanimity, i.e. there is stability in fame or defamation, victory or defeat, heat or cold, simplicity or grandeur – it is what it is.
- Have the courage to remain light and avoid sulking and isolating yourself. When an enemy wants to attack they first isolate, and then conquer. This is how, what we call *Maya*, illusion, works. Stay around good company even if you do not feel like it, especially the company of small children and animals.

Peace

"The peace pulse is the soul of the soul ... it beats gently, constantly, peaceful, stable, rhythmic, neutral, unblamable ... extremely experienced & absolutely innocent."

Anthea Church, Inner Space

In 1983 I gave a talk to the Members of Parliament at the Philippine National Assembly, Batasang Pambansa. One of the participants asked me to define peace. Fortunately, Lucy, my translator, used the word *kalinaw*, meaning 'clear mind'. She explained that the root, *linaw*, referred to calm and tranquil, as in a still body of water. Until today I have not found a better definition of inner peace.

Before visiting another country I would always check what word was being used to translate 'peace', as the translation was often 'no war'. I was living in Hong Kong at the time and it was said to have the highest rate of peacelessness in the world, second only to Beirut where a full scale war was raging.

Peace is often seen as passive, weak and defeatist. I once asked a group of businessmen in Korea whether they wanted to be peaceful and they responded unanimously that of course they want to be peaceful. I then asked, "As businessmen you want to make a lot of money right?

Do you think you can be peaceful and also get rich?" They all felt that this would be impossible. I asked, "So, what will you do?" and they responded, "Get rich and then we can be peaceful!" I wished them luck. Many do not make it with all the stress in business and the follow on impact on relationships and health.

Being able to keep my mind clear is the power of peace - not to react to anything. With a clear mind, I can stop, think, and then act. Those who can remain clear in crisis are who we like to choose to be leaders. This is what constitutes a powerful leader. When we react with fear and anger, we are lowering our energy, creating confusion in the mind, and losing our vision.

The Brahma Kumaris use the greeting, "Om Shanti", and are often known as the 'Om Shanti people'. Shanti means peace, and also silence.

* * * * *

6

Making Asia Home

Charity Begins at Home
"Your one step of courage will bring 1,000 fold help from God."

Bapdada

After just over three years of studying Raja Yoga, Tom and his brother Robert, who had also taken it up, set off for Malaysia to open a Brahma Kumaris Meditation Centre. They arrived at their parent's home in Ipoh expecting to start there, however their Mum would have none of it. Their parents felt it disrupted 'normal life' and wondered why their sons were not living a life like others. They had sacrificed and worked hard to send Tom and Robert to school in Australia in order for them to study for a profession and earn a good living for a good life. It was very understandable for them to react like this.

Tom and Robert packed all their belongings in a taxi and headed for Kuala Lumpur. On nearing the capital city, which they did not know at all, the taxi driver asked where they wanted to go. "Any suggestions?" they asked, and this is how the work of the Brahma Kumaris started in Malaysia. Together, they had a lot of faith that they would be guided, and within a few weeks that was certainly the case. Robert found work in an advertising agency and they found a good place to rent to establish the Centre.

On one of my trips to India I had contracted typhoid. This kept me in Australia for a while. It must have been due to my high mental energy, but I really felt great, although physically I could do no more than bathe myself and get dressed. I took advantage of being in hospital and learnt to read and write Hindi, which I had been picking up during my trips to India. It helped that I was considered contagious and was given my own room!

I had already left my job in anticipation of joining Tom and Robert, but whilst waiting for them to settle into Kuala Lumpur I was asked if I would go to Hong Kong for 3 months to help with Brahma Kumaris work there. I sold my car, packed my belongings and arrived in Hong Kong. The address given was Golden Crown Court and I expected a very grand building. It turned out to be a very small apartment of 800 square feet, and in it were two elderly ladies who did not speak a word of English. I began exploring what I could do in Hong Kong. Sharda, from Ahmedabad had also arrived and we were to start an English-speaking Meditation Centre on the Hong Kong side of the harbour.

We were offered an apartment in the fishing village of Aberdeen ... rather too close for comfort to the Fish Market for us vegetarians! This area had just started to be developed. Sharda helped me with my Hindi. If I wanted a newspaper in English, I would need to get to the stall early, as there were only a couple delivered each day. The apartment overlooked the sea and we would get a *kai do*, a small boat, if we wanted to go out to one of the islands. The MTR, Mass Transit Railway, had not been connected to the rest of the island so traffic kept most people at a distance.

Japan and Didi Manmohini
"I leave my body outside with my shoes."

Picasso

Within the first few months of living in Hong Kong, the Additional Administrative Head of the Brahma Kumaris, Didi Manmohini, visited. I could feel her powerful energy and enjoyed her presence. However, not speaking much Hindi I was not able to glean as much wisdom from her as I would have liked. I was invited to join her on her trip to Tokyo for four days and jumped at the opportunity. Four days became three months as I was asked to stay on to follow up with all the interest generated by her visit. Japan had gone into winter by this time and all I had taken with me was a small travel suitcase with 4 sets of summer clothes!

The Centre was a traditional wooden Japanese house where no cars could access the narrow streets. All the interior walls could be removed to make one large area, which was very convenient for public programmes; however the beautiful, rice paper walls and woodcarvings were not built to keep heat in! The house was however, built to withstand an earthquake and there were tremors almost daily, which we became used to. A neighbour practised the *shakuhachi*, Japanese flute, every day, and so in spite of the cold, I delighted in this whole experience. I also got used to eating, and cooking, seaweed and the many wonderful and unique Japanese delicacies.

There was an obsession about wearing the right slippers in the right areas and absolutely no shoes were to be worn inside. After removing your shoes outside, someone would generally take the time to neatly face them in the right direction for when you left. If only we paid so much attention to leaving our ego outside and straightening our attitude!

I attended many different meetings in an effort to get to know the people. Once I gave a talk titled 'Can and Should Japanese Overcome Workaholism?' I saw these people were returning home at 9 or 10pm at night, so it seemed like a good topic. At the end of the talk all agreed that they should overcome workaholism, but they said they couldn't do it! It was interesting speaking with the Japanese in English. They used very 'proper' English words - many I was not comfortable with. When I told them I was in Japan to teach meditation, they asked if I was a 'missionary' ... "Oh no.", I replied, "I am not a missionary." (Am I?)!

Everything was written in Japanese and when I needed to go to the supermarket to buy the most simple things like salt or plain flour, I needed help from someone to write it down. The train stations sometimes only had Japanese signage.

Someone from India once told me the story that when he visited Japan, he was advised to get off his train at an exact time and he would be met there. In India, time is a little more flexible. He hesitantly followed the instructions and to his amazement, at exactly the minute he alighted his friend was there waiting. No need for station names!

How did I know if someone understood English? I would just stand and look lost and wait for someone to offer help! Fortunately the Japanese are very kind and courteous and would go out of their way to help, sometimes walking with me for quite a distance.

Malaysia (Again)

"Dadi Janki has the most stable mind we have ever tested."

Medical and Science Research Institute, University of Texas 1978

From Tokyo, I flew to Kuala Lumpur. Meanwhile all my things were still in Hong Kong! Dadi Janki, was visiting Singapore. Robert, Tom and I drove to Singapore. It was a 6 hour drive, and when we arrived we were asked why we had not arranged a program for Dadi in Kuala Lumpur. We took up the challenge; after a quick lunch we drove straight back to KL to organise a program for Dadi!

Tom and Robert had 2 mattresses, 2 cups, 2 plates, 2 sets of cutlery and 2 cushions! Fortunately I had my superannuation pay-out from Australia and in just three days, we furnished the whole house with a refrigerator, beds, curtains, dining set, chairs and all that was needed. We booked a room at the local Hindu temple, contacted the media and cooked sweets for 300 people. To our surprise more than 300 came. The press had done an article on Dadi Janki titled 'The Most Stable Mind in the World'. It attracted all manner of people interested in meeting this great personality, including face readers, palm readers and mystics. In the middle of the programme I asked someone to go out and bring back a big hand of bananas for all the people crowded at the windows!

We had never looked after a senior teacher of the Brahma Kumaris and there was no one to guide us. We did not know how to cook the Indian food that Dadi was used to but she enjoyed the Sweet and Sour Walnuts with rice! Perhaps not as much as we thought though, as she opted to eat fruit from the trees for breakfast!

What was meant to have been a short transit for me in Kuala Lumpur turned out to last a month. I stayed on with Robert as Tom had planned a trip to India, and after the evening with Dadi, over 50 people wanted to do the meditation course. Today there is a very big BK Retreat Centre near the KL airport and over forty meditation Centres throughout Malaysia. It is very fertile ground for spirituality.

Singapore
"People with long hair can expect to be served last."

A signboard at the local post office in Singapore in 1981

I could not find work in Malaysia so I went to our Centre in Singapore. There, with the help of a very well-known headhunting agency called Business Trends, I easily found work within a few days. The owner of the business, Lalita, was a nineteen-year-old Indian lady who had the support of her father and friends. Her father was an astrologer and did my numerology and horoscope. From that he knew I would be good for the business. When I mentioned to Lalita that I only wanted to work part time because I wanted to be available to help at the Meditation Centre, she insisted on giving me the same salary agreed upon for a full time position. I used the company car to go all over Singapore to meet clients and quickly felt very much at home. It would have been good to have also had use of the car to drive home as it seemed that the time I finished work was exactly when the monsoon rains would come. I got drenched on my way home almost daily. However, with the heat in Singapore I did not actually mind!

Singapore was very conservative in those days. I found that nearly all secretaries were the same in appearance, skills, age and ability. It was hard to tell one from the other, but easy for employers to choose a few when a vacancy arose. It was in Singapore that I thought deeply about 'new souls' and 'old souls'. Singapore was modern, clean and had great shopping and clubhouses. Generally the people were very kind and polite, good and efficient. I felt at that time that many were new birth souls ... perhaps not with the experience of having lived through many lifetimes. In comparison, my experience of looking into the eyes of people in India, was that *many* were old souls.

I had a great time working in Singapore and Lalita was very supportive of what I was doing. If I had press interviews or talks she would give me time off, or even provide her office for interviews, and she would pay me when I travelled to Malaysia to help with the activities there. Unfortunately the government was not keen for me to work and refused to renew my work visa after three months. As predicted by Lalita's father, I was lucky for the company and they were reluctant to let me go, however being a corruption free country, a law was a law.

Our Regional Co-ordinator then asked me where I would like to go next. I am a bit of a country girl so Hong Kong was my last choice. Of course, that is where I was asked to go!

Meanwhile, Lalita employed Dee from our Centre in Singapore, and Dee ended up working there for over twenty years as the receptionist. Having grown up in a *kampong*, Dee was very simple and just wore a simple *kurta* to work. Although it was a high end establishment, Lalita accepted Dee as she was, and so many clients said that if Dee ever left Lalita, they wanted to employ her. A great example of just being one's self!

* * * * *

7

The Long Haul!

Hong Kong

"Few leaders realise how little they have to do."

John Heder, Tao of Leadership

Hong Kong Friends: Dr Simon Chau (Greenwoods Raw Cafe); Jenny Wong Deli (HR Consultant), Ruby Ong (Reflections Bookshop); Wendy Kwok (Foodlink Foundation); Maureen Chen; Dr Chou Wah Shan (Dreams Possible); Diana Lin (TVB Presenter); S C Mar (Silver Age Laughter Team)

This time, I was not to leave Hong Kong for another 21 years! It also meant that Tom and I were finally the 'monk and nun' we had planned to be as we hardly met up after this move. The Raja Yoga Centre had now moved to Causeway Bay, nearer the city area, into a building called Pearl City Mansion. Again, although it sounded grand, it was even smaller than Golden Crown Court! We held meditation classes in the small sitting room where we could fit a maximum of four people. We had to plan our exit from the room because if we all stood up together we were not able to move! When we invited guests for dinner it had to be just a tablecloth on the floor in the classroom.

We were on the 14th floor and we hung our washing outside on long poles. If any of it dropped down we would need to go into the restaurant on the ground floor to retrieve it from their terrace. Roslyn had now joined me and we had a great time together. The apartment was furnished with a double bed and I drove her crazy at night with my antics ... talking and giving lectures in my sleep, and even bringing things into the bed. She was very good-humoured about it all.

We also shared a job, and for many months the Chinese staff there did not know that we were two different people. We all look the same to them! Our boss was a student at the Centre, and though not a wealthy man, he employed us because he wanted our good energy in his office. He also knew that the Centre needed money. He would not let us do any real work because he did not want us to get stressed, so we used the office for planning activities for the Centre. This was very opportune because Roslyn had had the grand inspiration to hold an Asian Women's Convention and we now had an office to work out of. The staff were all very cooperative as well.

There were just the two of us. We were young and inexperienced, and neither had organised a large event before. It was perhaps just as well because we had no idea of what was needed. Otherwise, we would not have had the courage to take on such a major event. We simply went along, keeping 'the vision'. We invited many speakers, both men and women, and they all agreed. It was like, "Oh we have too many speakers for one day, we will need three days!" And so it grew like this!

The day of the program came and we ended up having VIP guest speakers coming from the UK, Germany, the Philippines, Indonesia and Japan. We hadn't even realised that meals, accommodation and transport also needed to be organised for all the guests. Fortunately our sisters, who were bringing guests from the other countries, stepped in to help us. They were as young and almost as inexperienced as us, but we were more inexperienced! We were offered the use of two five-bedroom luxury apartments with maids, drivers and cars ... thank you God!!

We also had a very large BK contingency coming from India, the UK and Australia, including senior yogis, Dadi Manohar Indra, Brother Nirwair, Didi Nirmala and Sister Jayanti. Most Centres would only ever host one of these guests at one time, but our students were honoured to house and care for them all.

The programme went along perfectly. In the middle of it, Roslyn and I looked at each other incredulously, as if to say, "Did we organise this?!" It was a great foundation for all the other big crazy things I have organised since, that have also been way beyond my capacity! This programme was held in a 5 star hotel and I am not sure to this day where the funds came from.

Hong Kong's Colourful Characters

*"If everyone would look for that uniqueness
then we would have a very colourful world."*

Michael Schenker

Hong Kong has that energy where it seems anything is possible, and I thrived in that environment. It was also the home to many colourful characters and when visitors came these characters were included on the 'must see' list. Our visitors were also treated a visit to Victoria Peak and the Chinese street opera in Mong Kok, the most populated spot on the planet. I became good at imitating the sounds of the opera; I did not use Chinese words, but rather just sounds ... trying to use words cramped my style.

Often our first stop was the home of Aileen Bridgewater in the countryside. She was a radio host for a talk back programme, RTHK. Through her conversations with people and her outreach, she founded *SANTA*, Spare a New Toy Appeal. This began when a guest on the programme mentioned, that as an orphan they had never received a new toy. So, each Christmas a large Christmas tree would go up in Central and people would donate toys and place them under it. The toys were then distributed throughout the Territory. Aileen also started the *Hong Kong Kidney Foundation* for kidney donation awareness, and *Helping Hand* which supported the elderly with a famous cookie bake-off every year. The British in Hong Kong seemed to have maintained the ways of the old land, and Aileen was elegant and charming.

She exemplified the saying "Love is recognition." Learning to notice the community helped me to love my new home and its people. She helped me to 'see' people, like the man who made crickets out of dried grass, the 'bag ladies' and all the wonderful characters going about their ordinary daily lives.

Next was Reverend Murray Rogers, a Methodist Minister. Murray had followed his friend, Charles Freer Andrew, a strong supporter of Mahatma Gandhi, to India where they lived in Gandhi's ashrams from 1950 – 1971. He lived with his wife, Mary and their long-term friend Heather, in the hills in Hong Kong, and they lived a Gandhian lifestyle. Although British, he wore an Indian style kaftan and the women wore saris. When I visited, we would go on silent walks in the hills and Heather would play her simple wooden flute which added to the beauty of the silence. We would enjoy hours of deep and sweet reflection ... and then afternoon tea at the little ashram they had created. Murray lived in deep contemplation, and every word he spoke carried a signal to the heart.

He was a good friend of the Vicar at St John's Cathedral, in the city. He had a key and open access, which was very Christian of the vicar! Sometimes I would meet him for lunch in the Vicar's house and we would have intimate discussions about spirituality. He had a deep interest and rich experience in interfaith work and I learned a great deal from him. Once, when I asked him about love, he responded, "I feel we cannot be too gentle these days. People need our gentle thoughts and feelings and not to be judged." As I travelled back home on the MTR, the local underground, and looked at people's faces, I could feel his words resonate deeply with my being. His words stayed with me for over a decade.

Then, there were Ron and his wife, Veronica, at the *Sek Jai* community in Tai Mei Tuk. After Ron retired from the Police Force, he and Veronica planned to return to England, but just days before their departure they stumbled across an old abandoned house where they found several books with hand written notes. Intrigued, they made enquiries with nearby neighbours and came to know that the house had been used by the *Sek Jai* Community, the Vegetarian Community. This community comprised a group of women who, along with being vegetarian, had discovered the hidden healing power of local herbs. A passion had been awakened. Ron and Veronica hunted down the owners of the house and moved in! They restored it and ran a goat farm.

It turned out that the leader of the Sek Jai Community had been married and experienced a terrible life of labour. She escaped, and in her days of survival, discovered many local herbs that she learned to use for healing. She would have visions of ingredients that could be used and discovered an orchid in the hills that had not yet been listed. A community of women gathered around her, and together they offered healing to the villagers.

In this lovely quaint area you can still see Hong Kong as it was a century ago. There are single clan villages where everyone has the same surname. When I asked an elderly lady how long she had lived there, she replied "Seven generations."

Still on the same route, was Simon Chau Siu Chong. The name on his visiting card just stated 'Activist', but as I observed his activity over time I noted that that truly was an understatement! Simon had set up the Translation Department at the Baptist University in Hong Kong and was working there as a Professor. He also wrote a daily column for a Chinese newspaper, presented a weekly program on radio, and had a very large and active organic community garden, a meditation group and later, a vegetarian society. Today he has a raw food café called 'Greenwoods'.

Simon is smart. He would cook for his weekly meditation group, but it would be *jook*, simple rice porridge. His philosophy was, he did not want people to enjoy it and eat too much; it was just to appease growling tummies so that they could meditate. I always learnt so much from him.

Some years ago, when he was still working full time, I asked if he could translate one of Dadi Janki's books within a month for a book launch in Singapore. His response was, "If I put everything else on hold I can." He did it. And not only that, he packed his backpack with home-grown organic vegetables and cooked for the press at the press conference also!

On Simon's 50th birthday, he gave himself the gift of slowing down. He achieved even more! After living in fast-paced Hong Kong for so many years, I then had to be very mindful when I walked with him. I am reminded of Carl Honoré's words, "Shifting the mind into lower gear can bring better health, inner calm, enhanced concentration and the ability to think more creatively", from *In Praise of Slowness: Challenging the Cult of Speed*.

Interfaith

"If we have no peace, it is because we have forgotten that we belong to each other. Not all of us can do great things but we can do small things with great love. Every time you smile at someone, it is an action of love, a gift to that person, a beautiful thing."

Mother Theresa

It was quite natural in Hong Kong to be involved with people of all faiths. I helped to establish, and became the Chairperson of two interfaith organisations - the first, *Unity for Peace*, and as the reunification of Hong Kong with China loomed over us, the second, a more official organisation, *Hong Kong Network for Religions and Peace*. We organised concerts and visits to the various mosques, gurudwaras, synagogues, temples and churches. We would also meet socially and became best of friends.

In between my work with these two organisations, the Brahma Kumaris also organised three international consciousness-raising programmes. The first was dedicated to the United Nations' International Year of Peace. Held throughout 1986, the *Million Minutes of Peace Appeal* asked for contributions in the form of prayer, positive thoughts and meditation, towards a world peace 'bank'. People in Hong Kong just could not get what we were talking about. A non-monetary bank?! We even had to seek the approval of the Monetary Authority of Hong Kong to place our 'bank' in the city so people could make their contributions. The Brahma Kumaris was recognised by the United Nations for organising the largest programme for the IYP and received seven UN Peace Messenger Awards. The Million Minutes of Peace Appeal reached 88 countries and collected over one billion minutes.

Two years later, *Global Cooperation for a Better World* was launched at the House of Parliament in London. This campaign collected hopes and visions for a better world from hundreds of thousands of people in 129 countries. In Hong Kong we continued the campaign on for another 2 years after its conclusion as there were so many great programmes happening under its banner with refugees, schools, companies and organisations. The Body Shop gave their staff leave for half a day every week so they could go to aged care facilities and orphanages, where they offered gentle hand massages and celebrated birthdays with the people in those facilities. Margaret Tancock, who held the Body Shop franchise, was delighted by the impact on her staff; they were The staff was surprised at meeting people who had lived significant lives, and were enriched hearing their stories. Margaret also organised a *Black Spot Tour* of Hong Kong's most polluted areas for the media, as well as many other great initiatives for this campaign.

The third initiative, *Sharing Our Values for a Better World*, explored what the key values of people were internationally. It then worked on raising awareness of the twelve main values that had been highlighted, and promoted their development at both individual and collective levels. Educators from all religions and all walks of life from around the world then developed the *Association for Living Values Education* which is now active in over 70 countries and is supported by UNESCO and UNICEF. ALIVE provides guiding principles for the development of the whole person including his/her physical, intellectual, emotional and spiritual dimensions. Books have been published in many different languages with activities designed for children from 3 years of age to young adults.

As each of these events culminated in Hong Kong, we organised fairs which attracted thousands of people. There were just a handful of us, but we organised companies to sponsor 40 stalls for different charities, a vegetarian food extravaganza, the painting of a bus, many side events including a Guide Dog demonstration, a Fire Engine display, First Aid training, and entertainment throughout. As Chairperson for these programs, I enjoyed working with a team of wonderful people - movers and shakers representing a very diverse range of backgrounds including environmental protection, business, fashion, education, finance and government. Many of these friendships continue until today.

The Hong Kong Cancer Fund
*"You beat cancer by how you live, why you live
and in the manner in which you live."*

Stuart Scott, Anchor at ESPN, Bristol

For over twenty years, the meditation Centre in Hong Kong conducted weekly classes for people living with cancer. On a monthly basis we brought in others who would offer their skills in various healing modalities. On one occasion, I asked the group, mostly consisting of English expatriates, to close their eyes and think about God and tell me what feelings arose in them. For the majority, the feeling was, "Why me?" or similar. We explored this further and I discovered that most came from a Christian background and had been brought up to believe that if they were good and prayed, nothing bad would happen to them. They felt betrayed and confused, and their faith was totally challenged by what they were going through.

In an endeavour to more deeply understand what these people were experiencing so I could help them without compromising their religious beliefs, I consulted a few priests. I'm afraid their words brought me no comfort. They only supported my own original reason for not believing in God those many years ago, that suffering was God's will. However, thankfully I did witness many Christians in the group strengthen their faith over time and rise above their physical and emotional suffering. Their faces began to glow and appeared transcendent.

I was called to visit patients in hospital and they would also come to our meditation Centre when they were well enough. It was a privilege to share these intimate moments with them. I would carry a few things with me to the hospital, and as if I had been guided in what I had chosen, I would usually have the perfect resource in my little bag of treasures. Sometimes they would ask me to take them 'beyond' with a meditation, and at other times they would want to be right here. On one occasion the perfect song for a caring partner was what was needed.

Meeting Princess Diana

"For those who seek to understand it, death is a highly creative force. The highest spiritual values of life can originate from the thought and study of death."

Elizabeth Kubler-Ross

Meeting Princess Diana

In 1995, Sally Lo, the Founder of the Hong Kong Cancer Fund, was organising one of her spectacular charity balls and invited Princess Diana as the special guest. I had the opportunity with about fifteen women who were living with cancer, to have a small private meeting with Diana. I was surprised that in turn, each one was expressing how they were glad to have cancer as it taught them the value of life and how to live. One of the women was a doctor, and she shared how she had never noticed the beautiful roses growing on her balcony, nor the taste of the coffee and toast she had for breakfast every morning. She began to smell, taste and feel everything around her and live in a state of awe and gratitude for what 'Life' offers. She shared that she was grateful that she had at last learned what it meant to live. Diana was sensitive and gracious and it was a very loving and touching meeting.

As we saw with the outpouring of grief upon her death, Diana had meant so much to so many people. In Hong Kong, people were surprised at their own distress on her passing. Many questioned, "What was it that connected people all over the world, from so many diverse cultures, with Diana?" No doubt it was many aspects - her 'rags to riches' story, her vulnerability, her connection with ordinary people through the many charities she was involved in, shaking hands with AIDS patients at a time when it was so greatly feared, or simply her model celebrity image.

It seems people need to distract themselves from their own lives by following the lives of others. But in this case, the Cinderella fairy tale ended in tragedy. Fairly or not, Prince Charles seemed to get the brunt of it, *"He kissed the princess and became a frog."* (Gaines 98)

Terry Fox Run

"I guess that one of the most important things I've learned is that nothing is ever completely bad, even cancer.
It has made me a better person. It has given me courage and a sense of purpose I never had before. But you don't have to do like I did... wait until you lose a leg or get some awful disease, before you take the time to find out what kind of stuff you're really made of.
You can start now. Anybody can."

Terry Fox

Another great experience I had working with the Hong Kong Cancer Fund, was helping with the *Terry Fox Run* fundraiser. Some of the proceeds from this fundraiser were donated to cancer research at the Brahma Kumaris Global Hospital and Research Foundation in Mount Abu, India.

Terry Fox was a Canadian athlete, humanitarian, and cancer research activist. His right leg was amputated in 1977 due to cancer, and in 1980, with a leg prosthesis, he embarked on an east to west cross-Canada run to raise money and awareness for cancer research. Although the cancer eventually forced him to end his quest after he had run 5,373 kilometres in 143 days, and it ultimately cost him his life, his efforts resulted in a lasting, worldwide legacy and Fox remains a prominent figure in Canadian folklore. His determination united the nation. During his run, families would rush home from school and work to turn on the radio for an update on his efforts. People from all walks of life lent their support and his memory inspires pride in all regions of the country. A 1999 national survey named him, "Canada's greatest hero."

The walk that I participated in covered three country parks from Victoria Peak, through Tai Tam Reservoir to Quarry Bay. Musicians from the Hong Kong Philharmonic Orchestra played at various stops along the way, and I was delighted to have raised one of the largest donations through my sponsors.

Coincidence

"When you live your life with an appreciation of coincidences and their meanings, you connect with the underlying field of infinite possibilities."

Deepak Chopra

Another interesting group I worked with on a monthly basis, was a group of 24 managers of two sister hotels. The General Manager had started to include a short talk or reading, as well as a collective prayer/meditation with them in their daily briefing.

I once asked the managers how they were able to smile and be pleasant all day and if they found it to be a strain. They shared that in their morning briefings, they were invited to share with their colleagues any challenges they were facing that day, like having a family member in hospital or some other challenge. They found that this act gave them a chance to mentally hold a colleague in their hearts with compassion, support them where possible, and not expect too much from them that day.

On one occasion, we took up the topic, Coincidence. To my surprise, all 24 managers were very sure that they had never experienced a coincidence. I clearly explained to them what a coincidence was and gave them 'homework', to observe if in fact it did happen to them after all. When we met again after a month, only one person who worked with me directly had experienced 3 coincidences all connected with me, and none of the others had experienced any. We explored why this might be, and concluded it was because they did not leave anything to chance. In a five star hotel, where people are paying for impeccable service, this was understandable, however I still encouraged them to be open to coincidences as it makes life a lot more fun, and generally achieves more than what our cerebral brain can organise.

After another year, I checked in with them, and by that time they could not imagine not having coincidences. They had become commonplace in their lives.

Etiquette

"No matter how educated, talented, rich or cool you believe you are, how you treat people ultimately tells it all."

Unknown

The hotel was a wonderful place to learn etiquette and I would often take other meditators for the experience. Australians are masters of casualness and equality, which has its own beauty, but it seems to me that manners have been sacrificed in their wake.

At the end of the meditation sessions at the hotel, there would be a vegetarian buffet for all the managers. The etiquette was for them not leave before me. I had been staying on chatting with the General Manager, totally oblivious of this until she pointed it out.

Once, I was playfully challenged to have an arm wrestle with a Brahma Kumari teacher who was visiting Hong Kong. She was also the President of the Philippines Aikido Association. I easily brought her arm down. Of course I realised, that out of respect she would never win over me.

More recently I have been living in Taiwan and trying to imbibe the etiquette of the people here. I find most people to be intelligent, and yet they do not share their opinion unless asked. When they see me struggling with my Chinese, they will stand by me and subtly indicate that they are happy to help if needed. They do not just jump in.

The population of Taiwan is as large as Australia and yet it is half the size of Tasmania, but it never seems to be noisy, nor have I felt crowded, nor experienced being pushed. People queue up patiently and there is calm order everywhere. I am not quite a 'senior', however because I have grey hair, they insist on me taking their seat.

I once observed a staff member on the underground train helping a visually impaired lady board and find a seat. At the lady's destination, another staff member came onto the train to help her alight and take her to the elevator. I have witnessed bank staff coming out from behind the counter to help a man in a wheelchair fill out a form with infinite patience. Even on entering Taipei, the staff at Immigration were extremely helpful and apologetic when my e-gate pass did not work.

Someone made the comment that I am becoming Taiwanese, and thinking of the manners the Taiwanese people have, I replied, "I am trying to be!"

Foodlink Foundation
"Replace Hunger with a Smile."

Vanessa Hwang, Founder of Food link Foundation

There was always a lot of food left after the buffet lunches with the managers of the two hotels, and I enquired what would happen to it. The General Manager told me that they needed to dispose of it all. It seemed to me that there would be enough for at least another 30 people and I was shocked. From this, *Foodlink* was born.

With my humble resources, I brought together a few friends with the idea to sponsor thermo boxes for charities and for each charity to be partnered with a hotel from which leftover food could be collected each day.

Upon investigating the huge extent of waste throughout Hong Kong, together with a serious need for hunger alleviation and nutritional support among lower-income groups, Vanessa Hwang, with the help of her family and friends, established *Foodlink Foundation* in 2010.

The foundation was registered as a charity dedicated to fighting hunger, building self-sufficiency, and fostering nutritional wellness among those in need, while simultaneously reducing food wastage in businesses like hotels.

Currently over 1.6 million people live below the poverty line in Hong Kong. Despite being one of the world's richest cities in terms of GDP per capita, Hong Kong has one of the world's largest wealth gaps. The vision at Foodlink Foundation is to ensure that every needy person has access to a hot, healthy meal by collecting safe-to-eat surplus food from hotels and food and beverage outlets all over the city and delivering it to charities who serve those in need. The role of Foodlink is to connect the supply to the demand as effectively as possible. The benefits are twofold - while reducing hunger they also reduce the pressure on landfills.

Foodlink works with over 112 donors and 100 beneficiary organisations to serve children, the elderly, low-income families, asylum seekers, and the homeless, among others. In 2017, it collected 620 tons of surplus food and provided 1.4 million nutritious meals to those in need, and positively impacted on the 3,382 tons of food waste that was disposed in landfills daily.

Unconditional Trust

"Trust is the glue of life. It's the most essential ingredient in effective communication. It's the foundational principle that holds all relationships."

Stephen Covey

As my term of 3 months in Hong Kong stretched into its 16th year, I was feeling that I could never become a part of the Chinese community. I didn't feel that I was trusted. I began to explore why this was and realised that there was actually a serious trust deficit within the community itself. I wondered "Was this because of the commercial nature of Hong Kong, or because of the Cultural Revolution in the mid-late

1960's where families were systematically turned against each other?" It became an issue for me.

I was planning to spend a weekend alone at the Franciscan Retreat Centre in Cheng Chau, one of Hong Kong's small islands. Coincidentally, a 3 day workshop was being organised by the *Foundation for Community Encouragement* and a friend had been asked to help financially support it. She called me and asked if I would like to attend as she preferred to sponsor people rather than just give cash. It just so happened to be at the same place that I was planning to stay! I had embraced the ideas of the FCE some years earlier when my own community was going through an upheaval, and I found it very insightful and helpful. In fact, I had been promoting their retreat, not realising it was where I was going to be!

Thirty participants were asked to sit in a circle together and only speak if we experienced sweaty palms or palpitations. My immediate feeling was something along the lines of, "Oh no, not more New Age mumbo jumbo!" The palpitations soon started and I was the first to speak... "I have lived in Hong Kong for 16 years and still do not feel trusted." The palpitations became stronger, in fact so strong that I felt others must be able to see them! "I feel hurt", I added. My heart became calm.

We sat in silence for the most part of the two days, and sometimes, perhaps out of boredom or impatience, someone would be tempted to break the silence. However, I could feel when it was not coming from the heart. My take-away, was a personal pledge to have unconditional trust. I realised, trust is a part of my original nature and that if I stopped trusting, I would only have to re-build trust again at a later time. Also, if there is not trust in a community I am a part of, I need to model trust and "Be the change I want to see", to quote Mahatma Gandhi.

Immediately, I was tested on my pledge. I returned to the Meditation Centre in the evening to find a note on the spike at the reception, where anyone could have seen it, "Joe has AIDS. He is in Queen Mary Hospital. Please call him. Tel # .... ". I was surprised - it was a breach of confidentiality, and until this day, neither Joe nor I have ever known who left the note.

I went to the hospital the next day. Joe was a young man of about thirty-five. He had had a very multicultural upbringing and spoke fluent Cantonese and English. His T-cell count was down to 19 and he had multiple lung abscesses, malfunction of the liver, his skin had broken out and he had chronic diarrhoea. Many of these symptoms were possibly because he was taking 112 tablets a day! The medical profession were very much in the experimental stages of medication for AIDS then.

Joe was vibrant, friendly and open. He was quite sure he would die staying in hospital with such a high possibility of infection. Not expecting that he would act on my advice, I suggested (quite irresponsibly, I realised in hindsight!!), that he drop the medication, check out of the hospital, become vegetarian and meditate, as he had nothing to lose. The next day he called me to see if I could suggest somewhere for him to stay. AIDS was new to the world and there was a lot of fear surrounding it. It was not easy asking anyone to take on a person with AIDS. I finally called Toby at the Humanist Association, based on Lantau Island, who really touched me with his response, "Sure, thank you for asking me."

I spoke with the other teachers and students at our Meditation Centre about the situation and asked if they were comfortable to have Joe around. They all responded, "If you say it's OK, then it's OK." I experienced their trust. We were just beginning to be informed that AIDS was not contagious and could not be contracted through shared utensils; however one of the teachers started to doubt this and insisted I ask Joe to use separate utensils. I could not agree and tried to explain that this would be discrimination. Over time all the students got behind the other teacher. They no longer trusted me.

Joe smoked and would apply aftershave before coming to the early morning meditation class. This was another test for everyone. Values of purity and cleanliness are cultivated at our Meditation Centres and many felt these were being compromised by his presence. They couldn't stand the smell and certainly did not want him sitting near them. Joe was gay and his larger than life personality also challenged the quiet sanctity that others sought.

Meanwhile, he was benefiting greatly from coming along. He had an experience of God's unconditional love in meditation and he shared that he could no longer hate his father - possibly a major factor in his illness. After this experience, his health totally improved. He was a great singer and he did some performing. He volunteered at our Centre and was sharing the benefits of meditation with his AIDS Buddy and the medical team looking after him.

I was faced with a dilemma. I felt that turning Joe away from 'God's door' was not at all acceptable and the reasons being given by the students were not substantial enough to warrant it. I was starting to feel stressed and consulted my naturopath. "I have heard of a monastery that employed someone like this and you have one for free!" was Graeme's response.

I began to wonder if I could trust my discernment. Money had started to go missing and many of Joe's stories were not stacking up. I began observing his karma, to try to suss out whether it was appropriate to have him around or not. He had very little in the way of clothing, and I asked one of the students if her husband may have some clothes he did not need. Joe ended up with Giorgio Armani attire! I introduced him to the Hong Kong Cancer Fund and he was employed to help with the Terry Fox Run. He won first prize in the Lucky Draw, a ticket for two to Bali!

However, I came to find out that Joe had been diagnosed as a pathological liar and that he had started borrowing considerable amounts of money from some of the students. I had to start dropping hints to protect other soft hearted students, "You know Joe is going through a hard time. We all want to help him but the policy at the Centre is that we do not lend or borrow money from each other. So in case Joe happens to ask you, please keep this in mind. If you do lend him anything, I do not even want to know about it as it has nothing to do with the Centre."

The next thing, I received a message that Joe was on remand for possession of drugs. He now had a partner and his partner told me Joe had tried to overdose on heroin in hospital. As he did not die he was charged with possession. More stress! I could not tell the students about this. I would steal away to the prison to visit him, making up some story about where I was going. Being dishonest was totally out of character for me and my stress levels increased even more.

It was my first experience in a prison environment and I found it very distressing. I sat amongst mothers, wives and children as they waited for their 15 minutes with their 'numbered' family member. I pondered how they could retain, or in many cases, rescue their relationships under these circumstances.

Prison was a great challenge for Joe as he was one of the first inmates with AIDS. He experienced blatant discrimination from the staff that were afraid of him. When he was released from remand, I organised for him to do a television interview to highlight the discrimination he was experiencing. I had realised how otherwise good people, discriminate against others when they are overcome by fear. It is not generally due to dislike or hatred.

Along with money, 'things' started to disappear from the Centre, and finally I felt I needed to ask Joe to stop coming. I maintained my relationship with him outside the Centre, but I could no longer expose everyone else to the risk. I was aware of how people let their guard down, feeling so safe in our rarefied atmosphere. I have since made it a point to encourage people to be mindful of their valuables even at our Centres.

During my next visit to Madhuban, I spoke to Dadi Prakashmani, the then Administrative Head of the Brahma Kumaris, about trust. We were driving and she responded, "We can trust most people 95%. For example, we trust that our driver will take us safely to our destination. However we need to check with him to see that he is OK, whether he needs tea, or to stop for a break."

I realised that we often give responsibility to others and then have high expectations of 100% delivery. It is kinder to care and support them in fulfilling their responsibility. I also realised that what Dadi said was realistic. When we say we do not trust, it is usually because we expect

100% trustworthiness and yet we ourselves are also not that trustworthy. I would prefer people to only trust me 95% and allow me some leeway, as I am not perfect.

When I returned to Hong Kong, I was told that a very close friend had said something unkind about me. Previously I would have thought, "See, you cannot trust anyone, even your closest friends." Instead, I thought "No problem, that is her 5%. I hope she will offer the same to me when I need it. "

* * * *

8

More of Asia

Philippines
*"In character, in manner, in style, in all things,
the supreme excellence is simplicity."*

Henry Wadsworth Longfellow

Just as I had travelled to Tokyo from Hong Kong for four days and ended up staying three months, I travelled to Manila, intending to stay for just two weeks, and stayed for three months, starting a BK Meditation Centre there.

Marge had come across the Brahma Kumaris whilst studying dance in San Francisco. On a visit home she shared what she had learned with her family and friends. They were interested to know more, so when I arrived from the airport we started straight away.

I stayed above a restaurant owned by Marge's friends, and soon Sister Rajni arrived. There was a hairdressing salon downstairs next to the restaurant and the staff who worked in the salon were from far away villages; they too stayed on the same floor as us. They cooked fish, which was a challenge for Sister Rajni and I. She had been vegetarian from birth, so it was particularly uncomfortable for her. She would cover her nose and go into the kitchen with a burning incense stick whenever she needed to get something.

The salon staff were kind and generous people. I used to sit with them and tell them about meditation in the evenings after they had come home, showered and changed into their pyjamas. I loved the family feeling and their sweet simplicity. I was concerned however, that they believed everything I said, and was aware of how vulnerable, simple and innocent people can be and how easily they can be cheated and used.

After Sister Rajni left, I transformed the downstairs *Tree of Life* restaurant into a vegetarian restaurant and created a new menu. I taught the cooks Chinese, Indonesian and Western vegetarian cooking. Vegetarianism was not popular in the Philippines at that time so it was not a huge success. However, the restaurant managed to stay open for a few years. The chefs were not vegetarian themselves, so they probably also lacked the passion for cooking. When the restaurant was closed for a day, all the staff would gather in it and have a great time together. They did not need to go out anywhere; just being together was enough joy for them.

I enjoyed going to a wide variety of places to teach meditation, including the Philippines National Assembly, the *Batasang Pambansa*. It was 1983, the Marcos era. Before we started the training, I introduced the lesson of the Eight Spiritual Powers to the Secretary General. As he stood in front of the picture I was using to explain, he said, "If I had realised this before, I would have lived my whole life differently." He then 'ordered' all 800 staff, from the gardeners to the members of Cabinet, to attend a three-hour session with me. Even their leave was cancelled for this. I also taught at offices, factories, department stores, organisations for the disabled and villages.

The Rebel Meeting

*"Every organisation should tolerate rebels
who tell the emperor he has no clothes."*

Colin Powell

On one of my visits to Manila in 1992, I was introduced to Gringo, Lt. Col. Gregory Honasan and other former Generals who had helped to overthrow the Marcos government in a peaceful revolution in 1986. The government had just granted them amnesty. They certainly changed my impression of what a 'rebel' is. As former high ranking military personnel, they were dignified, intelligent and well mannered. Not at all what I had expected of rebels. We met in a house outside the city and a few of the Generals were on guard, as they were still not feeling secure. Gringo asked me, ... yes little me! ... "Should we overthrow the government? The people are asking me to do it. They are suffering because of corruption even more now than they did under Marcos. It is not that Ramos is worse, but he is not removing the corruption, and it just grows by itself. We have tanks. We can do it if we choose to."

"But who is without corruption? Who could lead the country? Why take the law into your hands when you cannot change what is. You have already overthrown one government, and as you say, nothing has changed." was my response. Gringo and his team had overthrown Marcos in the People's Power Revolution. The people on the street presented flowers to the soldiers. For the most part it was without violence. In fact, Gringo claimed that less people died than in Gandhi's revolution.

I spent several hours with the officers and we had an in depth discussion as to what would happen if they were to remove the current political party. We agreed that there was probably not anyone capable of removing the corruption, and also no one better to lead the country. I implored them to capitalise on the spirituality of the people to work towards nonviolent change.

By chance, that morning Senator Leticia Shahani, the sister of President Ramos, had come for breakfast. She had gifted her brother, President Ramos, with the *Moral Recovery Program* and was trying to help him dismantle some of the corruption, which had become so endemic in the society. I understood how hard it was to remove corruption as a friend had been working with President Vincent Fox in Mexico aiming to do the same there. The Ministers were receiving threats on their families by the big cartels and it was a huge uphill battle. I understood the challenge.

South Korea

*"Wisdom is knowing we are all One.
Love is what it feels like
and Compassion is what it acts like."*

Ethan Walker

I have had the fortune of visiting South Korea on several occasions. It is a beautiful country and when the people are thirsty for spirituality, they are really thirsty. On my first trip, around 1984, I conducted a two-day retreat and about sixteen people sat cross-legged on the floor and listened to me for two days! I was amazed. The BK sister, who translated, also cooked morning tea, lunch and afternoon tea, all in between translating. It was like magic. How did she do that?!!!

If I had been conducting the retreat, I would have had the vegetables chopped and the refreshments pre-made. I was amazed that at the end of the day, we would shop for the next day without any pre-arrangements. It was so cold that the vegetables would freeze sitting in the car overnight. I was grateful for the wonderful under-floor heating system inside! Jenny seemed to manage everything so easily and lightly. It left me thinking that perhaps some of us think and plan too much. She just flowed with everything, as I often see people do in Asia. And it all seems to work!

On another occasion, I was invited by the Manhae Foundation to an interfaith conference in Seoul. The conference was supported by the government and was mostly attended by Buddhist leaders from Vietnam, Mongolia, Taiwan, Sri Lanka and all the countries in between. We were treated as VIP guests and accommodated at the five star Lotte Hotel. Buses took us to temples all over the country where we were greeted like royalty. At one temple, hundreds of Korean women dressed in colourful *hanbok* (traditional dress), lined both sides of the street and applauded as we drove in. We discovered on the last day, that we had been over-endowed with our titles. I was being introduced in Korean as the 'International Leader of Yoga'. Another participant, not even a priest, was being introduced as a Bishop!

I have a great respect for Buddha as a teacher. His teachings give a lot of clarity about the workings of the mind, and I have gained a lot from various Buddhist teachers. I was easily able to share my enthusiasm for the teachings with the Buddhist masters at the retreat and I became known amongst them as Buddha's daughter!

'Coincidentally', the day after this particular conference, Dadi Janki arrived in South Korea. I enjoyed helping out with her visit. My responsibility was to take notes. Having gone to bed after 11pm, she came to me after our meditation at 4am the next morning. I thought she would be taking rest, but she wanted me to 'catch' the depth of her morning's insight about karma. "When a karmic situation is presenting itself, do not let it catch hold of you, move on", she explained. I understood then how it was, that even when she was very ill, she could pick herself up and fly to the other side of the world to address large gatherings of people. At 103 years of age, she was still doing this.

On yet another occasion, I was invited to a United Nations NGO-DPI conference calling for a civil-society-led 'Coalition for Global Citizenship'. The concept of Global Citizenship finally put the BKs into the mainstream of UN engagement. We had often felt that due to our spiritual perspectives, we were on the fringe. At the conference, the response to questions about global concerns like poverty, was that we need to see ourselves as a global community. It was agreed that this was the way the 17 Sustainable Development Goals adopted, would be met. The realisation we belong to each other and are one family is at the root of spirituality and is the message of most spiritual organisations.

Below is the list of the 17 Sustainable Development Goals. We still have such a long way to go to realise them...

1. No Poverty
2. Zero Hunger
3. Good Health and Well-being
4. Quality Education
5. Gender Equality
6. Clean Water and Sanitation
7. Affordable and Clean Energy
8. Decent Work and Economic Growth
9. Industry, Innovation, and Infrastructure
10. Reducing Inequality
11. Sustainable Cities and Communities
12. Responsible Consumption and Production
13. Climate Action
14. Life Below Water
15. Life On Land
16. Peace, Justice, and Strong Institutions
17. Partnerships for the Goals

The Brahma Kumaris World Spiritual University in India and its affiliate programs around the world have been working on many of these issues for decades, engaging people in various ways including professionals from twenty specific fields like Education, Media, Health, Women, Science, Agriculture, and Youth. Some of the programs have included conducting free meditation in prisons and schools, health camps including eye camps, values education, training in organic farming and yogic farming, promotion of road safety awareness in villages, towns and cities all over the world, and drawing on the spirit of volunteerism.

The principles of Global Citizenship have been particularly evident in the construction of one of the Brahma Kumari's flagship projects, India One, a 1MW thermal solar power station constructed in Abu Road,

Rajasthan. Funded by the German and Indian governments and donors from all over the world, this solar site provides the energy needs for 25,000 people who attend the Brahma Kumaris residential programs in Abu Road as well as delivering electricity off the grid for a further 10,000 residents of the Abu community. It was accomplished with the help of volunteer engineers, project managers and solar power experts from all over the world and provided employment for local people. The project specifically supported people in acquiring technical expertise, performance capability and managerial competence.

Working closely with its sister organisation, the World Renewal Spiritual Trust, the Brahma Kumaris were recognised as a Scientific and Industrial Research Organisation by the Indian Ministry of Science and Technology in 2011.

I was inspired by Golo Pilz's courage. India One was his brainchild. A carpenter by training, and yet he actually helped to direct a lot of the construction of the solar sites. He dedicated almost 20 years to the development of solar energy in the main campus as well as in Retreat Centres and Centres throughout India. If any Centre in India wants to install solar power they contact our Solar Department and our brothers travel there and install it at the Centre's cost. I was grateful for this as so often there are power failures throughout India. Wherever solar power was installed I was always guaranteed hot water, and at least basic amenities. In contrast to this, I was having a root canal filling with a dentist in Jaipur. When the power failed he continued with a torch!

* * * * *

9

The Happiest Time of My Life

The Right Place, The Right Time
"There is never just one thing that leads to success for anyone. I feel it is always a combination of passion, dedication, hard work, and being in the right place at the right time."

Lauren Conrad

Wilton, The BK Centre for Spiritual Learning, Illawarra, Sydney

In 2002, I was welcomed into Sydney by not just one, but two rainbows stretching across the sky; a spectacular sight from the plane! I was returning to Australia. After 22 years based in Hong Kong and travelling throughout Asia I wondered if it would take time to settle back in. Surprisingly, not a bit! In 2002 I had been asked to coordinate our Retreat Centre in Wilton, on the edge of the Southern Highlands, around 1.5 hours south of Sydney CBD.

After the pollution and noise of Hong Kong, it was absolute bliss! The smell of the eucalyptus, the sound of the birds, frogs, crickets and cattle, fresh air and early meditation by the open log fire followed by freshly brewed chai made with freshly ground spices was a delight to the body and soul. It could not have been more of a contrast to life in Hong Kong. Stopping to smell the roses became a practical experience for me and I would become intoxicated with their rich, deep scent as I walked the small stone path to the dining room.

There had not been a gardener at the Retreat Centre for some time, and they had suffered a severe drought, so the gardens looked very stressed. I felt like a Communist as I strongly urged everyone to put down their pens and take up a rake or shovel! In return for our small gesture, a 'garden gnome' arrived who planted thousands of native plants, trees and grasses. This would ensure that much less water and mowing would be required.

Robin also took on the job of renovating the Centre, which included restoring the main dining complex which white ants had been living on for years. The main hall, which had only been used for Irish *Ceilis*, social gatherings, and was occupied by a ghost, came next. The hall was transformed into a beautiful space with under-floor heating, stage and theatre lighting. Having the capacity to seat 250 people, it has put the Retreat Centre 'back on the map' and has been busy every weekend since.

Besides all this work, we organised a few concerts, two of which were titled, Euphoria. It was how we all felt, living as a community and working in unison for the greater good of whoever would benefit.

The UK music group, *Bliss* came in during their Australian tour and we worked day and night to get the outdoor stage and grounds ready.

I had to go to a hire company for a pneumatic drill. What a sight - me in a sari teaching the brothers how to use it! I remember being brought to tears when I stood back and saw the way in which we were all working together, with so much harmony and bliss. There were wonderful cookies and cakes, great coffee, and each and every one was putting in 100% of themselves.

In order to raise money to build a stupa at their nearby Retreat Centre, a group of Buddhists came in to cook vegetarian food. They then offered chanting from the stage which mesmerized everyone. Greg, our architect, had a queue all day for the 'gold coin chai', and Matthew freely gave out his delicious sticky buns. Others were doing Virtuescope readings, bushwalks, organic gardening, lectures and cooking classes.

With all this good energy, the retreats we offered were over-booked. Not only did the Retreat Centre thrive, but we did too. I could not stop having laughing fits, even during our classes, but the Centre residents were all very patient and happy to wait while I composed myself.

My time there was the happiest time of my life. For the first few months, I felt so light. I had been away for a long time and it was as if my karmic slate was clean; every interaction was light and easy. I kept feeling that something amazing was going to happen, then after several weeks I realised that something amazing **was** happening!

I put it down to being in the right place at the right time. It felt magical. It had been my best experience of community, and each moment was being surpassed by the next. If I was working in the office, I would get a call from the kitchen, "Coffee?", "Juice?" There were cakes made by beautiful mums who had volunteered to keep the chai and cookies coming for the workers, and homemade ice cream made of fresh liquorice or mango.

Dadi Janki also visited, and we had an outdoor lecture and an awesome sunset meditation program. She was driven around on a golf buggy, Sister Jayanti standing behind her, her sari blowing in the wind. It was a lovely sight.

And then, Dadi asked me to return to Hong Kong. Ohhh!!!!! I was not ready for that! In fact, I had been thinking how much I was going to enjoy this place now that all the renovations had been completed.

* * * * *

10

Boomerang Back to Asia

Cambodia

"Money is like love; it kills slowly and painfully the one who withholds it, and enlivens the other who turns it on his fellow man."

Khalil Gibran

I returned to Hong Kong for another year. However, it really seemed that my time there was over. From 1997, I had been visiting developing countries in Indo-China, Vietnam, Cambodia and Laos. I had begun to find living in Hong Kong challenging. Observing the disparity between the wealth of that country and the lack of wealth of poorer countries had become hard for me. Resources were being wasted in Hong Kong, whereas in poorer countries, the people made use of every small item.

In my teenage years, I avoided wealthy people, believing them to be rich at the expense of the poor. It was destiny that I ended up living in Hong Kong amongst many of the wealthiest people there. The majority of them were kind and caring, and often did a lot to help those in need. In fact, some of the people I met in Hong Kong are among the best people I have ever met. There was no doubt that they were wealthy because they had been great donors of wealth in the past – that is the Law of Karma!

I left Hong Kong and moved on to Phnom Penh, Cambodia. Our Centre had been operating there for just 5 years.

During the genocide carried out by the Khmer Rouge regime, Cambodia lost a quarter of its population of 7 million, mostly the educated. In fact anyone who could read and write was a target. Many more fled as refugees. I worked with a wonderful group of young people while I lived there. At hardly 25 years of age, these young people worked as headmasters in schools and colleges and filled positions way beyond their education and experience. They rose to a challenge, and through overseas scholarships were able to contribute greatly to Cambodia's development. They would wear t-shirts quoting Gandhi, "Be the change you want to see."

We stayed in a traditional Cambodian wooden house and I enjoyed sitting on the balcony watching the monsoon rains, especially the children who would innocently take their clothes off and play.

In Phnom Penh, the Brahma Kumaris catered to a relatively small population and were already fairly well known, so eventually I decided to move on to Siem Reap. Meanwhile, Tom, my husband, who had also been helping at the Wilton Retreat Centre in Australia where I had been based, arrived in Cambodia to replace one of the teachers. She then decided to stay on, so Tom and I set up activities in Siem Reap together.

Siem Reap

*"Traveling – it leaves you speechless,
then turns you into a storyteller."*

Ibn Battuta

There is a huge tourist population in Siem Reap. It has a deep spiritual history, so we were encouraged to open a meditation Centre there. We arrived with just a suitcase each, but were fortunate to know

Sambo, who had worked with UNESCO and organised sponsorship of training for Khmer teachers, of the Living Values Education Programme. At the time, Sambo lived between Phnom Penh and Siem Reap.

The Khmer Rouge had moved into her hometown, Phnom Penh, capital of Cambodia, in 1975. At first the Khmer people were happy to see them. The civil war had ended, the Americans had left, and these were their own people. They innocently assumed that order would return. However within hours, the 3 million inhabitants were ordered to leave their homes and go to the countryside to grow rice, even though it was not yet the season for this.

Sambo had recently graduated as a lawyer and married. She had no idea of the terror the family were entering into as they joined the throngs of people on the road. She wore her nice shoes, packed noodle packets to distribute on their journey and was in a good mood. The reality slowly became obvious to her. For the next 4 years, in order to stay alive, she had to play dumb. The Khmer Rouge targeted the educated. When given something to read she would look at it upside down. She was not able to let on that she was literate. All people with glasses were executed. Her father was asked to build a fence. He built it straight. This made the Khmer Rouge suspicious and he was tortured and killed in Sambo's former secondary school in Tuol Sleng, which had been converted into Security Prison 21. Her happy memories have been overlaid forever.

In spite of this, in 2006 through UNESCO, Sambo opened her heart to the opportunity of working, together with Valerie from France, with former Khmer Rouge soldiers in Koh Sla, Kampot Province. They were the last stronghold to surrender. After 25 years of isolation, only one person in the community of 650 was literate. They were grateful for the willingness of the facilitators to travel so far, stay with them, and help them move on from their trauma.

Siem Reap is at the centre of the Hindu-Buddhist Empire. It was known as the Angkor Empire from 802 – 1431. From the 11th – 13th centuries it was the largest pre-industrial urban centre in the world and spanned Cambodia, Laos, Myanmar, Thailand and Vietnam. More than a thousand temples in Siem Reap Province surround Angkor Wat, the City of Temples. It was originally constructed as a Hindu temple dedicated to god Vishnu. However, it was gradually transformed into a Buddhist temple towards the end of the 12th century.

Charities in Siem Reap

"When we want to help the poor, we usually offer them charity. Most often we use charity to avoid recognising the problem and finding the solution for it. Charity becomes a way to shrug off our responsibility. But charity is no solution to poverty. Charity only perpetuates poverty by taking the initiative away from the poor. Charity allows us to go ahead with our own lives without worrying about the lives of the poor. Charity appeases our consciences."

Muhammad Yunus

Having been exposed to the poverty and other needs in Cambodia, I was keen to make a difference, especially where NGOs appeared to need greater assistance. I shared my experiences with friends and many began to contribute funds through me. However, after 3 years I realised that things were not as they seemed. The 'needy' NGOs were often being kept that way in order to draw in more cash. It was a mistake.

A vast amount of charity is given in Cambodia, and there are over 350 NGOs in Siem Reap alone. I often hear people say they wish to give to charities most in need. But, I have realised it is all a ploy. There are some amazing NGOs in Cambodia run by people with big, kind and strong hearts - They need strong hearts! In my experience, these were usually the ones that were doing well and used contributions honestly.

I worked directly with NGOs, providing volunteers and training. Later, I discovered there were paedophiles in NGOs run by foreigners who I had come to trust, and huge amounts of money were being misappropriated in some of the Khmer run NGOs. It was heart wrenching to pull away, knowing that nothing could be done to help the children that were being used as pawns in adult games. I felt there was absolutely nothing I could do. Corruption is endemic in every sphere of life there. My eyes had opened.

> *"When I give food to the poor, they call me a saint. When I ask why the poor have no food, they call me a communist."*
>
> Dom Helder Camar

On the positive side, I did manage to start two small enterprises. One was a mushroom farm in one of the orphanages that would then supply to hotels. The other was the *Khmer Independent Life Team, KILT*.

Khmer Independent Life Team creating 'Jewels of Peace'

I had come across Bel and a group of people who had been affected by land mines. They were performing at some five-star hotels but were being managed by someone who pocketed the generous donations they received and barely kept them alive in terms of providing food and accommodation. I invited a friend from Hong Kong to come over and teach them Chinese knotting, a craft she had taken up as a hobby. She brought with her some semi-precious stones and strings, and we rented a hotel room as a workshop. We then rented a house where the artists-to-be built a workshop. We also bought nice clean clothes for them, and arranged exhibitions for their creations in a few hotels. The 'Jewels of

Peace' were really beautiful, sold well and brought dignity to these new entrepreneurs.

Although they found it hard to maintain relationships with the hotels without me supporting them after I eventually left Cambodia, they had developed creative skills and adapted their talents to local resources, and today are still selling their creations at the local market.

The Peace Café
"Avoiding meat and dairy is the single biggest way to reduce your impact on Earth."

The Guardian, 31st May 2018

Peace Café, Siem Reap

Whilst in Siem Reap, I received another chance to transform a restaurant, making it completely vegetarian. The Singing Tree Café was almost vegetarian. Along with holding regular meditation sessions at the Café, I worked with the owners on many wonderful projects including organising a climate change event in 2009. This was another of those magical events where things just happened against all odds.

Only a few weeks out from the annual 350.org awareness-raising week, Tom and I decided we should do something to support the project. We agreed on a ride with 350 cyclists from the town to Angkor Wat, finishing at the Singing Tree Café for refreshments. Normally there would have been a $20 surcharge for foreigners to enter the Temple area, but with powerful positive thoughts, we managed to get permission for all participants to cycle to the entrance of Angkor Wat. It was a very grand event and it was great to get Cambodia on the map for this international event.

Climate Change Event with 350 Cyclists, Siem Reap

Some months later, tired of dealing with all the irregularities within the charities we had been working with, we decided to take over the Singing Tree Café. The former owners wanted to sell. We used the balance of contributed funds, and made the Café available to all charities to hold their events. A Fair Trade shop was opened for the really great enterprises that were working with local artisans to re-develop skills lost during the genocide, and we renamed the café, the Peace Café.

Behind the Café was a two-bedroom house. I set up an outdoor kitchen for Tom and me as we preferred to cook our own food. An old monkey used to come and steal my chickpeas and other tasty morsels from the cupboard, so until I bought a lock, I had to be on the lookout! We also learnt that a water pistol was enough to scare him away. Tom, being an avid bird watcher, built a huge aviary behind the Meditation Hut for singing birds that would delight everyone with their beautiful melodies. I would not normally like to have caged birds but there were boys everywhere with slingshots, so the birds were safer, and they had a very large area in which to fly. We taught an Asian Myna bird to talk.

He was not interested in going anywhere. Even when we took him to the huge Butterfly Garden so he could fly free, he would just sit on our shoulders and chew our ears. We didn't mind, but when he sat on other people's shoulders, some were freaked out!

The Peace Café became a venue for Living Values Education training, permaculture training, performances by the Khmer Independent Life Team, and a disco for older children who were being cared for by some of the charities. Being young teenagers, they wanted to go out at night, but there was nowhere safe for them to go. Brad, a volunteer from the US, offered to organise a dance evening every Saturday night and 40-50 young people enjoyed dancing and half priced ice-cream and cookies.

Monk Chat
"Three things cannot hide for long, the Moon, the Sun, and the Truth."

Buddha

Monk Chat: Me with the Monks, Siem Reap

I was very comfortable interacting with the monks. I taught meditation in some of the spas of five-star hotels, and asked some monks to partner with me. I felt that tourists would expect a more authentic

Khmer experience with a local Cambodian and to learn about Buddhism. Most of the monks had been killed by the Khmer Rouge and I found that I was needing to teach Buddhism and Buddhist meditation to the monks so that they could then share their teachings with the guests.

At the Peace Café, we held a weekly 'Monk Chat' and invited Buddhist monks to share their knowledge of Buddhism and their Buddhist life. Sometimes visitors to Cambodia became confused seeing the monks eating meat or smoking in the Café. This has become a regular practice in Asia. But before judging, perhaps we should reflect on the cultures of other faiths where religious leaders also smoke and drink. I am not sure why we expect Buddhists to be any different.

Living in a small place, it did not take long for us to become a source of information and networkers for people moving to, and visiting Siem Reap, especially being in the Café. On one occasion, I was asked to organise a meditation session for a well-known American company. As usual, I felt it was good to partner with a Buddhist meditation teacher and to hold the program at a temple. One of the monks told me about a nun at a temple 25 kilometres from the town.

We made an appointment to meet at the temple the following week. When I arrived there was a coffin in the middle of the meditation room. A rather amusing conversation followed ...

"Someone has died?" I enquired.

"Yes, the nun who teaches meditation has died. I forgot to tell you. You can meet her wife."

"Wife! She was a nun, a woman?"

"Yes."

Hmmm ... what was going on? "Oh, you mean 'Vice', as in Vice-President?"

"Yes."

OK, so that was cleared!

"How long will the coffin be here?"

"For one month. People need to come from far away to pay their respects."

(I doubted the body was still inside as there was no smell and no ice.)

"I do not think the American visitors would be comfortable to have a coffin in the meditation room."

"Oh that is OK; we will remove it straight away!"

… I do not know what happened to the paying of respects!

Actually, when I say 'nun', I need to explain that there are actually no ordained nuns in Cambodia. There are many communities of women, mostly older women and widows, living adjacent to the temples. They are called *dounji*, but they are not ordained. They have their hair shaved, dress in white, and observe eight or ten Buddhist precepts. Even though their devotion to the Buddhist path is strong, they generally perform various menial temple functions, including sweeping the temple grounds, cooking and washing the monks robes.

In Buddhist countries there are monks, laymen and laywomen. In some Buddhist countries, and in some Buddhist sects, there are ordained nuns. In most Buddhist countries women work hard to be acknowledged for being worthy of ordination, just as many women in the Catholic and other faith traditions do. Although many claim there has never been a tradition of ordained nuns in Cambodia, Laos or Thailand, there is much evidence to the contrary. An ordained nun is required to ordain a nun, and so some temples allow, and sometimes even encourage, their nuns to travel abroad for ordination.

Love … or Torture?
"Please don't kill me with your kindness."

Jagdish Chander

I am eternally grateful to my parents for providing security for me throughout my life. Had it not been for their acceptance and love I could never have lived such an adventurous life.

A comfort zone is a psychological state where things feel familiar to a person, where they are at ease and feel some control over their environment; the experience of anxiety and stress are minimised. In the back of my mind I was aware that I always had a home to return to where I would receive every kind of assistance that I needed. Without being conscious of this, it has provided me with the security to be carefree and to take risks, even up until today. I am over sixty years of age and many at my age are starting to question their future security as their health begins to deteriorate. As I have never had thoughts of insecurity, it has not come to my mind yet to think like this. My blessed good health is of course also a major factor in this thinking. I am still as adventurous as ever and am stretching my comfort zones more and more.

Another reason I feel I have been so open to adventure, is the concern I've felt about being attached to comfort zones. I realised that these could easily grow if I did not keep moving out of them. Too often I have heard people turn down wonderful opportunities because it is too hot, too cold, too noisy, too many mosquitos etc. I appreciate the independence gained by staying beyond comfort zones.

I was however, once really tested in this. On an invitation from a Thai sister with whom I had lived while in Hong Kong, Tom and I travelled to Thailand. Before reaching paved road, we travelled for eight hours by bus from Siem Reap to the border. Because of regular heavy monsoons, the road was full of potholes and vehicles would drive where the holes were shallower, regardless of the on-coming traffic! There was no air-conditioning and as it was the dry hot season the road was superdusty. We had to keep the windows closed otherwise we wouldn't have been able to breathe from the dust.

On arrival at the border, my white clothes were brown. We passed through Immigration by foot, and then hopped on a bus towards Noi's home. To get the next bus we had to cross the highway with our luggage in tow! Finally, as we neared our destination, we called to see if Noi had arranged accommodation at a hotel as I had requested. "You must stay with me and my mother", she lovingly pleaded. "No, I am really dirty, hot and tired. I need a clean and comfortable room with air conditioning", I said. She insisted, "You will be very comfortable in my home!!"

When we finally arrived around 10pm, we discovered her house had been demolished!! That's right ... no house at all! We stumbled across the rubble to find there was one bed in a makeshift tent, from which she had removed her old mum. I was to sleep there, even though I insisted that it was not right. Using the light of our mobile phones, we stumbled to the bathing area; a cement tank of water and a scoop. Tom went soft on Noi's loving hospitality and did not want to upset her by going to a hotel. But when we went to bed the second night, I found her mum's false teeth in my bed!! In the morning I got my way and we moved to a wonderful cottage in the National Park ... Aahhh!!!!!

On another occasion, in Patna, India, many years later, there was a complete electricity failure and I was wondering how I was going to sleep in the very hot weather in a room on the balcony where it was not safe to open the door or windows. I thought I would suffocate. I was contemplating asking the sisters in the Centre if I could go to a hotel, which I already knew would not be a good experience. As a last resort I tried the air-conditioner which was on Phase 3 electricity. Miraculously it worked, even though neither fans nor lights were working! Some fairy was looking after me.

Pakistan
"Haji Ali taught me the most important lesson I've ever learned in my life ... We Americans think you have to accomplish everything quickly. We're the country of thirty-minute power lunches and two-minute football drills. Haji Ali taught me to share three cups of tea, to slow down and make building relationships as important as building projects."
Greg Mortenson

Visa photo for Pakistan

On a study trip to India from Cambodia, I was invited to spend some months in Pakistan to see how the people there responded to our meditation. Although hesitant, I trust my own good karma and this helped me to accept the invitation. Of course, we never know what past karma we have with a certain place; however, I checked in with my intuition and felt it was clear. There had been many kidnappings in Karachi, which was where I was to stay. I rationalised that it was good to have this experience in order to build my resilience as the world is moving more and more towards a state of insecurity.

I stayed with one of the few Hindu ladies living there who had taken to the practice of Raja Yoga. Sheila was a doctor. She taught doctors and was very smart. She organised for me to teach meditation at a few colleges and it was well received. Because she was a little nervous of my going out alone, my limit was the small shopping area near our apartment.

Karachi was once a thriving international metropolis. I found the Pakistani people to be sweet and gentle. They welcomed me with enthusiasm and were very helpful. After living in Cambodia, a land of smiles, it was hard to suppress my smile. It is not really in the Pakistani culture for women to smile at strangers, but when I did, they looked relieved that they could be 'normal' and they would usually give me a broad happy grin.

Having read *Three Cups of Tea: One Man's Mission to Promote Peace ... One School at a Time* by Greg Mortenson, I was not surprised by their kind and gentle ways. In his book, Greg talks about his transition from being a registered nurse and mountain-climber to a humanitarian committed to reducing poverty and elevating education for girls in Pakistan and Afghanistan. It may sound naïve, however one wonders whether his suggestion of supporting the people living in remote mountainous areas in Pakistan, rather than bombing them with drones, would have prevented some of the terrorism that now spans the globe after the bombing of that area.

On my first day alone in the apartment, Sheila had arranged for three people to visit. Having stayed in Malaysia I was anticipating the 'call to prayer'. I was also ready and waiting for my guests. However, no one came. I later found out that what I thought was the call to prayer was the doorbell and I had not answered the door. I was waiting for the usual 'ding-dong'!

Teaching meditation in Pakistan required sensitivity. I generally used to sit in silent meditation with a picture of the light, and only answered questions that the students asked, rather than 'teaching' anything.

I was to attend a talk by a Hindu man at a community centre with Sheila. He became ill and I was asked to speak instead. My talk on Raja Yoga generated a keen interest and about ten people came to Sheila's home the next evening to learn more. They were due to come again the next night, however one man came early and the others came very late. It is against the law in Pakistan for a woman to be alone in a house with a man they are not married to, and I realised I had gotten myself into 'a situation'. To make things worse, there was a blackout, which often occurred in Karachi. I had learnt where to find the backup light, however I did not want to bump into this man in the dark so I just stayed quietly where I was not being able to see a thing! He seemed like a decent man and I was not too worried, however I was relieved when the light came on and the others arrived!

I was cautious to not use any Indian references when I introduced meditation to the local people. When I was asked what the practice was called, I told them it was Soul Conscious meditation. I made a mental note that this was its new name! When asked where it came from, fortunately I could truthfully say, "Pakistan!" As much as possible I tried to blend in. Hindi is very similar to Urdu, so I spoke Hindi when I was out. I also wore a *shalvakameez* with a head cover. But still, people would refer to me as "Madam". Our lovely Muslim home-helper would call me, "Pakistani Madam."

The Muharram festival was coming up. I had seen self-flagellation before in the Philippines and in Malaysia, so I chose to avoid it. We also wanted to avoid the animal sacrifices, which were to happen on the streets. Instead, we organised a small retreat in someone's spacious home and hid ourselves away for three days of silence. Muslims and Hindus dropped in over the holiday period and joined us in our sweet silence.

The origins of yoga and meditation are said to be a small seal in the museum at Mohenjo-Daro, and I was keen to visit. The seal is of someone sitting cross-legged. By chance the lady I was staying with came from a village nearby and I managed to get a ride there from Hyderabad after attending her cousin's wedding on Christmas Day. I was in Pakistan on Christmas Day teaching Christmas carols to Hindu children at a Hindu wedding in a Muslim country!

Mohenjo-Daro is said to have been built around 2500 BCE, and was one of the largest settlements of the ancient Indus Valley civilisations. It was one of the world's earliest major cities, contemporaneous with the civilisations of ancient Egypt and Mesopotamia. It was abandoned in the 19th century BCE as the Indus Valley civilisation declined and was not rediscovered until the 1920s. Considering it the place of origin of meditation, I tried to sit and meditate, but instead, I became a bit of a spectacle.

At the small airport, ready to leave, a flight delay was announced. I started to engage with the other passengers. One young boy was related to the Prime Minister at the time, and was very astute. Another was a huge man with a big beard. "What do you do?" I enquired. "I am a hunter," he responded. "Oh, I am a vegetarian!" It could easily have been a comic strip as he was so big and I so small in comparison.

When I took my seat on the plane to fly back to Cambodia, I breathed a sigh of relief... Three months, and I did not get kidnapped!

* * * * *

11

A Big Project

The Future of Power
*"World power has shifted from country to country.
For a long time it has been in America,
and is now shifting back to Asia. We first concentrated this project in India to deeply explore its historical use of soft power – rich in spirituality,
value and cultures. The question is whether Asia can bring back soft power
now and what will happen globally
if it does not. Hard power, the use of force and unmitigated growth,
is just not sustainable."*

Nizar Juma

The Team at the Taj Mahal

Having settled Tom into the Peace Café, I was now feeling that I wanted to be back in the mainstream of the BK world. With Tom's blessings, I decided to leave Cambodia.

I did not know what was next for me on my journey; however I was scheduled to attend a teachers' retreat in the Philippines. I packed up and left Cambodia for good. When I arrived in the Philippines, my yogi friends were asking, "How is Cambodia?" to which I responded, "It is going well but I have left." Them, "Where are you going?" Me, "I have no idea!"

I had a ticket back to Australia but I did not feel that was to be my next stop. Then the day after arriving, I received a call asking if I would go to India to help with a project called, *The Future of Power*. To the surprise of my seniors, I agreed immediately. I could think of worse places to go than India. They could have asked me to go anywhere! A friend of mine once said, "Surrender is easy, it is just being available." Being available is pretty open, which can be scary!

The Future of Power project was just in its inception. India was emerging as a world power. Although India has been occupied by the Moguls and British for thousands of years, its culture has hardly changed. However, with more and more exposure to commercial values and the prosperity borne from them, India is quickly changing its ways.

Seeing this, the initiator of The Future of Power, envisioned bringing Indian leaders together to dialogue on 'soft power'. Soft power is inner power based on virtues and values, whilst 'hard power' is external, that of guns and money etc. In dialogues, leaders would be asked, "Could India bring back soft power; the power it once knew so well, that of values, spirituality and true leadership?" This would be a challenge as corruption is now rampant and commercialism has taken a firm grip.

My role in this project was to invite 40-50 leaders from different professions in each state of India to join the dialogue. It ended up being held in sixty cities throughout India. The Australian Indian Institute in Melbourne hosted a conference on "India the Reluctant Superpower." I think we would all prefer a reluctant superpower than one an eager one! The inviting cities carefully selected the participants on the basis of their values. Most of the people I met were good candidates for the re-emergence of soft power.

Our definition of a leader was, 'When they speak, others listen.' This brought me in touch with some amazing people. The current Indian Prime Minister, then serving as the Chief Minister for Gujarat, Narendra Modi, was one of our chief guests for a public program which was held separately to the intimate dialogues. Sachin Tendulka, the Indian cricket superstar, was also invited to attend a dialogue. In fact, I spent time with many members of the Indian Cricket Team at their hotel in Bangalore where I introduced them to Raja Yoga meditation. Once, on my way up to see them I met the Australian captain, Ricky Ponting. I asked him who I should cheer for in their match that day. He said, "Just good cricket", an answer I thought reflected the soft power of the sporting world!

I still have connection with one of the members of the cricket team, Shikhar Dhawan. We share a wonderful exchange; 'the Warrior and the Yogi'. There is much to learn from each other. I once drove him to our Retreat Centre in the Blue Mountains in Australia for a silent retreat. While out exploring the mountains, it started to rain and I thought we would get good shelter and exploration at Jenolan Caves. The road was narrow and winding and the rain was pouring down. He was playing the Semi Final against Australia the next day, and I realised what a big risk I had taken to take this drive. I cannot even imagine how I would have faced his fans if anything had happened. In hindsight, it was probably not a wise thing to have done!

Other invitees included royalty, police superintendents, doctors, professors, scientists, dancers, film directors, musicians and magicians. I was most impressed with the doctors, who I found worked for half the day for their income and spent the other half, or more, tending to the poor and needy. Many of them had built speciality hospitals for those who cannot afford healthcare. I was deeply touched by a top psychiatrist when I met him at his clinic surrounded by very poor patients. He was the head of psychiatry for the north of India and could have been making a lot of money from the rich and famous, who would have been equally in need of his help. When he looked up, his face was blissful and it reminded me of the joy of serving. He was what I have come to describe as a 'gamma person', one who lives on a high. I have seldom met such people with this kind of energy outside of India.

I stayed at BK meditation Centres all over India, in more than 50 cities. I would spend 10-30 days in each city organising both the dialogue and the evening program that followed. We gained a lot of experience and all that the local team needed to do was follow the formula that we had found worked. I really take my hat off to the local teams; neither myself nor Nizar are from India, and they showed great humility and trust in us.

I speak enough Hindi to get by, and after so many years living in Centres in Australia and Asia, I could adapt to just about any culture. The project was a good fit for me, and I for it, and I enjoyed the experience for over four years. I lived out of a suitcase with 15kg domestic travel allowance and learned to manage it very well. At one point, as I am an organised kind of person, I longed for some drawers. I was to stay in that city for a month, so I bought a small set and had them set up in my room. The next day, I fell and twisted my ankle and had to move rooms. The drawers could not come with me! Soon after I ended up staying in a hotel room, which was quite rare. I was so happy to have a cupboard and drawers. I put everything neatly away and went to bed.

Knock knock!!!! "Your visa has expired, I am sorry you will have to move out of here, right now." Oh well, I got the message and gave up on the drawers! I had applied for the visa extension months before and, "It was coming"!

The stories of this period could fill a whole book and it is hard to choose which of all the wonderful experiences I had on this project, to include. One of my favourite experiences was when I stayed in a Centre connected to a BK Girls' Hostel in Indore. Fifty young girls rose at 4.00am, meditated and studied, got ready for school, helped grind flour, cooked, and booked trains, among other things. The older ones mentored and stayed with the younger ones and they were so happy. They were excellent dancers and were often called all over the country to perform during their school breaks. It was a fun place to practise my Hindi and gain confidence, and just as their teachers encouraged and brought out their skills, they also brought out mine. Following this visit, early in my stay, I became proficient enough in Hindi to read the morning class from the Hindi script in Centres all over India.

I also had the chance to visit Madhuban, our headquarters in Mt Abu in between programs and get to know how things operated, and then to visit Australia and some other countries during the monsoon months.

One lesson I learned from my visits to Madhuban, is to be "Ever busy, ever free." On one occasion, I went to the tailoring department to get a small repair done. The brothers there insisted on stitching clothes for me, even though piles of cloth waiting to be stitched almost hid them from view. It was a great lesson to take on; we are almost always busy, but let's always be free enough to do what we really want to do, and what is important - this keeps us alive.

It was interesting for me to meet members of India's royal families. After giving up their entitlements for the sake of unity at the time of India's independence, they are all coping in very different ways. Many have turned their palaces into hotels, some are working for the benefit of the society, others performing their religious duties as 'servants of the Lord' in various temples, and one King I met was off to England to sue

Queen Elizabeth for personal jewellery that was to be returned to India but is still on display in Buckingham Palace. Others are very engaged in community service.

Throughout my involvement with Future of Power my days were spent being driven around in cars meeting participants. I was never keen on visiting the toilets and often too shy to ask, so I did not drink. I was lacking exercise and became concerned about my kidneys and my health in general, so I decided to withdraw from the project.

In Australia, a new building for our National Headquarters had been purchased in Sydney and I was asked to return to coordinate that Centre. To be nearer to my mum who is now in her 80's also felt right. She lives 600 kilometres north of Sydney and I managed to visit a few times a year.

* * * * *

12

Bhutan and Nepal

Bhutan
"Time does not hurl itself forward at breakneck speed here. Change happens very slowly. A grandmother and her granddaughter wear the same kind of clothes, they do the same work, they know the same songs. The granddaughter does not find her grandmother an embarrassing, boring relic."
Jamie Zeppa, Beyond the Sky and the Earth: A Journey Into Bhutan

During my extended period in India, I had the chance to spend time in Bhutan and Nepal. The Consulate General of Bhutan in India had attended our Future of Power dialogue in Kolkata and invited me to his homeland, waiving the requirement of the usual tourist levy of US$250 a day. He wanted me to explore the possibility of hosting a dialogue in Bhutan. Many people dream of visiting the land where Gross National Happiness trumps GDP! Although I spent only a few days in both Thimpu and Paro, I learnt a lot about this little Himalayan Kingdom. I even had the chance to spend an evening with young teachers as I had called a wrong number and thought to ask the lady I spoke to if we could meet anyway!

I had travelled to Bhutan with Lakshmi from Kolkata, and we arrived in Paro just before lunch. We learned from the English newspaper that comes out every two weeks, that there was to be a farewell for the Ambassador of India at 2pm. I knew about the Ambassador and had shared gleanings from his book *Being Indian* with many friends. We arrived a little late and the only seats still available were at the front. We did not realise we were sitting with the Ministers! We were impressed by the depth of the speech given by Pavan Sharma as well as the interaction with the audience, which besides the Ministers, included university students. They asked very intelligent questions, and having received their education from some of the most prestigious boarding schools in India, spoke perfect English.

After the session, we met with some Ministers and an Indian representative from the Trade Office who was very informative. He had lived in Bhutan for some years. Although delighted with the people and his life there, he had no illusions about the place we all dream of as being a heaven on earth. Having few natural resources and very little industry, Bhutan is probably more dependent on India than the people would like. However, India is willing to support Bhutan as a protected state, although not a protectorate; Bhutan acts as a buffer between India and China. The Bhutanese are not allowed to speak Hindi, however all the shops we visited were enjoying Hindi movies. We could also communicate in Hindi and use Indian rupees.

Lakshmi and I considered trekking to Tiger's Nest; however even on the small hills we were a little short of breath due to the altitude, so weren't sure if we could do it. We could not stop laughing when we got to see where it was. Clearly we were not fit enough for the excursion! Our driver was the driver for the Consulate we had met in Kolkata; always very polite and impeccably dressed in the compulsory national Bhutanese dress. He must have thought we were very unrealistic even considering it, but never commented nor discouraged us.

Bhutan truly is a travellers' paradise. It is traditional, has natural beauty and the people are friendly. Lemongrass oil was used for daily cleaning in the hotel we stayed at – it beats those chemicals! I now use lemongrass oil myself for cleaning. It is especially useful in Asia with all the mosquitos.

At the time of our visit we did not have a BK Centre in Bhutan, so we felt a Future of Power program would have to wait. Today however, there are many Centres all along the border, and I believe there are even some BK activities held inside Bhutan. So, we will see if the invitation comes again.

Nepal
"Aim to fly and touch the moon together."

Popular Nepali Quote

We held two Future of Power events in Nepal, both in Kathmandu and Pokhara. I was fortunate to spend quite some time in Pokhara. Scenically, it is very beautiful. I enjoyed looking out at Fishtail Mountain whilst hanging my clothes on the rooftop, and also from the dining room. We walked up the mountain to watch the sunrise on a beautiful and fresh clear morning. Unfortunately, I missed a paraglide experience over the mountains and lake because I took too long to think about it!

The dialogues went very well. Although it is close to India, the culture and feeling in Nepal is very distinct, mostly due to the blend of Buddhism and Hinduism. The government had been very unsettled for a decade, and the conversations were deep and important to all who were there.

Shopping in Nepal reminded me of my hippie days and my previous visit in the 1970's. The same colourful long woollen socks, boots and jackets were for sale. These days my attire is much more sober. I always wear white or cream even when I am not wearing a sari. I purchased a woollen sweater, which I paid for by weight!

Sadly, there has been a lot of devastation of the beautiful Pashupatinath temple complex. Miraculously, the sanctum sanctorum was untouched during the earthquake in 2015. Nine thousand people died in the earthquake and thousands were injured. I was in Sydney at the time and we had many Nepalese students. When I asked a couple if their parents were alright, they said that they were fine, but later I came to know that they were living on the street because it was too dangerous for them to go back indoors. The Nepalese have great resilience and there is much to learn from them.

Before the tragic massacre of the Nepalese royal family, I had visited Nepal for a very big BK program which was attended by the King and Queen. The massacre was a very painful experience for the Nepalese people. The King was seen as a god-like figure before democracy. When I managed the very large Centre in Sydney, it was always the Nepalese I would call on when there was really no one else to help with something. They are a nation of people close to my heart as they know how to help at a time of need.

* * * * *

13

Home Soil

Transitioning
"If you can take it you will make it."
Louis Zamperini

Innerspace, National Headquarters of
The Brahma Kumaris Australia

After 33 years living away from Sydney, I was returning to my hometown.

In India there is a saying, "A guest is like God". I was treated very well in India, and with so much love. Often when I would go out to meetings, just for the day, all the sisters in the Centre would come to the car to wave me goodbye. Nothing was too much trouble for them. It was hard to come back to earth!

Having had such diverse and often exciting experiences during all those years, I was not able to settle back in Australia. I could not find my place, my passion, my tribe, or ways to meet my longing for connection. Some years before, when I had returned to Australia and lived in the Wilton Retreat Centre for three years, all these needs had been met. It was strange.

According to psychology, we are hardwired for connection, and even though I have developed a strong connection to the Supreme, on a human level, I enjoy connecting and creating with others. For whatever reason, I could not achieve this at this time. I am very content being on my own, however when I am interacting with people I need genuine connection.

I felt that no one else could 'see' me and eventually I found it hard to even recognise myself. It was the toughest time of my life internally, though I was enjoying the beauty and comfort Australia offered. I have never been one to consult astrologists, but someone told me I was in my 'Saturn Return' and I would have gone through this wherever I was. In his book *Falling Upwards*, Richard Rohr speaks of the need to go through a hard time to transition into the second half of the spiritual journey, and I am now seeing that is true. Another friend suggested, "We have to get catapulted to where we need to be!"

It was good to be nearer my mum, but she did live 600 kilometres away, so I would only see her 2 or 3 times a year. She is so well. She says she can't help it! Her only complaint is that 'they' have taken her license away from her, "Just because I am 88!"

During my challenges at this time, I reached out to the work of Marshal Rosenberg on Nonviolent Communication. This work validates the fulfilment of needs and feelings as a means to explore our essence. Amazingly 'the teacher' came all the way from Hawaii in response to my mental call. Out of the ether, not having had any connection with the BKs previously, he wrote to me to see if I was interested in connecting with him during his holiday to Australia. Like many in my own community, he was interested in exploring the world, but more interested in meeting people than seeing the sights. This seeded a regular monthly practice group at our Sydney Centre for the next few years.

A particularly wonderful connection I made during my time in Sydney was with my Italian neighbour. He helped me cultivate the practice of 'connecting' first, before communicating. We worked on some projects together and whenever we met I would often immediately start talking about the project. In contrast, Luigi would pause, meet me through the eyes, kiss me on both cheeks, and only then would he be ready to talk.

He was always coming up with creative ways to use his talents to help promote our newly established Centre in this Italian neighbourhood. One of his creations was vegan gelato which he called Yogilato, and he very generously donated the income generated from it to the Centre. When asked to participate in the Italian Food Festival, he cooked vegan food and called it Peasant Fare, emphasising veganism is not new; it is common Italian food for everyone and does not need to be expensive.

After struggling to fit in for four years, an inner call to open a meditation Centre in Taiwan drew me back to Asia and it felt right to follow it. With the blessings of our Regional Coordinator, I was catapulted on to yet another adventure.

* * * * *

14

Chile

Becoming Whole Again
*"We all face crossroads in our lives where we can
retreat into ourselves, or we can hit the dance floor."*

Sebastian Lelio, Chilean Writer and Director

Interestingly, before I felt the call to Taiwan, I had agreed to go to Chile for two months to look into the possibility of serving there. This became yet another gift in the drama of 'My Life.' Immediately, I felt connected. Within twenty-four hours, and without any Spanish, I was out and about on my own and felt a connection with the people.

On the metro, and on the streets, the Chileans were kind and caring and took good care of me. I learnt to say "yes" when someone offered to carry my bags up the stairs, otherwise there would be another and then another offering to take them. A lady who had come to the Centre just once, offered to teach me Spanish. She wanted to get to know me as a friend, rather than a student. At least now I understand, *"Un poco de espanol"*,... a little Spanish.

My Australian friend, Caroline Ward, had lived in Chile for almost twenty years. By nature, she does not fit the mould of an 'institutionalised' person and had created a wonderful BK spiritual community there. Through her love, generous heart and her intelligence, she had manifested a house for the Centre, together with a lot of support. She is a 'connector' and everyone was able to find their place in this community. Her example has become the model of a BK Centre for me - serving the needs according to the present times.

We were at a women's program where the former president of Chile, Michelle Bachelet, was speaking. Caroline is an author and Mrs Bachelet had written the forward for Caroline's latest book, *My Courage Your Courage*, which has so far only been published in Spanish. Caroline had not had the opportunity to meet her and was a little shy, but I was determined they should meet, so we waited to catch Mrs Bachelet as she was coming out of the hall and even got a photo of them together.

My Courage, Your Courage was a program that Caroline and her colleague, Anjelica Fanjul took from the northern tip of Chile, Parinacota, over the Andes, to the very south, Aguila Islet. The program helps women to see their courage; the courage needed in hardship, and from this, the resilience they build in their lives. Courage is often seen as masculine, bravery, and many women are not aware of their own courage. Earthquakes shook Chile soon after this program and I am sure many drew on the strength they had now realised was within them in abundance.

One of the first words I learnt in Spanish was *palto*, meaning 'avocado'. Chile has some of the best avocados in the world. Visiting Petorco Valley, as far as the eye could see, there were avocados upon avocados. A lady had organised for me to give a talk in the city at a community centre and there was standing room only on the night. Then, we travelled to Vina del Mar for another program and a stroll through the colourful town of Valpraiso.

During another trip out of Santiago, I flew to La Serena and was driven a few hours north to Vallanar to speak on women's empowerment. It was very dry in Vallanar as we were just south of the Valley of Death, the driest desert in the world. Although it is near the coast, there is a cold current that creates this phenomenon. I was able to see some of the great contrasts in landscapes in Chile, although I will have to visit Patagonia and the Easter Islands another time.

One of the many blessings in my life has been music, although I have not always appreciated it. My father could have pursued a profession as an opera singer, however with four children he opted for a more stable income. My parents met in a musical society and my mother also has a great voice. My father was forever singing and playing the piano at home. As a teenager I preferred other music, and this may have served to turn me off classical music. However, it seems that wherever I go in the world I get spoilt by performances of the highest-level classical music.

In India, I was in Bangalore when Hariprasad Chaurasia and Shiv Kumar Sharma played together. In Mumbai, I saw Shiv Kumar's son, Rahul Sharma, playing at an open air concert, and was given a front row seat in Gwalior for their annual four-day music extravaganza, the Tansen Music Festival. The festival in Gwalior celebrates Tansen, one of India's greatest artists. He fused Indian classical music with that from Persia and Central Asia. There are many stories about Tansen's music and its effect on nature and animals. However, he has become such a mythical figure no one is sure what is myth and what is reality. But isn't that true about all of life!

In Chile, Angelica and Caroline, through their Curatoria de Talentos, organised a stunning musical experience at the beautiful Las Majadas Palace. In an elegant glassed room surrounded by old trees, Felix Olschofka played violin and Eugenio Urrutia-Borlando accompanied him on the piano. Prior to their performance, I attended an interesting workshop with Egidio Contreras who educated me in an appreciation of the classics. We struck up a great conversation without even knowing each other's language. We connected instantly and regretted not being able to communicate more.

Although I did not think I was ready to teach nonviolent communication, I had the chance to travel to Argentina where I conducted Nonviolent Communication workshops in a prison and a drug rehabilitation centre. I also did a workshop at a company in Chile as well as many at the Centre. I spent two healing months in South America, becoming whole again, and then I was on my way to my new adventure in Taiwan.

* * * * *

15

Taiwan

The Next Chapter
*"We are like islands in the sea,
separate on the surface but connected in the deep."*
William James

It had been during an early morning 4am meditation that I heard an inner voice, "Go and open a Centre in Taiwan." The BKs now have Centres in over 130 countries, and yet not in Taiwan. Didi Nirmala, our Regional Coordinator was due in Sydney just two days later. Her response was a little cool when I told her, as we normally wait for an invitation to open Centres in other countries so that we can be given support by local people. She probably wondered how it could work. I should have wondered about this myself! However, she kind of agreed and I immediately called our Centre in Hong Kong to inform them I was going to Taiwan to open a Centre. I was envisaging myself arriving at the airport with all my belongings, with just a smidgen of Chinese, knowing no one and just enough money to last for a month or two.

Rohini, who looks after our Centre in Hong Kong informed me that a Thai lady was offering to sponsor a Centre in Taiwan! My next phone call was to a wonderful Taiwanese lady whom I had taken to India as a guest some years back. "You are the only one who can do it!" she said with confidence. "OK, then come with me," I replied. We fixed the date, the Summer Solstice. She took leave from her work and met me at the airport and took me to her family home in downtown Taipei where her brother and sister-in-law now live.

We spent a busy and fascinating week together. My previous trip to Taiwan had been for an interfaith conference marking the opening of the Museum of World Religions. I had been invited to the opening by Master Hsin Tao. As it turned out, an inauguration of the expansion of their services was being held just two days after my arrival and I was invited as a special guest. I met many wonderful people connected to the Museum, as well as Master Hsin Tao. He had been an orphan, and then a child soldier for Chiang Kai Shek's army in Burma. From a young age, he had seen so much death and suffering. However, his experiences created compassion in him and led him to becoming a Buddhist monk. Usually he wore maroon robes and on one occasion I saw that he was wearing yellow ones. When I enquired about this he told me the Chinese monks had arrived and they wore yellow. He then told me when our gathering comes he will wear white! It was delightful to re-connect with him.

My friend and I travelled to Tainan and Kaohsiung in the south to meet three women who had attended a silence retreat at our Retreat Centre in the Philippines at the same time I had 'heard the call' to Taiwan. We totally connected and felt a very high regard for each other. Two of these women are from the United States but have lived in Taiwan for over 20 years. The other is a local who speaks very little English. I speak very little Chinese, but our hearts connected and she immediately offered a place for us to start our meditation Centre. I suggested that I stay with her and an interpreter for a few days so that we could get to know each other more.

An Indian lady, who has received spiritual sustenance from a visiting BK teacher from the Philippines for many years, arranged an apartment at a cheap rental right next door to her apartment. Together with her husband and son, she helped me in every possible way. She brought people who were interested in our classes, her son helped with social media and general guidance, and her husband helped to open a bank account. The apartment was a little far from the city but was comfortable and in an area popular with expatriates, so it was a good place for settling in to this new land and culture.

Within one week I had cleaned and furnished the apartment, and classes began. The Taiwanese are very spiritual, and Taiwan is a vegetarian heaven, although many vegetarians are surprised to be served eggs! The people are very friendly, helpful and sensitive. Even though I often got lost and was challenged when I shopped because everything is written in Chinese, there was always someone there to help with a lovely sensitivity, which was not at all imposing.

I arrived in the middle of summer and it was like living in a sauna. Some students from Hong Kong took care of the fledgling Centre for two months whilst I travelled to Indonesia. Fortunately, when I returned the temperature had dropped. I am appreciative of living in a place that has four seasons, and delight in each of the seasons in Taiwan and the different flowers, fruits and vegetables on offer at various times of the year. Shopping in the market, rather than a supermarket, we always know what is growing in the fields because that is all we can get.

After one year, a Buddhist nun, an acquaintance of a friend of a friend, offered her retreat house and a large temple, with accommodation, over an hour from the city of Kaohsiung. I showed her a book about the Brahma Kumaris and when she saw the people in the book she asked, "Are these all ours?" I was so touched by her inclusion. Although younger than me, she later said, "I am Taiwanese, you have had courage to come here and I will protect you." She offered the retreat house for us to stay in; however we decided to rent an apartment in Kaohsiung.

Not only have we now been offered a retreat house and a temple where we can hold retreats, but we now have two teaching locations in the city of Kaohsiung. All of this has been possible as a Korean teacher, Asha, joined me here in Taiwan. They speak a lot less English than in Taipei. Asha speaks at least enough Chinese for us to get by and is popular for her expertise in Korean Tea! There is a very strong tea culture in Taiwan. In fact, an American asked me if I had come to Taiwan for anything other than tea!

I am overwhelmed by the openness, trust and generosity of the Taiwanese people. Just walking onto the street I am greeted by everyone, and those who know a little English engage with me. It is all about *guanxi*, connection. Here in Taiwan, I am experiencing the purest form of *guanxi*, which I did not realise still existed on the planet. Perhaps it is my ears. I have long ear lobes. These are often referred to as Buddha Ears and are seen to be a sign of being spiritual, trustworthy and wise. I am touched and looking forward to the next chapter of my life here.

* * * * *

Practical Spirituality - My Thoughts and Experiments

16

Relationships with Myself, Others and The World

Perfection and Balance
"The more perfect we are the more gentle and quiet we become towards the defects of others."
Joseph Addison

We enrich relationships by respecting each other. My parents were the first to model this for me. They have been vegetarian off and on over the years, however before becoming vegetarian, and out of consideration for me when I visited them, they would eat early and burn scented candles to remove the cooking smell. They would also clean out the fridge of any meat. I did not ask them to do this nor expect them to. They wanted me to be comfortable and this was a way of expressing their love and acceptance of me. In return, I was more comfortable in the house and would want to stay longer and use the kitchen to cook for them and so respect was reciprocated.

It is a beautiful harmonious dance to learn to adjust to each other respectfully. My siblings had learnt this from my parents as well, and were always respectful and considerate in this regard. They have never challenged my choice of lifestyle, except when they felt I neglected the family in some ways. I accept this has happened, especially in the early years as I sought perfection in my practise.

I have learnt, sometimes painfully, that perfection is balance, and not 'up there' somewhere. Very often we move toward one extreme or another and lose the sense of balance in our quest. We need to hold a pair of opposites in our mind like a balance stick and walk the tightrope between them - neither using too much force nor being too easy. The balance of being detached and loving is one of the most challenging. Balancing love and detachment is not being loving one moment and detached the next. It is to constantly love, yet to love according to the many natural laws of love, not being possessive, controlling, exclusive and limiting.

If we all reached a state of perfection we would not be like clones. Perfection is a state of complete contentment. We would each be uniquely different as each ones 'content' is in fact different. We are each filling ourselves with different qualities and to varying degrees. Even plants take from the same soil what is meant for them, some filling with Vitamin A, others with Vitamin C. We can no more make comparisons with each other than we can with abstract and still art - they are intrinsically different and not meant to be compared.

Perfection may sound too high and lofty, however the word exists so there is no doubt such a state exists. We experience it in moments when someone does something that just seems so 'right' that we transcend the judging critical self. It can be something very small such as an *ikebana* flower arrangement, a meal or a work of art. There is a feeling of delight and connectedness at that moment as if you and the image of perfection have become one.

Experiment: *Think of a personal experience you have had of perfection. Capture the feeling.*

Oneness – The 'I' Within The 'We'

"A person experiences life as something separated from the rest - a kind of optical delusion of consciousness. Our task must be to free ourselves from this self-imposed prison, and through compassion, to find the reality of Oneness."

Albert Einstein

Many of us who have travelled and embarked on a spiritual path may consider ourselves to have embraced oneness. However, it is often rather superficial. We may embrace and delight in the variety of costumes, colours, and even beliefs. However, we are often challenged when it comes to different values.

I wrote earlier about the challenge in our community with Joe who was gay, smoked, wore strong aftershave, and perhaps did not share the same hygiene habits as others. In my experience, 'dirty' is often used to describe people whose hygiene habits are different. While in Hong Kong I would often hear Indians describe Chinese as "dirty" because they took a bath at night rather than in the morning. Likewise, the Chinese would say the Indians were "dirty" because the spices that they cooked with smelled.

Later in this chapter I refer to the documentary Kanyini. Being a vegetarian, I watched it a number of times to desensitize myself to watching an animal being roasted and eaten. It made me reflect on how meat is presented in such a sanitised way in our supermarkets and how equally inhumane the treatment is of raising animals and then slaughtering them in abattoirs. For each ones own reasons, both the indigenous aboriginals and those of western cultures would probably consider the other to be 'dirty and cruel'. I could easily label both of these groups in the same way, and create an 'us' and 'them' attitude.

The national motto in Indonesia is 'Unity in Diversity' and if practised it could be the key to creating harmony within our beautiful, colourful, diverse tree of humanity. It is a high goal, and as Deepak Chopra once said, "Separation is now just holding on by a thread."

Much of humanity has tired of division and is deeply moved when people of all ages, races and religions come together in song, art, or in one voice, standing for justice or simply, survival. Time is calling for each of us to be true to our individual core values and live those to the best of our ability whilst contributing our 'completeness' to the whole. To quote D. H. Lawrence, "The opposite of love is individuality." We now need to move in reference to the whole.

In science it is said that a cell with an absence of ease becomes 'diseased'. Not having a reference to the 'whole', an unruly dis-eased cell destroys everything in its way until it destroys the whole, along with itself. Similarly, when one individual acts destructively towards another it is because he/she has no reference to the whole, there is no feeling of belonging and therefore no inner harmony.

In her book *Creating We: Change I-Thinking to We-Thinking and Build a Healthy, Thriving Organisation*, Judith E. Glaser writes of insights gained in her struggle to survive cancer. "When I compared healthy and unhealthy cells and cultures, I noted several parallels between cell behaviour and organisation behaviour. First, cancer depletes life energy from a system. Cancer cells behave as if they are in survival mode (I-centric); Healthy cells are in a growth mode (WE-centric)." Her secret to re-instructing a cancer cell to become a healthy cell again is revealed in three principles: Open, Healthy and Transparent. In an organisation, when there is open, healthy and transparent dialogue, shared tasks become the centre of one's attention rather than the self. People then become sensitive to the needs and aspirations of others and adapt to new ways of thinking rather than being entrenched in their own point of view which saps energy and creates blind spots and biases.

The Sanskrit phrase from the Maha Upanishad, *Vasudhaiva Kutumbakam* translates as 'the world is one family'. Also from the Upanishads came the sound *Om*, perhaps the most broadly used representation of oneness. It is interpreted in many different ways, however the simplest description is the totality of sound, existence and consciousness. It is used in Hinduism, Jainism, Buddhism and Sikhism in prayer, song and chant.

The ancient practise of greeting each other with hands put together goes back to the ancient Indus Valley Civilisation and has been adopted by most of Asia as a respectful greeting. In many countries it is accompanied by the word '*Namaste*' which has many derivatives. Mahatma Gandhi explained Namaste as, "I honour the place in you, which is of love, of truth, of light and of peace. When you are in that place in you, and I am in that place in me, we are one."

Reflective practices including meditation, journaling and connecting with nature are now taught in some companies and colleges. These practices have proven to facilitate an emergence of inter-connected orientation - to care for the self, for others and the world. In *Flourishing Enterprises: The New Spirit of Business*, research done by Chris Laszlo, Judy Sorum Brown and their co-authors reveals that an increase in spiritual awareness is fuelling a passion for contributing to the wider good. They stress the need to flourish rather than be satisfied with just sustaining the world we have. They say, "The emerging beliefs we see today include a sense that complete well-being is more important than material success alone; to care for others is an essential quality of what it means to be human; cooperation is a powerful basis for business success; happiness is a more desirable societal goal and measure than gross national product; and the earth is a fragile, exhaustible, living system entrusted to our care ... As we are now faced with an unprecedented threat to our very existence through environmental degradation, little can be achieved without the support of the business sector and spirituality is now being seen as the vital link towards a flourishing world, and has become the new wave in management theory."

In *Megatrends 2010: The Rise of Conscious Capitalism*, Patricia Aburdene goes so far as to say that the focus on spirituality in business is becoming "today's greatest megatrend." And in the *MIT Sloan Management Review*, Ian Mitroff and Elizabeth Denton say, "Spirituality is becoming the ultimate competitive advantage."

This shift in consciousness has also been captured in Frédéric Laloux's book, *Reinventing Organisations: A Guide to Creating Organisations Inspired by the Next Stage of Human Consciousness*. Laloux discovered companies operating in very different industries and geographies, who without knowing of each other's experimentations, developed similar structures and practices to create more soulful environments in business. They were addressing the situation where managers or leaders who had been through an inner transformation, often left their organisations because they could no longer operate in environments that were inhospitable to the deeper longings of their soul. The stories of incredible success of companies who have stepped away from job descriptions, targets and budgets are inspiring.

Far removed from corporate world we can look at Oneness from the perspective of the Australian aboriginal people, custodians of one of the oldest cultures in the world. In the documentary, *Kanyini : Being Black*, by Melanie Hogan, Aboriginal elder, Bob Randall, explains ..."Kanyini means inter-connectedness; love with responsibility, to care for, to support, nurture and protect. The principles of Kanyini have held us strong and will allow us to rebuild our culture now that our culture is being recognised as having meaning, wisdom and durability. Within Kanyini is the 'Dreamtime' - belief system, inter-connectedness; spirituality - developed by adhering to teachings that particularly resonate and empower the individual in their most difficult times; family - expanding outwards from one's human family to all living things and Land, our 'songline' of the Earth, which is our powerbase, our security. We belong to all that there is, and all that there is belongs to us."

'Ubuntu', a similar concept in Africa, was popularised by Nelson Mandela and Bishop Desmond Tutu. It is often used to mean 'the belief in a universal bond of sharing that connects all humanity'. Tutu captured the meaning beautifully when he said, "A person with Ubuntu is open and available to others, affirming of others, does not feel threatened that others are able and good. Based from a proper self-assurance that comes from knowing that he or she belongs in a greater whole and is diminished when others are humiliated or diminished, when others are tortured or oppressed, Ubuntu is the essence of being human. Ubuntu speaks particularly about the fact that you can't exist as a human being in isolation. It speaks about our interconnectedness. You can't be human all by yourself, and when you have this quality – Ubuntu – you are known for your generosity. We think of ourselves far too frequently as just individuals, separated from one another, whereas you are connected and what you do affects the whole world. When you do well, it spreads out; it is for the whole of humanity."

To Taiwan's first transgender official in its executive cabinet, Audrey Tang, Ubuntu implies "everyone has different skills and strengths; people are not isolated, and through mutual support they can help each other to complete themselves."

In the Brahma Kumaris, the first lesson we learn is about soul consciousness. We often say that this is also the last lesson, because it is so profound; all other lessons are found within it. In my experimentation, soul consciousness gives the experience of oneness - being connected to the self and also every other thing. Although I only have glimpses of this full state of being, I know that my daily practise is unravelling the many layers of consciousness that create the illusion of being separate.

Experiment: Practise looking at the centre of the forehead when you meet people and being aware of the soul within that being and not the body. (Of course, you need to be discreet in this and not stare!)

Institutionalisation
*"Institutions will try to preserve the problem
to which they are the solution."*
Clay Shirky

Being an individual can be lonely and isolating and when people find themselves in chaos, they often seek out a spiritual teacher in an effort to sort their lives out. I've seen many people at a stage where they've lost confidence in their ability to help themselves and are grateful to have someone tell them what to do and what to think. They can also welcome becoming institutionalised in their quest for relief, as it is easy to gain acceptance and feel a sense of belonging.

However, after some time it is quite normal (and healthy) for people, as they begin to get in touch with their deeper selves, to question what they are doing and why. In Raja Yoga, I have seen new comers often want to wear a sari and then after a few years ask, "Why am I wearing this? Is this really me?"

In his book, *A Different Drum*, Scott Peck noted, "The greatest mistake of the Church was to suppress doubt, which has kept people institutionalised." It is important for people to be able to question and come to their personal understanding of the practices they have taken up and knowledge they are learning for them to evolve from being a 'believer' to a kind of 'mystic'.

I have greatly appreciated the space that I have been given by my teachers at the times I've questioned what and why I'm doing something. Time and space have given me freedom to work through my questions and doubts, and also helped me learn the difference between doubts that are healthy and those that are unhealthy. I've learned an overactive intellect that has lost touch with extra sensory perception needs to see to believe rather than believe in order to see. I've also learned that doubt can come from having a limited awareness, being judgemental, self-protection, fear, and also being influenced by others. It's important to be able to recognise the causes of our doubts as they can bring us closer to both clarity and ourselves.

Though necessary, when a spiritual organisation creates an institution around itself, its heart can be sapped of its lofty, idealised beginnings. None of our great spiritual founders created a religion; they lived to inspire truth and higher thinking. Over time however, as followers increased in numbers and properties were acquired for practise and lodgings for teachers, organisation was needed. However, it seems that organisation ultimately tends to overshadow teachings and hierarchy and management become entrenched. Often people in 'position' who are appointed for their ability to manage are not necessarily the ones who can inspire and lead on a spiritual level and yet they tend to hold the power.

The Brahma Kumaris organisation is referred to as a '*yagya*', meaning a sacrificial fire for sacrificing all attachments in order to strive for a higher good. The first Westerner to become a BK was Denise Lawrence.

She does not have a title or position within the institution, and yet she is one of the most sought after speakers amongst the Western BKs. Her words "I do not belong to an institution, I belong to the *yagya*. The Brahma Kumaris is a *yagya* and it has an institution, just as I am a soul and I have a body. I am no more merely a part of the institution than I am a body" encapsulate the attraction we feel towards her teachings. For me, I surrendered my life to the *yagya*, not to an institution and when I remember that, I am in touch with my highest ideals and aims.

The most successful spiritual organisations have worked out the balance between their management and the heart of their mission.

Experiment: *Is there any hidden doubt that I would do well to explore? Do I need the cooperation of someone to explore this doubt in a healthy way? If so, identify a person who would not try to influence you, but would help you to fully explore your feelings.*

Community

"A real community is immune to mob psychology because of its encouragement of individuality, because individuals feel safe to speak their minds and buck the trend."

Scott Peck

There is a middle path between individuality and institutionalisation, and that is community. The path of community requires us to stretch both our hearts and our intellectual comfort zones to adopt the mindset of 'and' rather than 'or'. It is a place where we can practice the balance of embracing oneness whilst owning our individuality.

Caring for the collective, each individual within the collective, and yet maintaining our '*swadharma*', that is, our own unique righteous way of being, is what I would call living in true community. Humanity desperately needs this - where everyone feels safe to be true to their own sense of self.

Pseudo-communities with people just being nice and pleasing others do not serve us. Nor do institutions where we all need to conform. Then there is collectivism which is about the greatest good for the greatest number – prioritising the good of the group over the welfare of the individual. There is a need for agreed communal laws protecting the rights of all individuals equally.

Building small communities wherever we are moves us slowly towards tolerance, understanding and acceptance ... one individual at a time. Yet it is a challenge to live in community. Relationships with others are often stressful, and so we can tend to avoid them. Losing our individuality and/or having our emotions triggered by others are big fears.

As part of my work with the Brahma Kumaris, it has been necessary for me, at different times, to live in Meditation Centres with any number of people of various nationalities and with all kinds of habits and idiosyncrasies. It has been a wonderful opportunity for me to develop myself and I've learned that love is inclusive. We do not extend ourselves spending time with people whose company we enjoy; those who are the same as us. There is nothing wrong with indulging ourselves being with people who we are comfortable with; it is a treat. However, true love, where we grow our hearts, is to include someone whose presence is a challenge. We extend our boundaries when we include someone whose presence demands our tolerance, accommodation and acceptance. When we extend our boundaries, the boundaries of the other are also extended and love grows. This is where the practice of soul consciousness is helpful. Going past the attributes and personality of the body, and seeing the spirit instead, saves time and energy and makes for a more equal connection.

I can see how living in community for so many years has hammered and stretched me for the better. Today, I have so many intimate friendships all over the world. I have been enriched by each and every one of them ... sometimes painfully, at other times pleasurably. Through both, bonds have been created and I am grateful I chose to overcome my fears of community and embrace it. However healthy boundaries are also helpful, or I probably should say, essential, when living in community!

Experiment: Think of a community you interact with. Do you feel alone or comfortably connected within that community? Are you also able to be yourself completely? Are you compromising any part of yourself to 'fit in'.

Comfort Zones
"Life always begins with one step outside of your comfort zone."
Shannon L. Alder

Many have said that I am courageous for living outside my comfort zones for most of my life. I don't feel comfortable in comfort zones; I am too adventurous to stay in them.

The sincere search for Truth and to stay 'North', pushes us out of our comfort zones socially. In the 1970's being a vegetarian was 'weird' and a challenge in social circumstances. When I lived in Hong Kong, I was invited to speak to expatriate women and to college students just because I was 'different'. When I walk down the street in a white sari, many people are curious and approach, others cross the road!

Often we do not appreciate our parents until very late in life. I realised only a decade ago that my parents deserve most of the credit for my being so adventurous. I always knew in the back of my mind that I could go home – nothing expected, no questions asked. Why not be adventurous when we are assured of security? I have also had the fortune of been born in a developed country that offers social security. And, I have always maintained good health. I am greatly appreciative of all the circumstances in my life that have allowed me to live a full life, a very rich life.

Reflecting back on all I have experienced and studied, I can see a pattern in what attracted me to spirituality. St Francis of Assisi comes to mind. Stifled by the comforts of his life of abundance, St Francis left everything to follow Jesus. He was compelled to live what he understood Jesus had taught. In the movie, *Brother Sun, Sister Moon*, one of the most powerful scenes for me was of St Francis stripping himself naked, placing his clothes at his father's feet and walking out into the wilderness in rapture. Another scene, when he was being beaten by his father yet was transported beyond the experience smiling in remembrance of God, had a great affect on me.

Nomads, like the aboriginal people of Australia have no concept of comfort zones. They accept what is and do not stay in one place long enough to get comfortable. Among other things, the wearing of clothes to define themselves is not important. These people have been labelled as 'uncivilised' however, perhaps we should stop and consider how we have been using this word. Is being 'civilised' merely having superficial etiquette and manners? The Australian aboriginal people, one of the oldest civilisations, have sustained their land and culture throughout millennia through an intricately developed wisdom based system which includes having respect for all things. In order to show respect, one needs to have self-respect. Perhaps this is a key to being able to be free of comfort!

A very recent book by Yongey Mingyur Rinpoche, a Tibetan Buddhist monk who left the comfort zone of his position, followers, his cocoon of a family lineage and supporters, to take up *sanyas* on the streets of India, has inspired me in my efforts to stretch my comfort zones even more. His book, *In Love with the World: What a Buddhist Monk can tell you about Living and Nearly Dying*, offers a running commentary about the Buddhist practises of emptiness and *bardo*, being between death and rebirth, in a way that has a very specific practical application of transcendence. Another layer of respect to what I already felt are very clear teachings on meditation has been added.

Experiment: Say 'yes' to the next thing that challenges your comfort zone. It may not end up being comfortable but you will have at least started to stretch yourself. Remember that our comfort zones are not permanent and will be taken from us sooner or later. It is wise to practise giving them up willingly.

Positive Thinking

"I may be wise, I may be otherwise."

Anonymous

"It is too easy. I know that." We may not say it, but we often think it. I had taken this position towards positive thinking. "Of course I know that; it is obvious." I've learned however, that this attitude blocks growth. It has its roots in ego.

There is so much we cannot learn when we think we already know it. When I viewed positive thinking with this mind-set, I overlooked the need to train my mind to think positively. I had not yet realised there was a difference between understanding, knowing and imbibing. I have seen this in others who say they believe in concepts like The Law of Karma and yet are unable to accept situations they find themselves or see others in. The habit of blaming is so strong that they cannot see reality.

Once in a long meditation sitting, I observed how a negative thought crept into my mind and took over. I lost control. Although I understood very clearly that the thought was not reasonable, nor based on truth, I could not stop the feeling it created in me. I noted that the feeling I was having was actually a habit I had developed; even though I did not believe in the negative thought I had had, the habituated feeling had taken over. This experience taught me that if I use my intellect to observe my thoughts, I will be more able to understand and realise what is really going on. When I am mindful of my reactions I am closer to ending habitual cycles of wasteful thinking and engage in positive thinking. I like to keep in mind the words of evangelical Christian pastor, Charles R. Swindoll, "Life is 10% what happens to you and 90% how you react." These words inspire me to be cautious about the quality of my thinking.

Generally, people are clear about the meanings of positive and negative thoughts. However, although we are aware we have so many unnecessary thoughts, the term 'waste thought' is new and even psychologists are not conscious of it. Waste thoughts are repetitive and unnecessary thoughts and they account for most of what is going on in our minds. Waste thoughts include excessive thoughts about things like what to wear, cook and eat, what others are doing and why something happened to me. Scientists have estimated that the average person has between 2,000 - 3,000 thoughts per hour or 60,000 – 80,000 thoughts per day. Of those thoughts, we would have thought 85% of them yesterday, and probably for the last 20 years! How boring!

In the Brahma Kumaris, we use the acronym 'SOS' – Stop, Observe, Steer. In my first lesson in positive thinking I learned to 'Check and Change', and created a habit of practising SOS – **S**topping, **O**bserving my thoughts and **S**teering them in the direction I wanted them to go. After a few months of checking and changing, I found I was mostly on course and could relax a little. If you find meditation challenging, I'd recommend starting with Positive Thinking training; it will help you to get your mind on track and will make meditation easier.

Thinking positively is powerful. For some time, I have been experimenting with holding an intention and have found that nearly every thought I have manifests. Joe Dispenza explains this phenomenon through neuroscience in his book, *Breaking the Habit of Being Yourself*, "Thoughts are the electrical charge in the quantum field, sending out an electric signal to the field. Feelings are the magnetic charge, drawing events to us ... Hold clear focused thoughts about your purpose, accompanied by your passionate emotional engagement and the signal will be strong enough to pull the potential reality you want to yourself ... you cannot think wealthy and feel poor and expect to draw wealth."

Being positive is not being in denial nor seeing through rose coloured glasses. When I was working in Hong Kong, I worked with a lady who was continuously complaining about our boss. I offered, "Yes, I can see that, but he is also good in so many ways." Frustrated, she responded, "The trouble with you is that you think everyone is an angel." "Not at all." I said, "To me he is OK. I have never met a perfect boss and I am not sure that they exist. If you think you can find one, good luck!" Positive thinking is not just about placating the mind with 'Pollyanna' type thinking, it is also being able to see through the 'illusion' to what is really going on. This is what frees the mind. When there is deep understanding the mind is stopped in its tracks.

Experiment: *Check and Change. As often as you remember throughout the day, simply observe your thoughts. Then consciously change negative and wasteful thoughts to useful or positive thoughts.*

Optimism
"The best leaders are infectious optimists and lead their teams to Discover greater optimism, resilience and self-mastery."

Victor Perton

"Good Morning!!" my father would chirp in the mornings as we slowly started to come to life. I would pull the covers over my head pretending to be asleep, and wait for him to go to work before coming out to the breakfast room. He was too bright! My mother too, was always singing doing the housework. I still remember the words to all those old songs like Nat King Cole's *A Bicycle Built for Two*. Was I really such a young grump when both of them were so positive and cheery!

Events that are beyond our control are closing in on us - like Climate Change and Corona Virus. It is hard not to feel the fear and worry and a general 'lowness' that seems to be seeping into society. Many of us have been trying to live consciously, avoiding misuse of resources, including antibiotics, in anticipation of these types of outcomes; however, there is only so much we can achieve without the willingness of 'bigger players'. Many are now at a loss at how to deal with these global crises, on top of their personal challenges. I fear that many feel overwhelmed.

In response, I have decided to ramp up my positivity and optimism and only share what can bring positive change. We do need to be aware of the innumerable injustices being inflicted on any living thing; however there is enough of that information out there already.

During my time in Hong Kong, I organised a programme for a project called *Images and Voices of Hope*. IVOP is an initiative of Judy Rogers, who with a background in Media, is mindful of the need to counteract the negative messages being blasted out from the 'media machines'. Whilst there are tragedies and untruths that do need to be reported on, positive and uplifting stories of resilience, forgiveness and survival also need to be shared so that people are empowered and given hope.

Australian, Victor Perton is often referred to as "that Optimistic man." Even though I contributed a quote for his book *The Case for Optimism*, I remained a little aloof on this whole topic. For years, my enthusiasm (that eventually rubbed off on me from my parents!), has been labelled naïve and immature. It is considered 'cool' to be little sceptical and reserved.

When speaking about the Centre for Optimism, which he founded in 2019, Victor says, "We are a movement supporting realistic and infectiously optimistic leaders to be beacons in the fog of pessimism and cynicism." Having had a diverse and illustrious background in politics, law and human rights, if Victor can still be optimistic after all he has been exposed to, anyone can! With his vast experience in leadership, he is committed to the belief that only optimistic leaders can truly lead.

Experiment: Ask yourself, what makes you optimistic? Write it down. Ask a family member what makes them optimistic? It may become addictive.

Creativity
"The opposite of war isn't peace ... its creation."

Rent, Jonathon Larson Broadway musical.

Some think that to be creative we need to be an artist of some kind. But there are many ways in which we can be creative. I was surprised when I was described as being creative when I worked on a renovation project with an architect, designer and electrician. "You can see the vision, and you make it happen" they said! I had not recognised my creativity in the process and realised that many of us have a narrow definition of creativity.

When we are not fear driven, we are naturally creative ... all the time. In fact, creativity is among the most important qualities we need in order to survive. When faced with difficult and even life-threatening situations we need our brain to stay active so we can find a way out. When we have an open mind, there are 360 angles from which an idea or answer can come. Fear creates tunnel vision where we only see one angle - danger! We go into survival mode and all our creativity shuts down.

To stem boring, repetitive and habitual thoughts, we can re-wire our neural pathways with creative thinking. At one time I was in a situation where I felt I was being 'pushed out'. For an hour or so I was caught up in this thought, all the while observing the sorrow I was creating for myself in thinking it. I had learnt enough to realise that if I maintained this stream of thinking I would attract more of the same, so I found an angle from which to free myself. I started thinking "I am being pushed up, *not* out" and immediately began to feel excited about what the next chapter of my life might be. Of course, I was offered an exciting opportunity within days!

A woman once told me a story. She had been sitting on the beach and was approached by a man who offered to take her to the mountains nearby. Normally she would not have gone along with him, however she was overcome by his charisma. As they were driving however, she noticed they were not going in the direction of the mountains, and momentarily she froze. Then something within her took over and in a very excited way, words began flowing out of her mouth, "Oh it's amazing you're coming along this road. I have a friend who lives here. Stop and let me see if she is in!" Her energy surprised him so much that he actually stopped! She went up to the front door and knocked. No one answered. She went to the back of the house and saw a woman in a car with two children. "I am in danger and need to get in!" Understanding the gravity of the situation, the woman let her in her car and as they drove out past the man, the driver yelled to him, "Just dropping the kids off. Be back in a minute!" She was married to a police officer!

When I tell this story during workshops there is usually at least one person who shares a similar story. Many of these people would perhaps be dead or badly harmed if they had not opened up to their creative centres. It works!

Until The Enlightenment, the word creativity was only used when referring to Divine creation. The Enlightenment acknowledged the greatness of human potential and challenged the fixed dogma of the Roman Catholic Church, empowering the common person. However in challenging people of faith, it seems we have thrown out the baby with the bathwater and lost sight of the mystical divinity, the mystical creativity that can be invoked.

I believe we are beginning to regain sight of mystical divinity – that pure and powerful energy that can be called upon in times of need. In the many stories that have been shared with me, it appears that it is almost divine intervention that has come to the rescue. I am not saying that this necessarily comes from God because I do not think there is such a clear divide between Soul and God, but it certainly comes from spirit. Creativity does not come from an intellectual dimension. It is in the soul, and perhaps we need to find ways to draw it out again and get more in touch with our mystical divinity.

Experiment: Grow Creativity. Do something new every day for a month whether it is a new route, a new dish or a new routine.

Exploring the Inner Dimension
"As soon as you trust yourself, you will know how to live."

Johann Wolfgang von Goethe

There has been a global resurgence of spirituality. In Australia, the largest growing 'religion' is non-religion. Many have, and are adopting some form of spirituality as they grapple with trying to find meaning, purpose and solutions. From around the 1990's, this led to what became known as the New Age Movement. In Hong Kong it was referred to as the New Wage Movement as it was noted that many people with little knowledge made livings from preying on others desperation and insecurity. In India they refer to this as 'The mouse who found a grain of turmeric and thought himself a grocer'!

The downfall of many disciplines is that there can be a trend of thinking that because one is a Master in one area, they are a Master in all areas. Masters with great wisdom may be able to help others to see through illusions and even be able to use healing powers, however some get carried away with their powers and begin to think they are God – or at least the next best thing! Coming under the illusion that they know everything becomes a slippery slope and has led to tragic consequences for some followers, who in their co-dependence followed anything they were told. For this reason many people are afraid of spiritual organisations.

Whilst the Church has quelled questions from believers, those who believe that science has all the answers are happy to ignore multitudes of anomalies in order to prove a point. In the last few decades, scientists have put a great deal of effort into researching the mind, working closely with spirituality as the physical and spiritual offer two very vast fields to comprehend and we can learn from each other's experimentation. Wars and other situations have brought spiritual teachers out of their seclusion, like the Tibetan Buddhists. This has enabled scientists to experiment on monks and yogis who carry centuries of wisdom and practise, and through rigorous scientific research the powers of a cultivated mind have been demonstrated.

However scientists do tend to look for subjects who fit the criteria for what they are trying to prove. Buddhism generally neither accepts the idea of the Soul, nor God. Recently a senior Brahma Kumari sister was tested in a laboratory and the scientists were amazed by the readings, however they could not decipher them. I am guessing the machines are not wired to look at things like the connection with God and Love.

In support of the theory of evolution, scientists describe the brain as evolving (said to have occurred through the evolution into birds and animals) from the brain stem, 'the reptilian brain', which controls the flight-and-fight response, to the limbic system which stimulates the impulse to nurture and other more developed emotions. The third stage is the neo-cortex, which has been connected to reasoning and planning, imagination and creativity. In my opinion, this is another example of fitting the theory to suit the belief. These three brains could have existed simultaneously from the beginning. Where is the proof that these states evolved?

Science has nevertheless, been able to determine that the mind has no physical form. What they have not yet been able to determine is what form it does have! It is akin to the *rishis* and *munis* of ancient India, who in their search for God were only able to say '*neti neti*', 'not this, not that.' At least they had the humility not to pretend that they knew.

Experiment: *If a scientist was ready to wire you up and test your state of mind, are you ready? We often deceive ourselves by 'looking good' in meditation, but what is really going on within.*

* * * * *

17

More About Power

Power and Love
"Power without love is reckless and abusive and love without power is sentimental and anaemic. This collision of immoral power with powerless morality constitutes the major crisis of our time. ... Power properly understood is nothing but the ability to achieve purpose."

Martin Luther King

After being involved in the Future of Power project for several years and witnessing the reactions people had to the word 'power', I developed a fascination with the concept of power and realised how important it is to re-define it. Just as Love is the currency between people, so too Power is equally prevalent in every decision we make. Every decision is based on our need to balance power and love in relationships.

Indian airports are a great place to pick up spiritual books and I had plenty of time at various airports and on flights to read them. Sure enough, I found what I was looking for, *Power and Love* by Adam Kahane, "Learning to employ both power and love is like walking. We can't walk on only one leg, just as we can't address our toughest social challenges only with power or only with love. Walking on two legs does not mean moving them both at the same time nor does it mean always being stable and balanced. It means moving first one leg and then the other and always being out of balance – being in 'dynamic balance'. That is, even when we are focusing on one leg, we must not forget the other. This is like yin and yang. When we are able to balance and shift between power and love, the two phenomena become one, we walk fluidly."

In hindsight I can see how my understanding of this was crucial as I navigated the next few years living in Australia. However, having learnt this so late in life, I have stumbled over Love and Power and the road has not been smooth. Dynamic balance? I often tripped over myself!

The word *power* comes from the Latin *posse*, meaning to be able. The most common understanding of power, is 'power over'. But what we need to work towards is 'power with'. So often we give power to another, allowing them to have power over us. "Relational power is infinite and unifying, not limited and divisive. It's additive and multiplicative, not subtractive and divisive. As you become more powerful, so do those in relationship with you. As they become more powerful, so do you. This is power understood as relational, as power with, not over," explains Edward Chambers.

There is a need for inter-generational dialogue for us to appreciate what each generation can bring into situations and I would say that elders need to lead the way in this. In ancient civilisations, and still today in many cultures, the elders are respected and honoured. However, in the West, as many have failed to step up as elders, we seem to venerate youth and be looking to them for wisdom. Whilst we are eager to empower the next generation, we cannot however expect them to be aware of how their power to self-actualise can impact on their elders. They are often blinded by their vision of where they are going and people whom they may feel are in the way can be overlooked, brushed aside, or even brought down. It is not intentional but can create casualties in relationships. This is often due to poor communication and an inner conflict between ambition and self-actualisation.

In his book, *Falling Upward*, Richard Rohr describes two parts of our spiritual life. Firstly, in our younger years we are creating the 'container', and as we mature we slowly let go of the container and focus on the contents that we have accumulated within the container. And as Carl Yung observed, "What is a normal goal to a young person becomes a neurotic hindrance in old age".

Rohr sheds light on what it takes to become an elder in the second part of life, rather than just elderly. He highlights the relationship between people in the two parts, "Juniors, on the first part of the journey invariably think that true elders are naive, simplistic, 'out of it,' or just superfluous. They cannot understand what they have not yet experienced. They are totally involved in their first task, and cannot see beyond it. Conversely, if a person has transcended and included the previous stages, he or she will always have a patient understanding of the juniors, and can be patient and helpful to them somewhat naturally (although not without trial and effort). That is precisely what makes such people elders! Higher stages always empathetically include the lower, or they are not higher stages!"

Paul Tillich offers some deep reflections on co-creating harmony as we strive to balance power and love:

"Where is the power here?

What is each actor trying to achieve and realise?

What are their positions, needs and interests?

Whose voices are being heard and whose are not? Where is the love here?

How are the actors separated and how are they united?

What is it that is being driven to be reunited? What is being kept united that is not driven to be? Which system patterns of power and love – of realisation and non-realisation, of connection and non-connection – are we interrupting or re-inforcing?"

Experiment: Am I in the first or second part of my spiritual journey? To create empathy, spend some time thinking about people in the part of the journey that I am not in.

Power and Innocence

"All weakness tends to corrupt, and impotence corrupts absolutely."

Edgar Z Friedenberg

In yet another book on power, I was attracted to the word *innocence* when I came across *Power and Innocence* by Rolland May. I expected to read that power was the corrupting force that marred our innocence. However May says that most of what we observe as innocence is in fact pseudo-innocence – a state of being naïve, having blinders on and not seeing real dangers, thereby colluding with danger, and often violence of some type. Unless we explore and understand our relationship with power, we will not be able to get to the root of violence which is tearing people apart all over the planet.

The Latin root of innocence, *in* and *nocens*, literally meaning not harmful, to be free from guilt or sin, pure. However as May explores in his book, pseudo-innocence is a common defence against admitting or confronting one's own power issues and has nothing to do with original innocence, "Innocence is generosity, especially in children, who can still believe and trust since they have yet to experience that betrayal which leads to cynicism. ... It is a way of perceiving life rather than a calculation. It is 'virgin' in that it is before the awakening to the vast possibilities in life for sensuality, tenderness, exploitation, and betrayal."

He says, "One is innocence as a quality of imagination, the innocence of the poet or artist. It is the preservation of childlike clarity in adulthood. Everything has freshness, a purity, newness, and colour and from this innocence spring awe and wonder. On the other hand, pseudo-innocence is a defence against having to confront the realities of power, including such external forms of power as the war machine or such inner forms of power as status and prestige.

"The fact that innocence is used for such extra-innocent purposes is what makes it suspect. Innocence as a shield from responsibility is also a shield from growth. It protects us from new awareness and from identifying with the sufferings of mankind as well as with the joys, both of which are shut off from the pseudo-innocent person. Deeds of violence in our society are performed largely by those trying to establish their self-esteem, to defend their self-image. It is important to see that the violence is the end result of repressed anger and rage, combined with constant fear based of powerlessness."

In my meditation practice, I do not often focus on innocence. I prefer benign. Similar in meaning, it resonates with my aim of being non-violent in thought, word and action, of not holding tight but lightly and gently allowing for what is.

Experiment: When has my 'innocence' resulted in anger, rebellion or even violence? Am I suppressing anyone's right to be?

* * * * *

18

Love

From Fear to Love?
"Fearlessness simply means that we do not give fear the power to silence or stop us."

Margaret Wheatley

In my 'major' on Love, I explored Love from many angles. From my explorations I realised there are two prime states: love and fear; all negative emotions are because of a lack of love, and where there is no love there is fear. Fear can be managed with love, beginning with understanding. When we understand, we can love. It is very difficult to love someone or something if we do not have an understanding of them. I have made the transformation of 'fear' to 'love' as part of my practise. I can recognise it most easily whenever the words 'should', 'must' and 'have to' arise in my mind. I can choose love in that moment.

I do not need to feel fearful in order to avoid danger – I just need a minimum of intelligence and common sense! As a psychological condition, fear has nothing to do with danger. Fear comes in many forms – worry, anxiety, nervousness and phobia, and is always about something that *might* happen, not about something that is happening *now*. For instance, someone may get very sick or hurt in our presence. The worry, anxiety and nervousness we feel is not because they are sick or injured, it is because we are fearful that they may get worse, we don't know what to do, or we won't do the right thing, etc.

Psychological fear is not rational and we tend to over-react to situations. After 9/11 many people were afraid to fly. However in America between 2002-2005, there were 30 deaths associated to accidents with planes compared to 128,000 road deaths.

It is probable that we will have acquired fear from our parents, an insecure upbringing or a traumatic event. Fear makes us feel vulnerable, insecure and constantly under threat, living in survival-mode and using ego, anger, greed or other self-destructive emotions as defences against the pain of it. We will want to become free from these patterns of behaviour and yet we cannot see why we are not able to. We need to realise however, that we always have a choice.

Sarah came from the UK to volunteer at our Retreat Centre in Australia. She fitted in well and loved being part of the community. The only problem was the spiders. Australia is known for its deadly spiders and snakes, and out in the country there are spiders everywhere! Sarah suffered from arachnophobia and would end up in a terrified state whenever she encountered a spider. She got very distressed to the point that she thought she would have to leave the place she had come to feel so at home in.

She decided however, to overcome her fear. Why don't more people do this? We can choose to face our fears and finish them once and for all, rather than be haunted by them for our whole lives. I learnt this from Sarah. She was very strategic in her approach and asked just the right person to help her.

George was patient and understanding and also had a very systematic approach. Step by step he helped her to face her fear. He stood with her while she watched a spider from a distance. She learnt to recognise the different types and came to realise the spiders she was encountering were not dangerous at all. Some of them even helped to keep the mosquito population in check! Eventually, not only did she get brave enough to press the button on a spray can, but she could catch the spiders herself by putting a jar over them, sliding a piece of paper under the opening of the jar, and gently moving them out of her room. Free FOREVER! She then went on to overcome her fear of swimming in the ocean. Again, she chose the right person, a trained lifesaver in fact. She delighted in the open sea. Free again!

Some years later, when I was in Cambodia, a lady of over 50 years in age discovered a tiny, squashed and dead spider under her plate, beneath the glass of the table. It was enough to drive her away from a training program that she had committed to deliver. I remembered Sarah and the choice each of us could make to be free, if we choose.

It takes courage to live and to love. The root in Latin, *cor* means heart. In Middle English courage was referred to as the ability to speak one's mind by telling one's heart. In this sense it relates to honesty, vital for true inner strength. Courage is also referred to as the quality of the spirit that enables a person to face difficulty, danger, pain, etc. without fear. Life without courage is tragic and at worst, can lead to suicidal tendencies as we try to escape rather than face difficulties in life.

It is understandable to have thoughts of ending one's life when there is no hope in easing physical and psychological pain. However, thinking in negative ways brings our energy levels down and drains power from the soul. It is absolutely vital to **en**courage ourselves, and others, whenever energy levels are dropping in this way.

Is suicide really a way out? This is where philosophy is tremendously important and not just a scholarly hypothesis. Before making such a huge life decision, we need to be clear about our personal philosophy of life.

If one believes in the philosophy of Karma, then losing our courage will certainly not make things better. (Please see the chapter on Karma for deeper reflections on this aspect of philosophy and also to explore the chapter on Death in respect of the evidence on Reincarnation.) There is a saying in India, "Our last thoughts lead us to our destination." The last thought in committing suicide is "I cannot face this any longer."

This would be perhaps, the worst state of mind to be re-born with. What is life without courage, hope and vision?

In all traditions great importance is given to the last moments of someone's life. However, we do not need traditions to realise how precious these moments are. Feelings of love naturally invoke the most healing responses during someone's final moments. It is often when the deepest and purest love between souls is experienced. Where there has been hurt and pain in a relationship; forgiveness, truth, and acceptance bring closure.

Another argument against suicide is the effect it has on others. Research reveals that on average one hundred and twenty four people are impacted with each suicide, including the first responders and health care professionals involved. We need to take whatever steps we can to prevent suicides. There has been a prevalent misconception that those who speak of suicide will not take that step, however the research tells us otherwise. Each of us is responsible to bring down the escalating numbers on the horrific statistics.

Not only can we lose hope in situations we find ourselves in sometimes, we can feel hopeless about ourselves also, not accepting our dark side. It takes courage to be open and honest in this way, but to do so with compassion is healing. None of us is perfect, yet. And then, it also takes courage to stand in our own light as this well-known poem by Marianne Williamson suggests ...

> *"Our deepest fear is not that we are inadequate*
> *Our deepest fear is that we are powerful beyond measure.*
> *It is our light, not our darkness, that most frightens us*
> *We ask ourselves, who I am to be brilliant,*
> *Gorgeous, talented and fabulous?*
> *Actually who are you not to be?*
> *You are a child of God.*
> *Your being small doesn't serve the world.*
> *There is nothing enlightened about shrinking*
> *so that people will not be insecure around you.*

We are born to make manifest the glory of God that is within us;
It is within everyone.
And as we let our own light shine,
We unconsciously give others permission to do the same.
As we are liberated from our fear,
Our presence automatically liberates others!"

Experiment: *In what ways am I holding back, afraid of the jealousy of others? Plan to step-up in at least one particular area of your life. What strategies do I need to put in place to support myself?*

Understanding This Thing Called Love
"Only a powerful soul can love."

Dadi Prakashmani, Spiritual Head of the Brahma Kumaris 1969-2007

During the years I was 'searching' I had been looking for a place where I could study spirituality and explore my inner world, not a place of worship or beliefs to follow. The Brahma Kumaris is known as a spiritual university, and in my early years of this study I took up Love as my 'major'. Love is the currency between us and can no more be avoided than money, yet it is one of the most misunderstood subjects in life. To initiate my study I asked people from all walks of life the question, "What is love?" I received many deep and insightful responses to take into my 'laboratory' to practise and experiment with.

One of my favourite responses was "Love is recognition." When I really 'see' something, or someone, my vision expands and this in turn opens my heart. One of our students in Hong Kong worked on the docks with a criminal organisation, the Triads. He was given this job because he was considered the toughest person in his department. In the early days of practising meditation he called me and asked, "What am I expected to do? I would normally just hit these guys when they act out. With this meditation 'thing', how am I supposed to manage here?" I shared with him my insights about love and recognition. After a few weeks he called me again, "I cannot function. I am loving everything, my shoes, my chair...." This was a guy who used to eat a piece of fruit with a big butcher's knife, sticking it in the fruit and holding it up to his mouth like a pirate!

We use the expression "He loves himself" when we talk about someone who we feel is arrogant. But actually, if someone loves himself he would not be arrogant. He would be secure in his own being. A person who truly loves their own being will accept who and what they are and will have the confidence to be humble.

Many confuse the idea of loving the self with being egotistic. Each one of us is no more important than anyone else, we are all equally important. This does not mean however, that we need to be a narcissistic. I have observed that those who are egotistic and narcissistic are never content. Brother Jagdish Chander, a senior brother at the Brahma Kumaris, and a prolific author until his death in 2001 once wrote "We all have love within. If we do not manifest that love in our interactions with others, it will turn inward and the love will only be for the limited self. When we love someone we want to give them everything they want. When we start to do this with our own selves, we can never be satiated because the love is selfish. We will do everything for our own selves and yet be discontent."

'Being' love and loving the self are very different things. In fact, to say "I love myself" is an oxymoron. How can I love my Self? I am Self. Who is it that is separate from me who will love me? The shortcut to mastering love therefore, is to **be** Love.

A man who no longer felt that he loved his wife and no longer had any feelings for her was told by educator and author Stephen R. Covey, that Love is a verb. "Love – the feeling – is the fruit of love the verb, or our loving actions." Covey advised, "So love her. Sacrifice. Listen to her. Empathize. Appreciate. Affirm her." By confusing love with a feeling rather than understanding it to be a verb, we confuse it with hormonal excitement. Our confusion starts in romance and we then transfer it on to the base instincts of mating.

In his book *The Road Less Travelled*, Scott Peck paints a clear picture of what love is not. When I presented his ideas to a group of women in a drug remand centre in Vietnam they were confused. "Everything we think love is, you are saying is not love; and whatever we think love is not, you are saying it is?!" I had shared with them that love is not possessiveness, jealousy and physical attraction, and yet we connect love with all of these!

Scott Peck's definition of love resonates with me the most. He says, "Love is to extend one's self for one's own or another's spiritual growth... Self love and love of others is indistinguishable. ... The most valuable thing you can bring into a relationship is your spiritual potential - the seed of your growth in love." About the phenomena of falling in love, he says "Falling in love is not an extension of one's boundaries; it is a partial and temporary collapse of them. Real love is a permanently enlarging experience, falling in love is not ... Love is effortful. It takes no effort to fall in love ... The myth of romantic love is a dreadful lie ... Love most happens when there is not a feeling of love ... Love is spiritual."

Being nice does not cause others to love us. In fact they will often take advantage of our need to please, and any other insecurities they detect in us! The need to be loved, to belong and to be accepted is a very insecure state to be in and it makes us vulnerable to abuse. As a psychiatrist in Hong Kong put it once, in broad generalisation, "Men give love to get sex, women give sex to get love." It is a sad, unhealthy and a co-dependent state.

Author, Robin Norwood helped many women to really 'see' what was going on in their relationships in her book *Women Who Love Too Much*. I have recommended this book to several women, suggesting they read a little at a time and slowly work through it. They have all found it rather confronting and were only able to deal with a little at a time, but it had a great impact, and seemed to be as effective as seeing a therapist.

After studying Love for over 20 years, I was delighted to find that the book *The Seven Myths about Love... Actually!* by Mike George summarised all that I had come to realise, and more. The myths are:

1. Love is acquired
2. Love is required
3. We fall in love
4. Love is exclusive
5. Love is lost
6. Love hurts
7. Love is attachment

It astounds me that we have been so misguided about Love.

Experiment: *Reflect on the above myths. Listening to songs and observing relationships, see if you can see the truth in them.*

I love you?
"I am love for you."

Mike George, The Seven Myths About Love... Actually!

If we considered that we are trustees of our children, rather than owners of them, as in "They are **mine**", we would play more observing and supporting roles in their life journey experiences than directive roles. Saying "I love you", sets a child up for a life of dependency, according to Mike George. An alternative would be to teach them "You *are* Love." When they behave inappropriately, we could remind them, "What happened? Are you not love?"

A woman once told me that saying "I love you" had become such a habit that she said this to a lady in the supermarket! We can do better. These words have had their place; by not expressing our feelings often, it is natural to regret not telling others that we love them, but perhaps we can move on to something even higher now. Imagine a society where children are brought up with the message that they *are* love, rather than they are loved? They would be empowered. I have always loved the wise words of Khalil Gibran about parenting ...

> "Your children are not your children.
> They are the sons and daughters of Life's longing for itself.
> They come through you but not from you.
> And though they are with you yet they belong not to you....
> You are the bows from which your children as living arrows are sent forth.
> The archer sees the mark on the infinite,
> And He bends you with His might that His arrows may go swift and far.
> Let your bending in the Archer's hand be for gladness;
> For even as He loves the arrow that flies, so He loves also the bow that is stable."

During my 'research' into the topic of Love, I found that many who have not been able to experience God's love, do not feel worthy of it. They have not felt love for themselves. Opening to God's grace, sensing God's love regardless of what we feel we deserve is a courageous step.

When I practised Buddhism I found that I felt worse about myself. It was not because of the teachings, I just could not live up to that level of truth and I gave myself a hard time for that. When I took up the practice of Raja Yoga however, I was able to bring about the changes in myself that I had hoped for. My love for the Supreme made it easy to do whatever He asked and I experienced being supported and loved along the way. I learned that Love provides the energy for discipline.

Experiment: *In your attitude set the practice – "I am love for you", rather than "I love you".*

Setting Boundaries

"People with boundary problems usually have distorted attitudes about responsibility. They feel that to hold people responsible for their feelings, choices, and behaviours is mean."

Henry Cloud

When we ask people, 'What is love?', their reply often includes the word 'unconditional'. Love needs boundaries however. Some years ago the term 'tough love' became popular, and is about setting boundaries with others so we don't enable inappropriate behaviours like addiction, bullying and violence. It can be very tough to set boundaries with those we love and often we tolerate inappropriate behaviour for far too long. Perhaps the question to ask ourselves in order to create the determination we need to maintain a boundary is, 'How harmful will it be to this relationship if I do not set the boundary now?'

Even after decades of my study of love and practising nonviolent communication, I am often disappointed in my handling of boundaries and the way I use words in applying 'tough love'. I am not always as respectful and compassionate in these encounters.

Small boundaries are good to start with, slowly moving up to tougher ones. For example, if an adult is living with me and is somewhat dependent on me for their living, I can at least set boundaries about sharing chores, basic costs that need to be covered and a minimum of communication. Once these are achieved I can then add other conditions to maintain a healthy interdependent relationship. Otherwise, I could end up supporting habits of wasteful spending, like smoking, drinking and gambling. We've all heard stories about the person who wastes their money and is never able to contribute to living expenses "because they have no money." Setting clear boundaries in the beginning prevents feelings of resentment later.

Another question to ask in this situation is whether my relationship with this person is based on love or fear? Generally we forgive ourselves for being the enabler in a codependent relationship because we feel that we are being loving. However, looking more honestly at our intentions, it is usually fear that prevents us from confronting another's inappropriate behaviour. We are afraid they will become angry, withdraw their love, or attempt to create shame or guilt in us. Fear is not strength and it is important to realise that to have fear is to be motivated by weakness. I need to empower myself, confront the situation and begin changing it.

When I am truly being Love the ability to set and maintain boundaries is natural. I protect myself from abuse whilst also nudging the other towards a healthier existence. If I am not, I become enmeshed and increasingly over-involved, over-responsible, frustrated, resentful and feel on-edge around the other person.

The author of the following *Personal Bill of Rights* is unknown, however the list is very empowering.

Personal Bill of Rights.

1. I have numerous choices in life beyond mere survival.
2. I have the right to discover and know my inner child.
3. I have the right to grieve over what I did not get that I needed, or that I got that I did not want.
4. I have a right to follow my own standards and values.
5. I have a right to recognize and accept my own value system as appropriate.
6. I have a right to say no to anything when I feel I am not ready, unsafe, or if it violates my values.
7. I have a right to dignity and respect.
8. I have a right to make decisions
9. I have a right to determine and honour my own priorities.
10. I have a right to have my needs and wants respected by others.
11. I have a right to terminate conversations with people who make me feel humiliated, and put down.
12. I have a right not to be responsible for other's behaviour, actions, feelings and problems.
13. I have a right to make mistakes and not to be perfect.
14. I have a right to expect honesty.
15. I have a right to all my feelings.
16. I have a right to be angry at someone I love.
17. I have a right to be uniquely me without feeling that I am not good enough.

18. I have a right to feel scared.
19. I have a right to experience and then let go of fear and shame.
20. I have a right to make decisions based on my feelings, judgements or reasons.
21. I have a right to change my mind.
22. I have a right to be happy.
23. I have a right to stability, to put down roots.
24. I have a right to personal space and time.
25. I have a right to be relaxed, playful and frivolous.
26. I have a right to be flexible.
27. I have a right to change and grow.
28. I have a right to be open to improve my communication skills so that I may be understood.
29. I have a right to make friends and to be comfortable around people.
30. I have a right to be in a non-abusive environment.
31. I have a right to be healthier than those around me.
32. I have a right to take care of myself no matter what.
33. I have a right to grieve over actual or threatened losses.
34. I have a right to trust others who earn my trust.
35. I have a right to forgive others and myself.
36. I have a right to give and receive unconditional love.

Experiment: *Is there a relationship in your life where setting a boundary would actually be an act of love? Strategically plan how you will go about setting this boundary.*

Not taking Sorrow

"You can see things with wisdom or woe, woe is to take things personally."

Caroline Myss

Most of us were brought up to be careful not to give sorrow, however without realising it our cultural upbringings have often ensured we take sorrow. As children, if I made a mistake I was corrected. It was often not until I cried and showed sincere remorse that it was understood I had gotten the message. Unintentionally, I was taught not only to feel sorrow, but to take it; to take things personally. I once heard personal growth author, Ken Keyes say "More suffering comes into the world by people taking offence than by people intending to give offence." One of the hardest lessons many of us have to learn now is how not to take sorrow.

On one occasion some years ago I triggered something in a friend. My words brought up issues she still held in her heart in connection to her relationship with her father. I was clear about what was happening, that her abuse was not meant for me but for her father, but when she exploded with an inappropriate tirade of insults and blame towards me I still took sorrow from what she said.

If someone were to offer us rotten food, would we eat it? We may need to politely accept it but we would then look for the nearest bin to dispose of it discreetly! We can strategically create ways to dispose of any sorrow too. Writing our feelings down on paper then tearing it up, or using visualisation and imagining it flying away are two examples.

A friend of mine worked with abused women, helping them to see that their partners did not actually believe the denigrating things they were saying to them. For example, if they were going out for an event and she dressed up, her partner might tell her she looked like a whore. My friend taught the women that because their partners felt insecure, they were afraid that someone else would be attracted to them. This helped the women see through the abuse and enabled them to disarm the attacks.

Sorrow that we hold on to has to go somewhere and sadly it is generally passed on to those we are closest to. At work our boss may be 'dumping' on us and it's difficult for us to respond, so we take it. We then go home and take it out on our spouse, our spouse takes it out on our child, the child kicks the dog and the dog bites a man in the street … and so it goes on! One of the most powerful things we can do to stop a cycle of violence, is to let it in one ear and out of the other.

A lady who came to see me in Hong Kong was ready to leave her husband. She could not take his daily abuse any longer. She was also in a stressful job and had their children's needs and the household to take care of. She began using the tactic of walking to another room, informing him "I am not here to be abused. I am in the other room, the door is open if you want to talk with me." Another woman took up painting and would go to her art desk. "How can you sit here painting when we are in the middle of an argument!" her husband would shout. Yet another woman would go into the shower and let all the abuse her daughter was still shouting at her, just go down the drain!

Experiment: Clean out your heart of any sorrow you have taken from anyone, and next time it is offered, just throw it in the bin, do not eat it!

Guilt

"Guilt is a useless feeling. It's never enough to make you change direction - only enough to make you useless."

Daniel Nayeri

A lot of guilt I experience is psychological guilt, meaning the action for which I feel guilty hasn't really affected a person or situation as badly or as much as I may have thought... and thought and thought!

Guilt is only useful when it instructs our conscience in what is right and wrong. As said previously however, our conscience has many voices that we need to clear away. We do need to admit error, but probably only need to spend 10 minutes in guilt so that we acknowledge our mistake and not appropriate blame elsewhere, and realise the consequences so as not to repeat it. Yet, we can sometimes spend decades feeling guilty about something we have done, often ending up taking those feelings to our grave. We need to learn to let that go. It has no benefit on any level.

Psychiatrist Dr David Hawkins points out in his book *Power versus Force*, that when we feel shame and guilt we operate on extremely low energy frequencies. Shame and guilt can often be used to motivate others. However, when these tactics are used, people are pushed into a low energy frequency. Consequently they will feel powerless to do what is wanted of them even if they tried. If we really want to get results from people we need to help them vibrate at higher frequencies and motivate with energies like acceptance and love.

According to Dr Hawkins, individuals who resonate in states below 200 - the level of Courage on his scale of levels of consciousness, are counterproductive to society. I find it fascinating that Courage is the turning point. Dr Hawkins scale (shown below) indicates how encouraging others, rather than shaming them into doing something is so potent.

- 20: Shame
- 30: Guilt
- 100: Fear
- 150: Anger
- 175: Pride
- 200: Courage
- 350: Acceptance
- 500: Love
- 540: Joy
- 600: Peace
- 700-1000: Enlightenment

Dr Hawkins Scale of Consciousness

Experiment: *Check if you are using shame or guilt to manipulate anyone into doing something.*

Death

"Only ten per cent have the wisdom to accept both life and death as facts and simply enjoy the dance of existence. After all, growth and decay are everywhere, all the time."

John Heder, The Tao of Leadership

I once saw a documentary about a man in Canada who would dress up as Death and go to shopping malls on a Saturday morning, shake peoples hands saying "Get ya later!" When we forget about the mortality of the body, our soul goes to sleep. I guess this was one way of waking people up perhaps!

A Swiss psychologist by the name of Bernard Crettaz organised the first Death Café in 2004. Since 2011 Death Cafes have been held in over 66 countries. Their purpose is for people to get together to talk about death and to aid them in preparing for the event, both emotionally and practically. However, it was Swiss woman Dr Elizabeth Kubler-Ross who has done more than anyone to create awareness about death and dying after she was appalled by the treatment of terminally ill patients in hospitals she worked at in the United States during the 1960s. Her book *On Death and Dying* published in 1969, explores the five stages most people experience facing their imminent death - denial, anger, bargaining, depression and acceptance. Kubler-Ross was a powerful force behind the creation of hospice care and in her later career also explored Near Death Experiences. The unknown creates fear and Dr Elizabeth Kubler-Ross has been instrumental in removing the fear of death and dying for many.

There are many different beliefs about what happens to us after death. One belief includes an understanding of karma and reincarnation. The soul does not die – it is eternal. It is only the body that dies. This realisation takes away the fear of death for many people. Some are not ready to 'leave' and fight tooth and nail to keep death at bay. Many have been experienced coming back from death by using their will. Others accept it calmly, and even cheerfully which helps to put others around them at ease. Each of us will face our mortality in our own unique way, and until we are faced with it we can never be sure how we will respond. We may just know that it is our time, or our inner awareness may tell us that it is not our time and we will fight it. Winning or losing the 'battle' is neither victory nor defeat. It is destiny.

It is those of us who are left behind who often suffer, but even this can be eased with honest conversations. One of the guarantees we come into this world with is that we will one day die, and yet death is often such a taboo subject that people cannot openly explore this part of life in an open and honest way. In her 70's, my mother would talk to me about death and how things would be if she died before my father, or if he died before her. This helped her a lot when after 49 years of a relatively happy marriage she faced my father's death and did so with acceptance. She had already mentally prepared.

Since beginning my spiritual journey I have lived overseas most of the time but whenever I have been able to, I have often talked to my mother about detachment. I asked her once if our conversations had helped her to accept my father's death. Over the years she has imbibed the ability to be detached at such a deep level so she responded "No I have always been like this". Although this had not been my experience of her in our earlier days I was so pleased that for her it had become so natural. Now that she is nearly 90 I asked her how she would cope if she lost one of her four children; if one of us passed on before her. "I will have to accept it" was her simple and wise response. And no doubt she has already thought about that too!

Having pets prepares us for death as well. Where I grew up we had a cemetery in our backyard for the numerous cats, dogs, turtles, lizards, rabbits, birds and guinea pigs that had been our pets. As sad as it was, we understood that when our pets died it was a natural part of nature. However today, as many people are detaching their hearts away from the hurts of humans and choosing less harmful creatures as companions, the death of an animal is often as hard to face as that of a close family member.

In India there is a fear of *Dharamraj*. Dharamraj actually translates as 'the king of *dharma*, or righteousness'. But Dharamraj has often been depicted as a man sitting in the sky waiting to punish us for our sins, similar to the Christian view of God. People who have had near death experiences however, do not describe *Dharamraj* as someone to be feared, but rather a love-filled light of truth. They often say though, that whilst in front of this Light they became distinctly aware of their shortcomings; that it was like being in front of a mirror. And, the more love they received from this Being of Light, the worse they felt. "It is like your best friend knowing everything about you" is how one person described it.

Upon realising the truth about themselves, people have shared that they regretted their own lack of integrity. So, it is *not* that God punishes. It is said, "The Lord is pleased with an honest heart" and the main basis of any relationship is honesty; it creates closeness. Most of the time, our excuses are lies and we deceive ourselves by making them. One of my favourite relationships with God is actually with *Dharamraj*. I would rather see myself in that mirror now than feel a distance between us when I no longer have the chance to get close. I have always imagined myself at that time being so clean and clear inside and just saying, "Hi, I am here."

Interestingly, studies of people who have had near death experiences show that many experienced regrets about what they did *not* do, rather than what they did. This is very instructional. How often do we fear stepping up into our 'light', taking a risk to live our passion, and share our feelings with loved ones?

Experiment: *You are at your own funeral. What are people saying about you? Write your obituary.*

* * * * *

19

The Power of The Other

The Other
"Once you label me, you negate me."
Soren Kierkegaard

Recently I was reminded of an expression I had picked up from school. Upon seeing graffiti on the walls of a bus stop one day I remember declaring "the Protestants must have done that!" Only recently, through my involvement in inter-faith work have I come to understand what a Protestant is and have wondered, who could have put that discriminatory attitude in my head? At that young age I didn't even understand it!

I used to wonder at the extent of bullying in schools and how children could be so mean. I am ashamed to say that when I was young I often heard adults and older kids calling some Europeans 'wogs' - a very derogatory term. I however, did not question this and followed. My friends and I considered it beneath us to mix with these people. Of course in my adult life I have very intimate friendships with many Europeans and greatly appreciate the feelings of family and their friendly, generous disposition. I now realise how much I missed as a child because of my discriminatory attitude. It stopped me mixing with them, befriending them and learning from them. I kept my little world so small.

Having been brought up in Australia under The White Policy I only had a brief encounter with one Asian in my entire student life. The one and only Chinese girl in our school invited us to her home after school. It was like entering another world – red lanterns, dragon carvings and sweets filled with black bean. It was only in 1975 that the Racial Discrimination Act was passed and more Asian migrants immigrated and settled in Australia. It is strange that in spite of not knowing any Asians, I remember in my mid-teens telling a friend that I would marry a Chinese! After marrying my Chinese husband, born in Malaysia, I remembered this and wondered how I could have known.

Immigrants were not the only ones discriminated against. Segregation was such that I did not meet an Australian aboriginal until I was 18, when I worked in the Aboriginal Employment Section of the Australia Department of Employment. Up until then, all I had learned about these deeply spiritual and sensitive people was that they threw boomerangs and ate witchetty grubs – as if that was worse than eating calves and lamb, chicken and fish!

White Australians may be proud of Charles Darwin's visit to Australia in 1836, however in *Origins of Species* published in 1859, Darwin's writings reflected the prevailing thoughts of society at that time. These were discussed in *Darwin, Race and Gender,* by Steven Rose who wrote of Darwin, "He was committed to a monogenic view of the human race and that the white races were evolutionarily more advanced than the black races, thus establishing race differences and a racial hierarchy." Perhaps then, it is time to change the name of the city of Darwin, a northern city in Australia with one of the largest aboriginal populations!

The 'other' can enrich our lives, and perhaps even our very survival as a species relies on the varied types of intelligence each of us bring to the world. Each one contributes their own innate wisdom and adds colour and beauty to the tapestry of life. "We are hard-wired to connect because it makes us bigger," states Henry Cloud, and this is why people love to travel and learn and feel such growth from experiencing the other.

I have had the wonderful opportunity to travel to over fifty countries and feel so blessed to have broadened my horizons through this. In ancient times students of the original, and at that time world famous universities, such as Taxila and Nalanda in India, were encouraged to travel in order to learn. People travelled from all over the world to study there.

Today, as we witness the largest refugee crisis of all times, we are challenged to stretch our comfort zones and make room for the other, and we need to be creative in the ways we do this. I like the words of Rabbi Azriel Azriel, "I would rather live in a scenario that I didn't choose and do not like but that takes you and your needs into consideration, than a scenario that I do like but that does not take you into consideration."

The *Uluru Statement from the Heart* was drafted by delegates to an Aboriginal and Torres Strait Islander Referendum Convention held near Uluru in Central Australia in 2017. I include it here in full as it is a beautifully crafted document created to help all Australians move towards reconciliation. *Makaratta* is an Aboriginal ceremonial ritual symbolising the restoration of peace after a dispute. It calls on all people of Australia to connect as one nation. As Australia celebrated the 250th Anniversary of the landing of Captain Cook in 1777, it was the opportune time to reflect on a way forward.

"We, gathered at the 2017 National Constitutional Convention, coming from all points of the southern sky, make this statement from the heart:

Our Aboriginal and Torres Strait Islander tribes were the first sovereign Nations of the Australian continent and its adjacent islands, and possessed it under our own laws and customs. This our ancestors did, according to the reckoning of our culture, from the Creation, according to the common law from 'time immemorial', and according to science more than 60,000 years ago.

This sovereignty is a spiritual notion: the ancestral tie between the land, or 'mother nature', and the Aboriginal and Torres Strait Islander peoples who were born therefrom, remain attached thereto, and must one day return thither to be united with our ancestors. This link is the basis of the ownership of the soil, or better, of sovereignty. It has never been ceded or extinguished, and co-exists with the sovereignty of the Crown.

How could it be otherwise? That peoples possessed a land for sixty millennia and this sacred link disappears from world history in merely the last two hundred years? With substantive constitutional change and structural reform, we believe this ancient sovereignty can shine through as a fuller expression of Australia's nationhood.

Proportionally, we are the most incarcerated people on the planet. We are not an innately criminal people. Our children are aliened from their families at unprecedented rates. This cannot be because we have no love for them. And our youth languish in detention in obscene numbers. They should be our hope for the future.

These dimensions of our crisis tell plainly the structural nature of our problem. This is the torment of our powerlessness.

We seek constitutional reforms to empower our people and take a rightful place in our own country. When we have power over our destiny our children will flourish. They will walk in two worlds and their culture will be a gift to their country.

We call for the establishment of a First Nations Voice enshrined in the Constitution.

Makarrata is the culmination of our agenda: the coming together after a struggle. It captures our aspirations for a fair and truthful relationship with the people of Australia and a better future for our children based on justice and self-determination.

We seek a Makarrata Commission to supervise a process of agreement-making between governments and First Nations and truth-telling about our history.

In 1967 we were counted, in 2017 we seek to be heard. We leave base camp and start our trek across this vast country. We invite you to walk with us in a movement of the Australian people for a better future."

Experiment: *Is there a practical way that I can be 'the other' for someone in need.*

The Power of The Other

*"Your willingness to look for the best in people
will subconsciously bring it forth."*

Marianne Williamson

I ordered the book *The Power of the Other* by Dr Henry Cloud, thinking it would help me with something I still struggle with ... being affected by the vision and attitude that others have on me. Words, I handle better as I can be rational, but the vision of others on me unhinges me. I was once cleaning some cutlery and became aware that someone who had previously been critical of me was watching me. Immediately I thought "I am sure she thinks I will not wash the cutlery properly." And even though I normally do wash the handles, in this instance I did not! If someone thinks I am disorganised I can usually prove that to them too! I try to take this as a lesson so I do not have the same type of effect on others.

Dr Cloud acknowledges the negative effects of vision and attitude in his book, but he talks more about the impact of the positive power of vision and words. He recounts the story of two aspiring US Navy Seals undergoing their final gruelling test to be accepted into this prestigious group. They were mates, having trained together for years. One finished swimming through the sea and stood on the shore and watched the other, after years of training struggle and then give up, unable to continue the final few hundred metres to seal his achievement. The one who had made it raised his arm and yelled, "You can do it!" and magically his friend lifted his energy and swam to victory.

I remember recounting this story during a retreat and a participant shared how in her fifties, she had joined a Zen teacher and several practitioners on a hike through the Blue Mountains. This woman had no idea what she was getting herself into and after several days hiking in rain and shine with little food and sleep, the group came to a ravine. Their teacher jumped it and instructed the others to do the same. Others jumped across, but this woman stood at the edge, exhausted. "If I try this jump there is a good chance I will not make it and I will fall to my death in this ravine. I cannot do it." Her teacher asserted "You *can* do it" and with that, the woman did not just jump but she soared across the ravine, taking flight with astounding grace and ease. She completed the remaining two days of the trek with high energy and felt buoyed by the power of 'the other'. Speaking less and speaking truth empowers our words and can be a source of strength for others.

I have lived with people from many cultures including Indian, Chinese, Filipino, Malay, Thai, French, English, Nepalese, Korean, American and German. Our different cultures have of course brought some degree of misunderstanding, however mostly it has been a joy to learn and grow from our differences. According to quantum physics, rather than being physical, we are 99% energy, so any differences are in reality infinitely minute. Our vision tends to focus however, on the most minute differences and we create so much chaos and enmity around them.

There is an ongoing debate as to whether humans are naturally good or whether positive qualities need to be nurtured. The word *culture* has its roots in the Latin *colere*, to inhabit, care for, till, and worship. To cultivate, is to be responsible for, respond to and attend to caringly. In Sanskrit the word *meditation* means to cultivate self. The ancient Roman orator Cicero, wrote of cultivation of the soul, *cultura animi*, meaningthe development of the highest possible ideal for human development. It alludes to the fact that the potential is there in each one and simply needs to be cared for and respected.

In the *Mahaparinirvana Sutra*, the *Tathagata*, is termed the 'true Self' or the 'great Self'. The Buddha tells of how he can see this hidden jewel within each and every being: "hidden within the *kleśas*, the mental contaminants, of greed, desire, anger, and stupidity, there is seated augustly and unmovingly the Tathagata's wisdom, the Tathagata's vision, and the Tathagata's body ... all beings, though they find themselves with all sorts of kleśas, have a tathagatagarbha that is eternally unsullied, and replete with virtues no different from my own".

In the teachings of the Brahma Kumaris, the one and only 'faith' we need is to acknowledge and believe in the intrinsic goodness of each soul. The original nature of the soul is understood to be of peace, love, happiness, knowledge, wisdom, bliss and power. When I realise myself as this, I can then practise maintaining the awareness that this is the nature of each and every one of us.

We also need to believe in the intrinsic goodness of ourselves. When we admire a quality in someone else, it is because it is already within our own Self. When someone compliments us, we must not deflect it and break the mirror. Powerfully mirroring that quality back to the other, and perhaps even reminding them that it is within them also - otherwise they would not see it in others!

Experiment: *Practise seeing the good in another and observe the change in their behaviour.*

Holding The Vision
"Angels don't worry about anyone, they believe in them."
Anonymous

Sometimes I worry about my family and friends when they are facing difficult challenges. However, worrying about something or someone disempowers both our selves and others. It is more important and helpful to *believe* than worry. Once, I was asked to coach a Captain of an Under 19s Cricket Team who had 'lost it' on the field. I advised him, that when he is questioned about what happened, just reply "Don't worry about me, just believe in me."

I'm sure we have all heard of stories about people who have been diagnosed with a life threatening illness and have chosen to take care of themselves, often healing through unorthodox methods including medicines, meditation or prayer, change of lifestyle and diet etc.

Meditation and prayer are powerful tools. Research indicates that prayer works just as effectively whether a person who is the subject of the prayer is in the same room as the one praying for them or, on the other side of the planet. It is the same when we meditate and have good wishes and pure feelings for someone. Of prayer, physician and author Larry Dossey says in his book *Healing Prayer*, "Prayerfulness is accepting without being passive. It is more willing to stand in the mystery, to tolerate ambiguity and the unknown."

He goes on to say "Every physician has a collection of bizarre observations, cases that do not fit the norm, that he or she files away secretly for years. High anomalies seem to have no possibility, even in principle, of being explained in the local, physicalistic, reductionist framework. Because they do not conform to our familiar constructions of reality, they cause immense intellectual indigestion in medical science and are commonly dismissed as the results of poor observation, mistaken interpretation, or outright fraudulent reporting."

In his book *Epigenetics*, Dawson Church suggests there is plenty of research the medical profession can look to for explanations for these types of anomalies. Epigenetics is the study of the signals that turn our genes on and off and it examines sources outside of the cell that control how genes express themselves. Church tells us that there is mounting evidence that invisible factors like our beliefs, feelings, prayers, and attitudes, play an important role. He says "In an epigenetic health cycle, we select positive beliefs, prayers and visualisations that support peak health. Each little brick can be helpful in tipping the scale of our health: Positive self-talk, nurturing beliefs, altruism, attitude, meditation, and prayer."

It has been said that prayer is like talking to God and meditation is listening to God. In Raja Yoga meditation we practise quieting the mind and 'tuning in' to The Higher Power. If there were one prayer I believed in though, it would be *'Thank You'*. No begging, bargaining and pleading. After all, as a child of God I have a right! I do not need to *ask* for peace, love, strength or understanding. I need only 'tune in' to experience and then radiate these qualities.

Most religions speak of two aspects of God; the loving being and the punishing one. For the sake of our health, studies are telling us that we are well advised to choose the loving God. Of Professor Gail Ironson's findings in her research on HIV patients, Dawson Church writes "People who view God as a judgmental God have a CD4 (T-helper) cell decline more than twice the rate of those who don't see God as judgmental, and their viral load increases more than three times faster. These beliefs predict disease progression even more strongly than depression."

In my twenties I noticed a lump in my breast and was advised by a doctor to have it removed. Not having faith in such an invasive approach, I didn't do anything about it until I came across a naturopath in Hong Kong who I believed in. I am not sure if he solved this particular problem but he kept me so healthy that I did not need to see a medical doctor for the whole time I was there. After more than twenty years the lump had not gone away, and in fact both breasts had become hard. I consulted a doctor and was advised to have them both taken off ... even more invasive! I thanked him and assured him I would take care of it.

On the advice of a friend who had recovered from invasive cervical cancer by taking raw food and having colonics, I decided to try a raw food diet. In just two months of raw food and manual lymph draining, my breasts had become completely clear. I enjoyed the raw food diet and chose to maintained it for another few months for good measure. Twenty years later I have no problems and my health is good. I still have raw food as much as I can.

Some felt I was being careless by not being more proactive. Others said I was in denial. But remembering the words of Dr Larry Dossey has kept my critics at bay, "Sometimes the approach of doing nothing works for healing. Not doing is also a healing. The quiet way of being flows from one's true centre. It is focused, authentic, genuine and accepting of any outcome. It is not contaminated by fear of death and contains no blame or guilt. It does not exclude any therapeutic approach and may involve using drugs or surgery as naturally as contemplation, meditation or prayer. It rests in the understanding that the higher self is immortal and eternal. People who use denial, have survived in greater number than those who face the facts squarely and honestly especially in myocardial infarction. It is thought that this is due to less anxiety, leading to lower blood levels of adrenaline, a calmer heart rate and blood pressure. In breast cancer those in denial fared the same as those not."

Experiment: Think of someone whom you are concerned about. Believe in them and see the difference it makes to both of you.

Peace-Monger Leadership

"In any type of institution whatsoever, when a self directed, imaginative, energetic, or creative member is being constantly frustrated and sabotaged rather than encouraged and supported, the person at the very top will be a peace-monger, a highly anxious risk avoider, someone more concerned with good feelings than with progress, someone whose life revolves around the axis of consensus."

Edwin Friedman

We often experience peace mongering with 'fence sitters', those who are averse to conflict. Wanting peace at all costs does not contribute to harmony and freedom. Fence sitters do not oppose, nor do they stand for what is right. They allow inappropriate behaviour, which brings increasing damage to a family or organisation. The fence sitter usually manages to stay on good terms with everyone as they do not say nor do anything 'to rock the boat'. However, their complicity enables others to continue inflicting harm. They watch as those who are willing to take a stand take the wrap, often assuring them how much they care!

I have reflected deeply on the words of Edmund Burke, "The only thing necessary for the triumph of evil is for good men to do nothing." My strong feeling is that it is important for us to do what is right, rather than what is popular!

In 1988 the Brahma Kumaris organised an international project called Global Visions for a Better World. Visions were collected into a book of the same name. One of the stories touched me deeply. This particular version of the Humming Bird story is from the Quechan people in South America. There are other versions throughout Africa ...

One day a terrible fire broke out in a forest - a raging wild fire suddenly engulfed huge woodland. Frightened, all the animals fled their homes and ran out of the forest. As they came to the edge of a stream they stopped to watch the fire and they were feeling very discouraged and powerless. They were all bemoaning the destruction of their homes. Every one of them thought there was nothing they could do about the fire, except for one little hummingbird.

This particular hummingbird decided it would do something. It swooped into the stream and picked up a few drops of water and went into the forest and dropped them on the fire. Then it went back to the stream and did it again, and it kept going back, again and again and again. All the other animals watched in disbelief; some tried to discourage the hummingbird with comments like, "Don't bother, it is too much, you are too little, your wings will burn, your beak is too tiny, it's only a drop, you can't put out this fire."

As the animals stood around disparaging the little bird's efforts, the bird noticed how hopeless and forlorn they looked. Then one of the animals shouted out and challenged the hummingbird in a mocking voice, "What do you think you are doing?" Without wasting time or losing a beat, the hummingbird glanced looked back and said, "I am doing what I can."

Finally an angel flew by and seeing the efforts of the little bird, brought a shower of rain.

Often we can be ridiculed or scorned for our naïvety; it takes a lot of courage to do what we believe is right. But it is in doing what is right that a higher force can comes into play.

Experiment: Check: Am I fence sitting, or being a peace-monger, with regard to some important issues that need to be addressed?

20

Compassion

Forgiveness and Compassion
"Forgiveness is the most irrational spiritual task because it stands in opposition of what you have been taught about fairness and justice. It is a mystical necessity."

Caroline Myss

Compassion is at the core of all spiritual traditions. I became a vegetarian when practising Buddhism. My understanding was that Buddha's prime value was loving-kindness. I felt that being vegetarian was the most practical first step. *Karuna*, the Sanskrit word for compassion, means placing one's mind in another's favour. With this practice we seek to understand the other from their perspective, and then we can have empathy.

Often religious teachings are quoted in ways that divide. In her book, *A Case for God*, Karen Armstrong states very clearly that no one can quote verbatim what any of the Prophets have actually said - the words were written by others, have been adjusted, and even doctored at various times, to suit those in power. Even the four books of the Bible, Matthew, Mark, Luke and John do not tally with each other in accuracy.

She proposes spiritual teachings be used as signposts for us to discover our own truths through them, rather than to hit each other with. This is perhaps also a practice many of us could take up within our own traditions, not only with other faiths!

Armstrong worked with many spiritual leaders from all over the world to develop the *Charter of Compassion* for which she was awarded the 2008 TED Prize. The Charter now has well over two million signatures.

The Charter of Compassion

The principle of compassion lies at the heart of all religious, ethical and spiritual traditions, calling us always to treat all others as we wish to be treated ourselves. Compassion impels us to work tirelessly to alleviate the suffering of our fellow creatures, to dethrone ourselves from the centre of our world and put another there, and to honour the inviolable sanctity of every single human being, treating everybody, without exception, with absolute justice, equity and respect.

It is also necessary in both public and private life to refrain consistently and empathically from inflicting pain. To act or speak violently out of spite, chauvinism, or self-interest, to impoverish, exploit or deny basic rights to anybody, and to incite hatred by denigrating others - even our enemies - is a denial of our common humanity. We acknowledge that we have failed to live compassionately and that some have even increased the sum of human misery in the name of religion.

We therefore call upon all men and women ~ to restore compassion to the centre of morality and religion ~ to return to the ancient principle that any interpretation of scripture that breeds violence, hatred or disdain is illegitimate ~ to ensure that youth are given accurate and respectful information about other traditions, religions and cultures ~ to encourage a positive appreciation of cultural and religious diversity ~ to cultivate an informed empathy with the suffering of all human beings - even those regarded as enemies.

We urgently need to make compassion a clear, luminous and dynamic force in our polarized world. Rooted in a principled determination to transcend selfishness, compassion can break down political, dogmatic, ideological and reli-

gious boundaries. Born of our deep interdependence, compassion is essential to human relationships and to a fulfilled humanity. It is the path to enlightenment, and indispensable to the creation of a just economy and a peaceful global community.

Studies have shown that a lack of empathy can inflict more suffering than physical violence. When we lack compassion we ignore or are disapproving of other people and an attitude of 'us' and 'them' arises. Atrocities arise from this. The basis for *ahimsa* or nonviolence therefore, is compassion.

Experiment: *Realise that when I am not seeking to get something from the other, forgiveness comes naturally. Apply this to a situation where I am struggling with forgiveness.*

Nonviolent Communication

"What happens to disconnect us from our compassionate nature, leading us to behave violently and exploitatively? What allows some people to stay connected to their compassionate nature even under the most trying circumstances?"

Marshall Rosenberg

I had not fully understood the meaning of compassion until I came across the work of Marshall Rosenberg's *Nonviolent Communication* known as NVC. The opening sentences in his book are quoted above. Compassion is about connection and the aim of NVC is to maintain connection with others. Rosenberg speaks of Emotional Literacy as a means to improve our communication skills because when we can no longer clearly express ourselves, we resort to anger, cursing and swearing. That is not the type of connection we want with each other!

I took an interest, read books on NVC and listened to Rosenberg's talks on YouTube. Then one day someone yelled at me. Because I did not know how to respond, I distanced myself. I was in Australia at the time and 'put out' the wish for an NVC teacher. To my surprise a random email landed in my inbox from someone from Hawaii looking for a community to engage with during his visit. I had had no previous connection to this person, nor did I know anyone who had! His visit to Australia brought together others interested in NVC and we formed a regular group practice which continued for almost two years. Soon after this, I found myself facilitating NVC in jails, drug rehabilitation centres, businesses and at some of our meditation Centres.

After more than thirty years of interest and practice, I still feel like a beginner. Rosenberg describes NVC as a language, and just like any language, it really takes time to become fluent in emotional literacy. The following words of Ruth Bebermeyer offer wisdom to reflect upon and have been helpful to me in responding to others.

Words are Windows
I feel so sentenced by your words, I feel so judged and sent away.
Before I go I have to know, is that what you mean to say?
Before I rise to my defence, before I speak in hurt or fear,
Before I build that wall of words, tell me, did I really hear?
Words are windows or they are walls, they sentence us or set us free.
When I speak and when I hear, let the love-light shine through me.
There are things I need to say, things that seem so much to me,
If my words don't make me clear, will you help me to be free?
If I seemed to put you down, if you felt I didn't care,
Try to listen through my words to the feelings that we share.

One of the practices in NVC is giving others we are communicating with feedback. The aim of this is to enhance connection through an open and honest expression of how their words and actions impact us. It is not accusing, blaming, reacting and name-calling. It is opening ourselves up so we can express the feelings that emerge in us as a reaction to what they have said or done. It does need to be thoughtfully processed though, so any blaming, shaming and accusing is removed.

Rosenberg's method for non-violent communication uses a four part approach: observation, feeling, need and request and it goes something like this:

When I (observation) ..... I (feel) ..... Because I am (needing) ..... Would you be willing to (request) .....

It looks simple, however keeping judgements and demands at bay can turn one inside out!

Another key aspect in NVC training is empathetic listening. When I conduct workshops on NVC, I begin by asking participants to pair up and listen to each other for five minutes, one at a time. They are requested to not bring in any judgements about the other person or what they say, nor interrupt, and to practice being fully present. At the end of each session I ask them to recall the last time that someone listened to them like that. Almost unanimously all agree it has never happened before! Interestingly, Taiwan has been the exception, although all the participants have felt that more empathy would indeed be helpful. At a Drug Rehabilitation Centre, one participant shared that he would make an appointment with his wife and listen to her for one hour. Another commented that it would be fair to offer his wife at least three hours!

A symbol used in NVC is the giraffe. The giraffe has the largest heart of all mammals, is not a predator and is vegetarian. Unfortunately these gracious creatures have just been added to the list of threatened species. Can you imagine a world without giraffes?

Experiment: *If there is a situation in your life in which you are feeling uncomfortable with another person and are not sure how to communicate, try to write out the situation using the NVC formula above and practise what you might be able to say.*

Gentleness and Grace
"What is the essence of your grace that is you?"

Caroline Myss

One simple meditation technique that I have found to be helpful is to hold in my mind a virtue that resonates with me and then let it gravitate towards the part of me that needs that quality. For many years I used the virtue of *gentleness*. Church of England minister, Father Roger Murray, gifted it to me one day. He was not able to attend a program we were holding in Hong Kong on Love and when I asked what he would have contributed to our discussion he simply said, "We cannot be too gentle these days. All people need our gentleness."

When people speak in a state of awareness their words can go straight to our heart. As I hung up the phone I picked up my jacket and headed to the station. On that train trip all I could see around me were people who needed gentleness and I sat absorbed in Father Murray's words. In those days, whenever I had nothing specific to meditate on, I held gentleness in my mind and it would always take me to a sweet place. It was also a word that I could practice at every moment in a practical way; in the way I walked, and closed doors. I was careful not to brush past a plant, allowing it space; and I preferred to wear soft shoes so that I made no sound on the earth. Dadi Janki once asked us to check how we walked on the Earth. "Do we pound the Earth in anger? Or stomp on the Earth with pride? Or, do we walk in gentleness?"

I was only about eighteen when I saw the movie *Brother Sun Sister Moon* directed by Franco Zeffirelli, and it was the beginning of a spiritual stirring for me. The gentleness and faith of Saint Francis of Assisi, and his ability to be beyond everything in his rapture, was a goal I sub-consciously set for myself. For many years gentleness was my go-to word that would take me into a place of contemplation and silence.

It is as if words choose me rather than me choosing them, and another word I accepted into my life was *grace*. It has so many meanings ... to forgive, to offer Grace before meals, and it is the root of the words *gracious, grateful, saving grace, God's grace and to grace someone with your presence*. According to some dictionaries, grace encompasses compassion, wisdom, patience, vision, endurance, humour, joy, resilience, forgiveness, hope, gratitude, ecstasy, generosity, fearlessness, bliss, creativity, and humility.

In her book *Entering the Castle*, Caroline Myss shines light on the teachings of Catholic mystic, St Teresa of Avila, "The power of a person devoted to truth becomes a channel for healing grace that benefits all humanity ... Truth has the power to heal ... What light do you hold in your soul? What is the essence of your grace that is you? ... Your particular light is your charisma, a type of grace unique to every person that embodies his or her spiritual essence ... Name your light ... Identify its forces of light ... Your charisma directs your life's path. Follow your charisma and you will find your soul ... You are measured by your ability to channel grace or withhold it ... Live in a field of grace and a divine well of grace is endlessly supplied ... Realise that you thrive more on truth than on fear."

Saint Teresa of Avila's Prayer
Practice illumination
Develop and share the gifts of your soul
Keep alert
Fly under the radar
Avoid power plays
Stop blaming others
Don't use the word 'deserve'.
Let your first response be 'what can I do?"
Do not assume a helpless posture.
Wait for your instructions to come through
to make you an invisible act of power.
Channel grace on a daily basis
Form a circle of grace with soul companions.
Live congruently
Be devoted to truth
Stay active in the world.
You are a source of healing.
Remain active in your castle
Let nothing disturb you
Let nothing frighten you

All things pass away
God never changes
Patience obtains all things
He who has god lacks for nothing
God alone suffices

Experiment: *Think of a word that resonates with you. Hold that word in your mind in your meditation or throughout the day and let it go to the part of you that needs it most.*

Humility

"I may be wise, I may be otherwise."

Anonymous

Grace and humility go hand in hand. Without grace, I have found it excruciatingly painful to be humble. Trying to be humble is like dying. Because the ego has become my identity and I have thought it is who I am, I have defended it for many years, in fact many births. Protective shields have been put up; they have become my masks and when I take them off I feel naked, exposed and vulnerable. Yet being vulnerable allows others to see inside me. It is powerful. It connects me more intimately with others.

Embracing humility opens us to the field of grace, and the experience of grace gets us through the required steps of humility. It is like exercise. Spiritual stamina is built through taking steps towards being humble. Challenges will come at every step and we will need to bow and move on. Just as it takes determination, dedication, devotion and endurance to become a great athlete, if we are to change, it takes the same kind of spiritual stamina and endurance to rise above the maze of causes and effects we are all trapped in so we can start to disentangle the karmic threads and become free. Humility is powerful. It is liberating. With humility we become masters of our selves and can stand in self-respect regardless of the vision, words and behaviours of others towards us.

A great fear that all humans have is to be humiliated. When we are humiliated we feel powerless, afraid and ashamed. Albert Einstein once said "Great spirits have always encountered violent opposition from mediocre minds" so, we could take humiliation as a compliment! We feel humiliated when the illusion of body consciousness clouds our ability to see and experiences ourselves as we really are. We are not matter, we are spirit and spirit is light, beauty and pure love. Thinking we are our body traps us into needing ego and anger to survive. Do we?

In the book *Wings of Soul,* a synthesised collection of hundreds of classes by Dadi Janki, she says, "You may have all the virtues however if you do not have humility, you will have the ego of having all the virtues." Dadi speaks of ego, impure ego and false ego, or *hubris*. Hubris indicates a loss of contact with reality and an overestimation of one's own competence, accomplishments or capabilities. It is also used when someone degrades another, under the illusion that doing so would elevate their own self. Hubris is thought to come from the Greek word *hybris*, meaning insolence, outrage and wanton violence. In classic Greek tragedies, hubris brings about the fall of heros, especially when they proudly challenge the gods. Pride is a breaching of limits.

Experiment: *Hold the word vulnerability in your mind and see where that takes you.*

* * * * *

21

Universal Laws

"We cannot break a universal law. We break ourselves trying to."
Stephen R Covey

Based on my studies, I have deduced for myself that there are just four Universal Laws to focus on. I invite you to add to these. What constitutes a universal law is that it cannot be broken. We will struggle until we realise and come into alignment with these laws. We will be broken if we cannot live within the wisdom of these laws, but the laws cannot be broken.

Universal Law 1: Eternity
"Everything straight lies. All truth is crooked, time itself is a circle,"
says the Dwarf before Zarathustra finishes his argument of the eternal return

I joined in a debate with other writers in the South China Morning Post in Hong Kong coming in with a third perspective and disrupting the common argument of Creation versus Evolution. Creation, Evolution or ... Eternity?

As mentioned earlier, I did not believe in God at all. How could a benevolent being create this world of sorrow? Why would God make some people healthy and wealthy and others poor and physically challenged? I adopted the attitude that I did not need God; God was for weak people who need a crutch. I could not see any benefit in believing in God, it didn't seem to help believers to worry less or act in a kinder way. In fact, many of the wars raging even now are based on religion. Sadly, religion often serves to make people more narrow minded and segregated. As Edmond de Goncourt stated, "If there is a God, atheism must seem to Him as less of an insult than religion."

Eternity is the concept of no beginning and no end. Was there a beginning in time, or has the world existed from eternity? If as Christians say, God is eternal, if there is such a thing as eternity, then why can't everything be eternal? If the world began with a Big Bang, are those gasses eternal? Has the world ever been created? Will it be destroyed? Or does it move in a cycle just as the seasons, day and night, and birth and death?

Christians tend to believe that God has created this world, and scientists in the Big Bang theory. When I heard the word Eternity, it acted like a *koan*, a riddle without a solution, used in Zen Buddhism to illustrate the limitations of reasoning. I felt my mind expand and the concept resonated as a Truth, a truth that I cannot prove with reasoning. One simple question yet to be resolved however is 'Which comes first, the chicken or the egg?'! Perhaps the following great men have the answer ...

Aristotle argued "everything that comes into existence does so from a substratum. Therefore the underlying matter of the universe could have come into existence only from an already existing matter exactly like itself; to assume that the underlying matter of the universe came into existence would require assuming that an underlying matter already existed. Material objects can come into existence only in place, that is, occupy space. Were something to come from nothing, the place to be occupied by what comes into existence would previously have been occupied by a vacuum, inasmuch as no body existed. But a vacuum is impossible, and matter must be eternal."

This viewpoint was disputed in the 13th century when some of the works of Aristotle, who believed in eternity of the world, conflicted with the view of the Catholic Church who believe the world has a beginning in time and a Creator. The Aristotelian view was prohibited in the Condemnations of 1210-1277.

Aristotle further explored the theory of an Eternal Return, also known as Eternal Recurrence ... "There may even be an eternal return, the universe and all existence and energy recurring, an infinite number of times" he said. This theory that the universe and all existence and energy has been recurring, and will continue to recur in a similar form, an infinite number of times across infinite time or space is also found in ancient India and ancient Egypt and was subsequently taken up by the Pythagoreans and Stoics. German philosopher, Friedrich Nietzsche also connected this theory to many of his other concepts saying, "If space and time are infinite, then it follows logically that our existence must recur an infinite number of times."

Nietzsche acknowledged that it could be a very depressing thought to think of this present life repeating identically if our present is painful. To accept eternal recurrence he embraced the concept of *amor fati*, love of fate, seeing everything that happens in one's life, including suffering and loss as good or necessary, the facts of life, whether one likes them or not. He is quoted as saying, "Only great pain is the ultimate liberator of the spirit ... I doubt that such pain makes us better; but I know that it makes us more profound."

Similarly, French revolutionist Louis Auguste Blanqui, claimed to have demonstrated eternal recurrence as a mathematical certainty. "Your whole life, like a sandglass, will always be reversed and will ever run out again, a long minute of time will elapse until all those conditions out of which you were evolved return in the wheel of the cosmic process. And then you will find every pain and every pleasure, every friend and every enemy, every hope and every error, every blade of grass and every ray of sunshine once more, and the whole fabric of things which make up your life, this ring in which you are but a grain will glitter afresh forever."

And German poet Heinrich Heine also wrote, "Time is infinite, but the things in time, the concrete bodies, are finite. They may indeed disperse into the smallest particles; but these particles, the atoms, have their determinate numbers, and the numbers of the configurations which, all of themselves, are formed out of them is also determinate. Now, however long a time may pass, according to the eternal laws governing the combinations of this eternal play of repetition, all configurations which have previously existed on this earth must yet meet, attract, repulse, kiss, and corrupt each other again."

The Greek philosopher, Critolaus, defended Aristotle's doctrine of the eternity of the world, and of the human race in general, against the Stoics, "There is no observed change in the natural order of things; humankind recreates itself in the same manner according to the capacity given by Nature, and the various ills to which it is heir, though fatal to individuals, do not avail to modify the whole. Just as it is absurd to suppose that humans are merely earth-born, so the possibility of their ultimate destruction is inconceivable. The world, as the manifestation of eternal order, must itself be eternal."

Universal Law 2: Entropy

"We think of GDP as a measure of the wealth that a country generates each year. But from a thermodynamic point of view, it is more a measure of the temporary energy value embedded in the goods or services produced at the expense of the diminution of the available energy reserves and an accumulation of entropic waste."

Jeremy Rifkin

I have always been fascinated by energy. What is it? How does it change? How does it work? Where does it come from and where does it go?

Following on logically from my thoughts about Eternity, the concept of Entropy caught my attention! Entropy is referred to in the second law of thermodynamics which deals with energy. This law of the physical universe states that the energy of an isolated system can neither be created nor destroyed. It is transferred from one location to another and converted to and from other forms of energy. Entropy refers to energy flowing from a state of orderliness to the disorderly and from the usable to the unusable. It explains why science and technology have only resulted in crisis, pollution and decay.

A very simple way to observe entropy is to drop a pack of cards. Picking up and putting this pack together again has no 'return on effort'. That energy has simply vanished. There are so many ways in which energy can just vanish!

As Meditation Teacher and Author, Ken O'Donnell explains in his book *Carousel of Time*, "In connection with a thermodynamic cycle, the net heat supplied to a system equals the net work done by it. The implications of this are considerable, especially if we consider the whole universe as one unique system and that everything in it, from an amoeba to a galaxy, is subject to the same laws.

If we just look at our planet, there is basically no new creation of air or water. We have the same atmosphere and amount of water that we have ever had. It has just been changed and re-changed, cycled and recycled ad infinita. If the law of conservation is true and nothing can be created from nothing and the total sum of the things that exist remains the same, we probably would have to find another explanation to either the Big Bang theory or even the idea that God, physically created all things from nothing.

In a sense, the second law and its measure called entropy, really just sums up ordinary human experience. For example, as the petrol in the car's tank burns in the motor, it loses its potential and the energy is dissipated in churning the pistons of the engine. That is, entropy increases. Some of the energy is lost through gases, some through heat and so on. As time goes on, the amount of energy that you can get out of the petrol becomes less and less as its stock is depleted, and so you have to go to the gas station and add more petrol.

At the same time, the spark of consciousness, which moves the energy of the body at an extremely subtle level, also loses its 'bounce', so to speak. The body becomes untenable due to age or accident. The spark of consciousness leaves the body, and the conscious energy that was holding the cells together leaves and the body dies. The molecules and atoms dissipate and the soul moves on.

The brain is a super-sophisticated computer, a part of which runs things in parallel. In other words, there are many things happening at the same time. Another part of the brain runs things in series, so that sequences of things can be sorted out. The conscious soul is the programmer of this computer, selecting, choosing, deciding and acting on what it perceives through the senses, while using both sides of the brain to do it."

Universal Law 3: Change
"The cause of all suffering is tanha, craving."

Gautama Buddha

Taṇhā is a Pali word originating from the Sanskrit word *trst*, meaning thirst, desire, longing, holding on, and attachment. In Buddha's Four Noble Truths, *tanha* is the cause of suffering and pain.

We know it to be true that one can never possess another or any thing, yet we cannot stop trying to hold on! We certainly feel ourselves 'breaking' when we do hold on to a possession, a loved one, or our appearance when it is disintegrating. We are often not conscious of our attachments until we are forced to let go of them. It feels so good to be attached, and then when a break or a loss comes, the heart wrenches and there is so much pain that we feel we are going to die! The same is true of attachment to our ideas and opinions, sense of identity and who/what we think of another's identity.

Denial seems to be the response of many to change. We are witnessing unprecedented natural calamities and almost weekly, we hear of new records being reached in heat waves all over the planet. Recently temperatures reached 44 degrees in Germany, the highest recording ever. Many deny that climate change is real, especially leaders who we now need to come on board so we all move towards a sustainable future.

Many are blinded by greed and choose not to see the seriousness of the situation. It has taken Greta Thunberg, a 15 year old girl with Aspergers Syndrome to speak the truth. She has said that being on the spectrum (of Aspergers) gives her an advantage "as almost everything is black or white." And, she has selective mutism, meaning she only speaks when needed. To her, speaking out about the threats of climate change became her greatest need. She started the school strikes that became a worldwide movement with children taking a stand on climate change on the grounds that there is no point studying if there is no future. Even Greta's teachers agreed that there is a need to be 'unreasonable' in the present situation, and she has gained the full support of her parents who became vegan and stopped flying on her insistence. Many countries have awarded her for her honesty and for taking a strong stand.

The Extinction Rebellion, a socio-political movement using nonviolent resistance to protest against climate breakdown, biodiversity loss, and the risk of social and ecological collapse, came to the forefront at the same time as Greta's movement did. These two movements have greatly helped to awaken the masses. However those who grasp their wealth and status are still very much in denial; only recently the Australian government approved the largest coalmine in Australia and one of the largest in the world ... it is just the beginning now that the Galilee Basin has been opened to mining! Naïvely I had thought there was still some sense in Australia! Perhaps the recent unprecedented fires there will help them to reconsider.

The only 'thing' that never changes is that which is beyond people, things and time ... God; constant and unchanging. This is the Power that we must reignite a connection with. This Being never changes in any sense; eternally, constantly, peaceful, pure, loving and blissful. It is comforting to know that however we are behaving, the love from this Being is unwavering. This is where the mind can rest.

Universal Law 4: Karma

"We are not punished for our sins but by our sins."

Elbert Hubbard

Karma is a Sanskrit word meaning action, work or deed. When we talk about the Philosophy of Karma we are also referring to the intent of that action. As Newton states in the third law of thermodynamics: *'to every action there is an equal and opposite reaction'*. So too, the effects of karma are equal as a consequence of that activity, as well as the intention of the actor behind the action. A good action creates good karma, as does good intent. A bad action creates bad karma, as does bad intent.

There are three types of karma:

Sukarma, pure action, performed without the slightest influence of 'body consciousness' - free of anger, greed, lust attachment and ego. These actions probably account for less than 1% of our actions. There is generally a trace of selfish motivation, even a slight one. When we give something in charity, it is often to ease our conscience, eradicate guilt, to feel good about ourselves or to look good in front of others.

Vikarma, actions influenced by some selfish motive. 98.99% of our actions would probably fall into this category if we were to be honest with ourselves. When there is any expectation for a return it would come into the category of *vikarma* as it is tinged with selfishness and ultimately brings sorrow.

Akarma, neutral action. These actions are so natural that we would not even be aware that we were doing right action. We would not look for the fruit of the action and not be affected by its outcome. In a perfect world, we cannot do any good for anyone. Eloquently describing *wu-wei*, Chinese for inaction or effortless action, Swiss Sinologist Jean François Billeter said it was a "state of perfect knowledge of the reality of the situation, perfect efficaciousness and the realisation of a perfect economy of energy". Chinese philosopher Chuang Tzu stated, "At the time of Perfect Unity, there was no action on the part of any one, but a constant manifestation of spontaneity." We could probably only give ourselves a .01% mark for this!

A vise, or vice, is used in carpentry; it is a tool used to grip or hold something fast. Vices like anger and attachment work in a similar way. We do not want to be angry or attached to an idea or person, yet we can feel 'gripped' by these feelings. The Greek word for sin, *hamartia*, originally meant error. Sin is a term that is also used in archery and means 'to miss the target'. And how easy it is to sin; how difficult to be accurate! To be appropriate in our words and actions requires skill. It is like walking a tight rope, our challenge being to maintain balance between opposite qualities like love and law, introversion and cheerfulness, intoxication and humility. We can normally inculcate any one of these qualities, however maintaining a balance between two is where we usually fall down, get hurt or hurt others. It is quite an art.

Let's look at the main vices, where they originate and their antidotes. It is more helpful to focus on the antidote rather than on removing the vice. As they say, "Where attention goes, energy flows and life grows." Vices are perverted virtues. They do not exist of themselves, as they are not original states. For example, stubbornness is the perverted form of determination and attachment results from a misunderstanding about love. In the same way, jealousy stems from laziness and laziness is a result a lack of self-respect.

Ego
"The real you is 99% beyond form."
Albert Einstein

The word for 'I' in Latin is *ego*. In Raja Yoga we understand that when we are suffering from ego we are identifying with what we perceive to be our external, material identity. Ego is often referred to as the false 'I' because anything that identifies with or is dependent on matter is in a constant state of change. This identification therefore can only ever be temporary – like our appearance, roles, external security and status.

Identifying with the body, i.e. 'body consciousness', causes us to measure ourselves with what can only be perceived through the senses. It is the great illusion of our times and leads to so much suffering as we find ourselves constantly competing and feeling 'not good enough'. Spirit is love. Ego is based on fear and insecurity.

"It's not easy to BE your self in a world where almost everyone wants you to be someone else! Even friends and colleagues often want you to be their version of you! We are surrounded and ambushed every day by a thousand images and voices calling us to invest our identity in their product, their brand, their label, their service. It's not surprising we all go through our own personal form of 'identity crisis'. Sometimes it lasts a lifetime! That's why who you 'think' you are, is usually who you are not!" writes Mike George in BEING Your Self: Seeing What's in the Way, is the Way.

I've noticed that people who embrace a spiritual path are not immune to the 'looking good' syndrome, and we see this across the board; also in our temples, mosques, synagogues and churches. In fact it can be an even greater challenge in our spiritual and religious places because there is a tendency for people to venerate and even blindly worship spiritual leaders. Spiritual growth is enhanced by respect and humility, but when it lowers our self-respect it is more akin to subservience.

During the time I lived at our Australian Retreat Centre in Wilton, most of the residents did not wear white clothes as is the custom of the Brahma Kumaris. They were often busy in the kitchen and helping with gardening and cleaning and felt that it was not practical. However, we did notice that guests who came to our retreats often forgot that they were on a spiritual retreat. The wearing of white by the Brahma Kumaris is part of our practice of simplicity and plainness – not being attracted to fashion and not attracting others to ourselves; often the very reason that fashion is followed! When we realised what was happening at the Retreat Centre we decided it would be better to wear our white clothes during retreats in order to maintain the atmosphere and raise the awareness of being in a spiritual place.

The self, the soul, is non-physical and innately who I am, eternally and originally. In Raja Yoga we term this 'soul consciousness'. In our practice, we endeavour to quieten all the voices that have told us (and may still do) that we should be a certain way, and spend time in self-reflection getting to know ourselves. From the day we are born we are labeled and given the burden of many expectations from many people. Appreciation of our 'true' self can come through many means like silence and meditation, and also reading; discerning what messages resonate with us and reminding us of our own Truth. I am so grateful for the many teachers and writers I have come across. They have offered me shortcuts to be able to understand deep aspects of myself and life rather than my having to work all these things out on my own!

There was a time when I particularly enjoyed educating myself on the more extreme states of delusion rooted in ego, namely Hubris and Narcissism. Hubris is an extreme form of pride where we become so blinded by our own view of things that we can no longer see reality. This often leads to a very great fall. In the Greek tragedies we read of examples of hubris in characters such as King Oedipus, so proud that he even defied the gods! Similarly, narcissism is an exaggerated feeling of self-importance. This often results in manipulative behaviour because a narcissist has no empathy for anyone else. Sadly narcissists thrive on vulnerability and are commonly found in charities and spiritual organisations. Upon realising this I was interested to know how I might protect myself and I came to learn that the best defense against a narcissist is absolute honesty.

Attachment

"Detachment is allowing, attachment is controlling,"

Deepak Chopra

Although it is not what we were brought up to believe, a state of detachment is actually closer to love than being attached. When we are not attached we can give another person space. *Niara,* Hindi for unique or 'to stand apart from', is translated in English as 'detachment', which is often taken to mean being aloof and uncaring. In the early days of my practice with the Brahma Kumaris there was a lot of misunderstanding surrounding this and our families bore the brunt of that misunderstanding.

Psychologists tend to refer to attachment as co-dependency. Before this phrase was coined in the late 1970's, psychologists would often get rather irate when attachment was referred to as something unhealthy. In co-dependency, we want someone else to take care of us and we lose our healthy boundaries. We allow ourselves to be abused and then blame the person we are following. Some of these co-dependent behaviours are rooted in attachment such as compromising our own values to avoid another's rejection or anger; remaining in harmful situations too long; tolerating inappropriate behaviour and lavishing gifts and favours on those we care about in a way that is in the long run, detrimental to them.

I remember a lady in Hong Kong who had suffered from depression for many years even though she had a lovely family, wealth and all that one could imagine would bring happiness. We were travelling to India together once and I could not find her at the airport. When I did find her she had been standing at a counter of another airline. Although she travelled very often, this was the first time she was travelling without her husband and she had no idea what to do. She confided in me that her husband would always do everything for her and I realised that this was the cause of her depression; she did not need to think. Her husband was 'loving' her so much that she actually had no power. After travelling to India, her parents who lived in South America, needed to sell a house and we decided that she really needed to go there to help them and to 'get a life', even to the point of travelling there alone.

Another woman I knew had lived in Hong Kong for just over a year. Her husband had been transferred there by his company and she gave up her own profession to be with him. As they had a small child she was unable to get work and felt alone, frustrated and unfulfilled as her husband was thriving in his profession and was always very excited about it. In an effort to entice him home from work early she would often cook his favourite meals, nevertheless he was generally late. Over time he began to feel resentful of her demands and even suggested she go back to her home country. She felt she loved him and he was neither responding to her nor being fair. When her and I reflected on this together, she realised that it was not love but need that was driving her. I suggested she take up some interests that she could become involved in and be more interesting to her husband when they were together. It worked and the marriage survived.

Khalil Gibran offered a guide for partnership when he spoke about marriage …

> *You were born together, and together you shall be forever more.*
> *You shall be together when the white wings*
> *Of death scatter your days.*
> *Aye, you shall be together even in the memory of God.*
> *But let there be space in your togetherness.*
> *And let the winds of the heavens dance between you.*
> *Love one another, but make not a bond of love:*
> *Let it be a moving sea between the shores of your souls.*
> *Fill each other's cups but drink not from one cup.*
> *Give one another of your bread but eat not from the same loaf.*
> *Sing and dance together and be joyous,*
> *But let each of you be alone,*
> *Even as the strings of the lute are alone though they quiver*
> *With the same music.*
> *Give your hearts, but not into each other's keeping.*
> *For only the hand of Life can contain your hearts.*
> *And stand together yet not too near together:*
> *For the pillars of the temple stand apart,*
> *And the cypress and the oak tree stand not*
> *In each other's shadow.*

How would a couple relate in a perfect relationship? What would be the basis of their relationship if there were no needs? They would simply celebrate each others life, sharing in each others joy of living, each one autonomous, free and clear.

Co-dependency has become so ingrained it is hard to imagine a world with perfect relationships. We do not even have words to describe a perfect relationship between two complete people. Words like trust or support would be obsolete. Today we become locked into each others needs. Women stay with an abusive husbands for security and men with an abusive wives for social status. Co-dependency is endemic in nearly all of our relationships.

Greed

"Need is limited. Greed is unlimited."

Bapdada

Desires are not inappropriate, however we need to check that by having our desires fulfilled, lasting happiness will be brought to both ourselves and others. "A healthy persons desires would lead them to happiness," states Deepak Chopra. When we have an intention on something great, all small desires fall away. It is easy to give up limited things when we set our sights on something higher. For example, someone who sets their sights on climbing Mount Everest needs to raise a vast sum of money. This need would supersede many small expenses previously thought to be necessary.

A need is something that is required for a safe, stable and healthy life while a want is a desire, a wish or an aspiration, and feelings are indicators of whether our needs are being met.

Need is limited, greed is unlimited. Look around you now; what could you say you honestly *need*? Generally we need a floor, a roof and air. Is it greed to have anything more than that? We are hardwired for aesthetics, however. Feathers, body paint, shells, rock carvings - human beings are aesthetic creatures. A world without beauty is unnatural.

When we feel we *need* things our mind can become obsessive, we then think too much and our peace is lost. For example we may feel that we 'need' a fancier car. Whenever we see fancy cars we notice who is driving them, we compare ourselves with them and want to be like them. Until we transcend the desire, we will keep thinking in this way. We may end up fulfilling the desire, however at what price? Perhaps we end up working for the car instead of the car working for us!

A wealthy businessman in Hong Kong once invited me out on his boat. He asked if I was enjoying the ride and I was feeling very relaxed and blissful. He told me he never felt relaxed because he could not afford to own the boat. He felt embarrassed that other people had boats that were faster and whenever they planned to meet up, the others would have to wait for him. On Monday mornings his staff would cop the brunt of his embarrassment because he would try firing them up to make him more money!

Greed is so serious that it has now brought us to the brink of destruction. It is worrying to see the mindset of some corporates who sincerely believe in greed as an evolutionary need. The film *Wall Street*, is a representation of this. In it, corporate raider Gordon Gekko states, "Greed, for lack of a better word, is good. Greed is right, greed works. Greed clarifies, cuts through, and captures the essence of the evolutionary spirit. Greed, in all of its forms; greed for life, for money, for love, knowledge has marked the upward surge of mankind."

As early as 1972 we received a warning with the publication of *The Limits to Growth*, commissioned by the Club of Rome and authored by Donella and Dennis Meadows, Jorgen Randers and William Behrens, representing a team of 17 researchers. It sold over 30 million copies. Not surprisingly there was a groundswell of negative reaction which the Italian economist Giorgio Nebbia observed had come from at least four sources: those who saw the book as a threat to their business or industry; professional economists, who saw Limits to Growth as an uncredentialled encroachment on their professional perquisites; the Catholic Church, which bridled at the suggestion that overpopulation was one of mankind's major problems; and finally the political left, which saw the LTG study as a scam by the elites designed to trick workers into believing that a proletarian paradise was a pipe dream.

In the early years of the 21st century, seeing the reality of the LTG predictions, opinions regarding LTG began to swing in a positive direction and these can be summarised in the views of influential energy economist, Matthew Simmons who said "In hindsight, The Club of Rome turned out to be right. We simply wasted 30 important years ignoring this work." We are still wasting time!

Lust

*"Falling in love is a trick that the genes play
on the otherwise perceptive mind
to hoodwink you into marriage."*

Scott Peck

The statistics of sexual abuse are rather horrifying. The final report of The Royal Commission into Institutional Responses to Child Sexual Abuse was released in Australia in 2017, and very few institutions came out clean. It is not surprising that many celibate spiritual people have been abusing others. In Christianity, chastity is an oath. I am not sure how much mentoring, coaching and spiritual training goes into assisting people who aspire to lead a spiritual life yet struggle with the disciplines. For this reason, many in society feel that a celibate life is inappropriate and would like to see priests and monks marry.

When we are engaged in spiritual practise accurately, the physical senses become cool and a sexual drive is absent. *Patanjali*, considered the father of modern yoga practises, included celibacy as one of the five *yamas*, social restraints. According to ancient yogic traditions, celibacy frees us from physical distractions and supports the yogic principles of truth and nonviolence. So often violence is associated with sexuality, even in marriage.

The ancient Indian science of *Ayurveda* advocates conserving body fluids as a way of conserving subtle energies, increasing concentration, vitality, character and health. Similarly, in Taoism, practitioners are encouraged to conserve spiritual energy that would usually be directed towards sexual pursuit, and directing that energy towards higher spiritual goals. It is considered that without this dedication achievement is compromised. In traditional Chinese medicine celibacy is referred to as *sanbao*, the three treasures: *jing*, nutritive essence, life force which nourishes and cools the body and increases longevity; *shen*, spirit, mind, soul, extracting nutrients from food and the air; and *qi*, energy, breath.

The spiritual teacher, Meher Baba, who at one point was a favourite of mine, described the differences between lust and love: "In lust there is reliance upon the object of sense and consequent spiritual subordination of the soul to it, but love puts the soul into direct and co-ordinate relation with the reality which is behind the form. Therefore lust is experienced as being heavy and love is experienced as being light. In lust there is a narrowing down of life and in love there is an expansion in being ... If you love the whole world you vicariously live in the whole world, but in lust there is an ebbing down of life and a general sense of hopeless dependence upon a form, which is regarded as another. Thus, in lust there is the accentuation of separateness and suffering, but in love there is the feeling of unity and joy."

The aim in any yoga practice is to become free of addictions and of course sex is often an addiction. As with any addiction, if you cannot abstain completely, then at least consider a 'fast' for a few months or even a year. It helps to clean out anything unhealthy that is hidden in this area. It is interesting that few speak about sex, and there are often deep and disturbing emotions tied up with it. Abstaining from sex, even for a while, is known to help awaken spiritual energy faster than any other discipline.

If you have ever been on a stallion when a mare is on heat, you will have experienced how addictive this drive can be in an animal. It does not feel safe to be on a horse in those circumstances; the rider is forgotten and the horse will jump over or break through fences or any other boundary that keeps them from their desire. Mahatma Gandhi who experimented with celibacy is reported to have once said "Life without celibacy is insipid and animal-like." In his practice, Gandhi developed a new measure of self-restraint and found increasing reserves of time and energy to devote to humanitarian and spiritual pursuits. "I realised that a vow, far from closing the door to real freedom, opened it" he wrote in his autobiography. "What formerly appeared to me to be extravagant praise of *brahmacharya*, celibacy, in our religious books seems now, with increasing clearness every day, to be absolutely proper and founded on experience."

Many modern day yogis advocate a compromise. However, as it seems perfectly right and normal to have sex in a married or steady relationship there is often not a true consensus in couples. There is a fear to offend or reject, many fearing they would be sending their partner into someone else's arms. This is usually not spoken about.

The other issue is contraception. It is not natural for us to take chemicals every day for many years, plus pharmaceutical chemicals add greatly to the pollution of our waterways! Sex is perceived as something people cannot live without and yet nature has designed sex for procreation, not for entertainment. In India there are still communities who, in keeping with the natural rhythm of life, become celibate after creating a family rather than further stimulating sexual desire.

Recent statistics on sexual violence in Australia show that 1 in 5 women and 1 in 20 men have been assaulted or threatened since the age of 15 years. It is not too different in other countries. When the vice, the grip, of lust takes hold of us, we cannot control the passion even when we are aware of possible consequences like contracting a disease, emotionally damaging our partner and/or children or bringing a child into the world in inappropriate circumstances. Many children struggle with the unresolved issue of not knowing a biological parent; no matter how much love they are brought up with, they still feel a strong urge to know their bloodline.

Some people choose to dedicate their lives to the service of others or to a cause rather than creating a family or even having a career. Their feeling is that having a partner would vastly extend their energy and responsibilities. Many highly successful people like boxers Mike Tyson,

Muhammad Ali and David Haye; Jiu-Jitshu legend, Rickson Gracie; scientists Sir Isaac Newton and Sigmund Freud; businessmen Nikola Tesla and Steve Jobs; philosophers Plato, Pythagoras, Socrates; artists, Michelangelo and Leo Tolstoy; and statesman, Winston Churchill have chosen to be celibate in order to direct passion towards a life goal.

In today's world the general consensus is if you do not have a high sex drive then there is something wrong with you and you should see a doctor! This does not even make sense; some people are foodies or sports fanatics. We are not all the same. Before taking up the practise of Raja Yoga, I thought there was something wrong with me too. I questioned if I truly loved my husband. However in books we both read, written by various gurus, especially Paramahansa Yogananda, celibacy was advocated for those seeking the ultimate spiritual quest. When Tom and I considered the aspect of celibacy it seemed natural. We both had the aim to truly love each other and we sensed that a physical relationship would mask a lot of issues with its 'kiss and make up' approach.

I am thankful I am part of a celibate community. I find the relationships between men and women are healthier. I have men friends who I am very close to, just as I am with women. It is just like an extended family with a lot of opportunities to explore the concept of unattached love. Relationships between brothers and sisters are some of the lightest we can experience. There is less expectation. Brothers and sisters are not meant to depend on each other, unlike partners or parents and children. I have also noticed that men become less macho when they are celibate and there is greater respect for women when they don't see them as bodies. Likewise, women become less feminine and have greater respect for themselves! Both move towards an androgynous balanced gender state.

Any woman reading this will relate to what it feels like to be constantly seen as a body. Besides being boring and insulting, the attention to body image also affects one's self esteem. Women look at women, comparing and competing. Although fashion is a form of art we can obsess about it as there is the illusion that we will be valued when we fit in. Women obsess about our bodies and looks to the point we totally forget who we really are. I remember as an eleven year old not wanting to go out unless I was allowed to wear what I thought was the fashion of the day. I so desperately needed to fit in and look 'good'.

Anger

"Anger and intolerance are the enemies of correct understanding."

Mahatma Gandhi

When my good friend Mike George was being pushed by his publishers to write another book, I urged him to take up the topic of Anger. I was meeting so many people who were feeling uncomfortable about their uncontrolled anger, and they wanted help!

We have to remember that angry people do not actually enjoy being angry. They generally feel regret, shame and sadness about their hurtful words and uncontrolled outbursts. In his book *Don't Get Mad Get Wise: Why No-one Ever Makes You Angry ... Ever!*, Mike talks about anger from a spiritual perspective rather than just seeing it as an emotion. This book has helped many of my friends.

I was once involved in a project with someone who was a self-confessed 'rage-aholic'. Their anger was based on a belief system that people need to fear you in order for you to get things done. This behaviour becomes a habit that runs, and often ruins, lives. Our jails house many who were not able to control their anger, sometimes even killing another person in rage. When teaching meditation in a jail in India, the gentle and polite brother who was setting up the room and playing the music told me he was in jail for murder. He had been in the army and had requested home leave for three years in a row. Upon being refused yet again, he was so angry he shot his commanding officer. If he had not had a gun, no doubt it would have been a punch. This is the danger of weapons! When we are angry we 'lose our mind' and are actually temporarily insane. Our intellect won't function – we can no longer judge right from wrong, we cannot form sentences and can only swear or hit out.

Passive anger is much harder to pinpoint but we often come across it in those who are 'nice'. Unable or unwilling to express their anger in obvious ways, they do so covertly. In one Meditation Centre I stayed at, the much-loved chef maintained control in the kitchen by being aloof. Volunteers who offered to chop vegetables would not be given a time to show up so would hang around until she appeared. Not me! I told her I was happy to help but needed to be given a specific time to do so. Even when chopping the vegetables, if I were to ask what we were cooking, she would say "I don't know yet."

In *The Celestine Prophecy* by James Redfield, four control dramas are explained. Being **Aloof** is one of them and is perhaps the hardest for me to deal with. One who is aloof controls others by not giving them any information. I remember asking someone one morning what time their flight was that day. His response was "I don't know." Actually, I did not even care, I was just trying to make conversation. I have learnt that the worst way to deal with an aloof person is to ask questions!

We all control others to some extent and an aloof person has often come from a home where the second type of control drama, **Interrogation** has occured. This type of control is when someone asks you excessive questions and then uses the information given to them to make you feel bad. They will make you explain and justify your reasons, decisions and behaviours to the point where you can feel you even need to justify your existence.

The next is **Intimidation**; threatening someone in order to control them. This could be in the form of emotional blackmail, threats of violence or withdrawal when you don't fulfil their wishes. This can be more obvious, but still not easy to deal with.

Lastly, there is the **Poor Me** control drama; eliciting pity from others in order that they do your bidding. I have fallen for this one often! I used to wonder why I did not want to help some people. I found my feelings were rather odd as I am usually very willing to help. When I read about the Poor Me control drama I realised that at these times I was experiencing a subtle awareness that I was being manipulated by the other person and I was resenting that.

It was interesting to read in *Power versus Force* by David Hawkins, that Anger vibrates at a higher energy frequency than Shame, Guilt and Fear. Anger stirs us into action; we are willing to do something to make a change. It is still a very low energy level but it acts as an indicator of something that needs to change. It is therefore helpful to be able to recognise and use the messages anger brings. We can then learn to express ourselves appropriately and connect with others in an authentic way. Some suggest assertion is a constructive way of expressing ourselves without hurting others, however I think it is best to avoid being too assertive as it can often border on bossiness - another subtle trace of anger! We know when we are angry when there is a feeling of a fire inside. Best to find a method to cool down before we begin expressing our feelings!

* * * * *

22

Spirituality, Religion and Superstition

Faith
"You can tell a person by their faith."

Bhagavad Gita

In life we can often be challenged to stretch our beliefs, trust and faith. In Hindi there are two words for faith; *Bhavana*, which is based on feelings and perception, and *Nischay*, meaning an intellectual faith and conviction.

I lived in India from 2010 to 2014 and during this time, the aspect of faith I came to appreciate most was bhavana. It was a great contrast to the type of faith I had been applying, *Nischay*. Wherever I went, I continually received loving feelings and I did not feel I had to do anything to deserve it. It seemed the Indian people were always looking for an opportunity to display their affection towards me. It was often done in very creative ways and included gestures like having the youngest girl dress up as a deity to say good night to me, a *rangoli* (sand art) created at my door, candle lit dinners, food carvings, decorating my bedroom with balloons and streamers, and perhaps the most outstanding for me, the cooking of eight dishes for each meal, especially for *me*, because I did not eat the food with chilli that they were accustomed too. I had to force them to cut this back to four!

Doing things with bhavana does take a little more time, but the result in terms of connection and relationship is worth every minute. How often do we meet friends who we value, and yet because of being in a hurry we do not stop to connect before getting into what we had planned to do or speak about? Bhavana is applying a 'pause' in order to connect and recognise the person I am with. Efficiency seems to be its enemy. A quality shared by many cultures, bhavana has almost been lost, especially where time has become very precious; more precious than relationships. When I speak to people about bhavana, especially in Asia, there is an awareness of this erosion.

A simple example of bhavana is, before offering a guest a glass of water, first consider the temperature of the water, the glass to be used to serve the water in and perhaps putting it on a tray with a napkin. It is adding love and care into our words and actions. I may fulfil a task for someone, but doing that task with love, happiness, and in peace, fills that action with an experience. Karmically, when I receive the return of the action, it too will be filled with feelings and not just help in a situation. It is clear to see how things 'go around' and the importance of infusing into our interactions and life in general, greater quality.

If I want to develop my faith in another person, it is important to create bhavana towards them and also have the right perception of them. A big part of my life has been receiving senior meditation teachers who visit and organising programmes for them to speak at. I remember one of these occasions when a senior teacher whom I did not have a lot of respect for visited; I expected more from her. I decided on this visit, that instead of 'seeing' her how I thought she was, I would see her how I would like her to be. It was an interesting experiment because her behaviour became much more centred and loving. I realised that the way I had been perceiving her had put her on the defensive, and she was not able to be the kind of person I liked to be around.

Growing up, I had not cultivated the kind of bhavana I witnessed in India. When I asked a group of Nepalese women what they felt when they remembered God, most had tears emerge in their eyes. The same evening, I asked a group of westerners the same question. They became very intellectual in the process! I would say we need a balance of the two, bhavana and nischay.

For centuries there has been a philosophical debate on faith and reason. Most religious traditions allow and even encourage some kind of rational examination of their beliefs. However, for some people this is not necessary. Faith comes to them intrinsically, and is usually based on experience. American theologian, James W. Fowler defined faith as "... an activity of trusting, committing, and relating to the world based on a set of assumptions of how one is related to others and the world." When I came across the Brahma Kumaris, I did not believe in God, and the idea of 'making effort to have faith', one of their teachings, interested me. Today I continue to put any idea to the test. If I experience 'proof' that it is true or right, I develop a strong faith in it.

For many years I have experimented with holding an intention. My experimentation had been triggered when I read *The Tao of Leadership*, by John Heder. I read the book twice and still only remembered one line, "Few leaders realise how little they have to do." This insight changed the way I operated more than any other idea. It aligned with *The Eightfold Path* in Buddhism, and I realised how simple and profound these teachings are; so simple that many overlook them...

Right Speech - non-hurtful, not exaggerated, truthful;
Right Actions - wholesome, avoiding action that would do any harm;
Right Livelihood - to not harm oneself or others; directly or indirectly;
Right Effort - an effort to improve;
Right Awareness - to see things for what they are with clear consciousness;
Right Concentration - being aware of the present reality, without

craving or aversion;

Right Thoughts – pure thought patterns; and

Right Understanding - understanding reality as it is, not just as it appears to be.

Likewise, the Bhagavad Gita (see **Actions Krti** in Chapter 25), speaks about modes of existence, *gunas*, and that harmony is achieved when we operate from the state of *satoguna*, meaning constructive goodness, and not looking for the return of the action. Simply doing the action because it is 'right'.

Belief
"You will see it when you believe it."

Wayne Dyer

When Dr Ian Stevenson left America for India to study reincarnation, he was mocked and ridiculed by other professors. Being a professor of high repute, they felt he was ruining his reputation in such ridiculous research. His obituary in the *New York Times* reveals that his detractors saw him as "earnest, dogged but ultimately misguided, led astray by gullibility, wishful thinking and a tendency to see science where others saw superstition." Yet, when he reached India and informed professors there of his research, their response was, "What is there to prove, we all know about reincarnation."

Up to 50% of the world's population have believed in reincarnation. Research into many ancient cultures and religions has found that from the Ancient Greeks, including Pythagoras, to the Norse people and the American Indians, reincarnation has been a strong belief. In recent years, surveys have shown that more than 20-30% of Christians believe in reincarnation. Yet, many scoff and label it a 'superstition'. Perhaps this is because many profess that the soul transmigrates into other species - which is much more difficult to believe!

In Tokyo in 2006, I met cellular biologist Dr Nemoto, International Secretary to the well-known scientist Masaru Emoto from Japan. Masaru Emoto authored many books about his experiments with water crystals. Following the directions set out in his book *The Message from Water – Children's Version*, I decided to try an experiment of my own without all the equipment needed to freeze and photograph water. I simply put cooked rice in two identical jars and closed the lids. Following the instructions exactly, on one jar I wrote, 'You fool', and on the other, 'You are beautiful.' After 6 weeks, the difference was remarkable. The one labelled 'You fool' had accumulated black fungus and smelt unpleasant. The one labelled 'You are beautiful' was golden and fragrant.

I lived in Cambodia from 2006 to 2010. It was extremely hot and humid there and I repeated this experiment three times, showing the jars in my talks on Positive Thinking. I thought it was a very good metaphor for what happens inside us when our self-talk is negative. The Khmer people told me many amazing things, like how a perfectly carved Buddha had been found inside a palm seed, but they found it hard to believe the results of this experiment! Belief is such a funny thing!

A Divine Intellect

"The power of a divine intellect is an extremely elevated power. Just as magicians of today show the cleanliness of their palms, so the cleanliness of a divine intellect brings all success into the palm of your hand."

BapDada

Sister Jayanti, a senior teacher with the Brahma Kumaris and author of many books, further elaborates, "The intellect is the vessel of spiritual understanding. Everything in human life depends on what is going on within the intellect. When we need to take a decision, we need to let the mind become quiet, keep spiritual wisdom in the intellect and stay connected with the Divine to receive power and clarity. When the intellect is without spiritual wisdom the conscience becomes dysfunctional."

There was a point when I became interested in the word *nous*. Though used often, I had never really thought about its origins. I discovered it is a Latin word, sometimes equated to intellect or intelligence and the basic understanding or awareness that allows human beings to think rationally.

Aristotle distinguished *nous*, the faculty for setting definitions, from *logos*, the faculty that uses them to reason with. Elaborating, he explained that the passive intellect receives the intelligible forms of things and the active intellect is required to make potential knowledge into actual knowledge, in the same way that light makes potential colours into actual colours.

There is also what is known as a 'cosmic *nous*', an ordering humanlike principle; a creator of order, and also a recipient. The Pre-Socratic Greek philosopher Anaxagoras, wrote "All other things partake in a portion of everything, while nous is infinite and self-ruled, and is mixed with nothing, but is alone, itself by itself. For if it were not by itself, but were mixed with anything else, the things mixed with it would hinder it, so that it would have power over nothing. It is the thinnest of all things and the purest, and it has all knowledge about everything and the greatest strength; and nous has power over all things, both greater and smaller, that have soul."

Socrates described people as being able to perceive more clearly because of something from outside themselves, something like when the sun shines, helping eyesight. He spoke of *anamnesis* whereby people are born with ideas already in their soul, which they somehow remember from previous lives. Socrates argued that nous in individual humans, must share in a cosmic nous, in the same way that human bodies are made up of small parts of the elements found in the rest of the universe.

Something to ponder on more!

Spirituality, Religion and Superstition

"Superstition is fear based, spirituality is love based, and religion is tradition which can shift back and forth from fear to love."

Maureen Chen, presentation to the HK Philosophy Cafe

In 2005 I attended a workshop conducted by Guy Claxton at the Hong Kong University. It was titled 'Spirituality in Social Work'. The outcome was interesting, considering the backgrounds of the participants. There were approximately 30 of us and of those, 25 were Christians/Catholics. (In Hong Kong you are either a Christian or a Catholic.) The following was captured from the workshop:

Spirituality	Religion
Free flowing	Structured
Androgynous	Male Dominated
Emancipating	Oppressive
Metaphysical	Conforming
Individual	Institutionalised
And	Or
Equality	Patriarchal
Liberating	Social Control
Transcendent	Culturally defined
Bringing Together	Separating
Applies to all	Applies to some
Inclusive	Exclusive
Flexible	Dogmatic
Expansive	Restrictive
Being	Ego

Later that year I presented my thoughts on superstition, religion and spirituality to the Hong Kong Philosophy Cafe. I thought it would be a good opportunity to test the theories I had developed in this regard.

On the scale between superstition and spirituality, fear and love sit at opposite ends. Superstitions are fear-based beliefs that are unrelated to truth. They may be found in religion when the foundation is fear and when we follow blindly. Spirituality however, is about living in the awareness of the non-physical self, experiencing inter-connectedness to all things. Religion can support this endeavour, but when we are not in a state of love our motives become fear based.

I have never thought of the Brahma Kumaris as a religion, although I probably appear to belong to a religious sect dressed in my white sari! I consider myself spiritual rather than religious. I make a tremendous amount of effort to discipline my mind because I believe in its power and how it can be used to help alleviate suffering - both my own and that of others.

Opening a bottle of wine, my father once asked me, "You are not allowed to drink this are you?" My response was that it was not a matter of being allowed or not being allowed, it was a matter of me understanding the effect of alcohol on my mind. Drinking alcohol was antithetic to my meditating; I aimed to pacify and manage my thoughts. Why would I make so much effort to manage my mind, including a daily practice of meditating at 4.00am, and then do something to contradict that effort?! I may as well sleep in!

I pursue my interest with dedication, just as professional teachers, doctors, artists, athletes or scientists follow certain disciplines *religiously* in pursuit of their goals. As in any profession, study is essential, and I actively engage in spiritual study to empower myself, gain insights and stay in a subtle awareness. To maintain such an awareness, essential to spirituality, I also follow various yogic disciplines like early morning meditation and a vegetarian diet.

Religious or spiritual traditions have passed down recommended disciplines known to aid people on those paths, and for centuries millions have practised them. However, it seems that at some point, the reasons for these disciplines can be forgotten and people begin following them as rules, without any deep understanding. Perhaps it just never occurs to them to experiment, to see if the disciplines prescribed to them actually make a difference. Then, there are also those who prefer to be followers, just as many would rather hand their bodies over to a doctor when they have an ailment rather than taking responsibility for their own healing and recovery.

Many institutions developed in the name of religion. People handed over their power, or in many cases were stripped of it, including the right to believe whatever they felt to be *their* truth. Religious leaders then claimed to be endowed with the authority of God or Truth and the right to judge 'the people'. Incorrect practise in early Christianity was called *vitia*, vice. Surely this would have included excessive devotion and fearful grovelling! Thankfully though, some have not been controlling, but have genuinely hoped that their people would experience the love and power of the Faith.

Scriptures have also been taken literally, but whose interpretation of the scriptures were people to follow? Often there would be such fear of being cursed if doubts were raised or questions asked. Many religious leaders were also afraid of losing control of the systems their institutions had introduced as means to maintain power. There was fear of losing followers, including their financial support.

Indigenous peoples like the Australian Aborigines have often had their spirituality characterised as a collection of superstitions and primitive myths. They were seen to be 'living in darkness' by Christian settlers. But how can we judge something to be superstition? James Cowan, author of *Mysteries of the Dreamtime* wrote, "I learnt to respect the uncluttered wisdom of their thought, their ability to derive so much spiritual knowledge from what appeared to be an uncritical respect for tradition. I soon learnt it was in fact, reverence. Their concept of sanctity I found to be far more complex and far-reaching than any we might find in the universal religions."

The belief that we are evolving has created an attitude that indigenous cultures are primitive and undeveloped and yet their sacred places and temples are the land itself - the earth, the rock-forms, trees, plains, mountains and the sky. Australian Aborigines see the land, insects, animals and humans all intricately linked in what they call 'the Dreaming', the time when the Ancestral Spirits progressed over the land and created life and important physical geographic formations and sites. There is no primacy in this; mankind and nature are co-equal partners. The Dreamtime conveys knowledge of 'the Primordial Event' and indicates the possibility of full participation in it by the individual. It is a state of mind – a return to the source.

Communities have conveniently tried to protect and preserve their traditions by calling anything that is different a cult or superstitious. Some cultures have been threatened by the non-economic worldview held by the nomadic indigenous who do not believe in possessing anything. The nomad carries his whole world within himself. Is this not a core spiritual law: that we can never own anything or anyone?

Traditionally, Raja Yoga has not been based on faith, but on knowledge and correct practise. The aim of Raja Yoga is to attain self-sovereignty. Practitioners are not encouraged to be followers, but to experience things for themselves. Truth is a personal experience, and experience is the highest authority. When we align our self with our truth we are then following our *dharma*.

In Hindu and Buddhist languages, the word 'religion' is often translated as *dharma*, meaning duties, rights, laws, conduct, virtues and the right way of living. The Sanskrit root, *dhar*, means 'to uphold'. *Dharma*, therefore means to uphold one's own righteous way of being, the freedom to be one's self and not be influenced by the atmosphere, someone or something. The word 'religion' comes from the Latin, *religare*, meaning to bind or connect again. It's a pity the original meaning has been lost.

Somewhere along the line we have put the fear of God into believers. Threatened with dire consequences if they break disciplines, many believe that this huge, all-powerful One would cast 'His' (it has generally been a patriarchal figurehead) wrath on them. Actually the fact is, breaking disciplines will have consequences. If an athlete does not maintain his diet and exercise routine there will be a loss. An awareness of self-responsibility for our actions needs to be restored in us and God needs to be removed from the punishing role - a role He/She has never taken on. His Holiness the Dalai Lama once said "Learn to obey the rules very well so you will know how to break them properly." Rules are guidelines for best practice, they are not meant to bind us in rituals and fear.

In the past, whenever I had to fill out forms that asked for my religion, I would write 'Peace'. However I was concerned, that upon seeing this others would think I was still a hippie! Now I write 'Nonviolence'. However, I do see Peace as the *religare*, the religion, of the soul - of every soul, that we need to connect with once again.

Raja Yoga is the practice of being true to one's self, getting to know one's self and being open to others regardless of their spiritual or religious practice. Many people maintain their own religion and yet comfortably practise Raja Yoga. They find it compliments their primary spiritual or religious practice.

* * * * *

Wider Views

23

Raja Yoga

Are These Brahma Kumaris a Hindu Sect?
*"Some churches, sects, cults or religious movements are
basically collective egoic entities,
as rigidly identified with their mental positions as the followers
of any political ideology that is closed to any
alternative interpretation of reality."*

Eckhart Tolle

Fearful of becoming enmeshed in a cult, Tom and I were cautious in our engagement with the BKs. The credentials of the Brahma Kumaris World Spiritual University sounded good; a non–government organisation with general consultative status with the Economic and Social Council of the United Nations, in consultative status with UNICEF, and affiliated to the UN Department of Public Information. Free of any religious affiliation and open to people of all backgrounds, today there are BK Centres in over 130 countries with over 9,000 Centres worldwide.

The organisation was established in 1937 with the aim of reviving the ancient teachings of Raja Yoga and exploring spirituality. Based in

Mount Abu, Rajasthan, since 1950, it now has three campuses, one of which is in Abu Road and can accommodate 20,000 people. The campuses have two main objectives: training BK teachers and students, and holding retreats and conferences for professionals to explore the connection between spirituality and the arts, medicine, education, science, the media, etc. Focusing on the area of human and social values, the Brahma Kumaris are widely perceived to be bringing a particularly ethical and spiritual approach to world concerns.

Louis Jolyon West defined a cult as "a group or movement exhibiting a great or excessive devotion or dedication to some person, idea, or thing and employing unethically manipulative techniques of persuasion and control designed to advance the goals of the group's leaders, to the actual or possible detriment of members, their families, or the community." Knowing the BKs inside out now for over forty years, and having served on their Boards, I am confident that they are not a cult. With over a million committed practitioners worldwide obviously there are differences in levels of commitment and practice, but overall BKs are good people.

Origins of Yoga

"Yoga is not a work-out, it is a work-in. And this is the point of spiritual practice; to make us teachable; to open up our hearts and focus our awareness so that we can know what we already know and be who we already are."

Rolf Gates

Yoga, originates from *yuj*, meaning, 'to join, yoke, connect or unite'. It is said to have been developed in the pre-vedic tradition around 1500 BC, and is mentioned in the *Rig-Veda*, the oldest Indian scripture. The origin of yoga is the connection between *atma*, the Soul, and *param atma*, the Soul beyond, Supreme. By being beyond, the Supreme Soul remains constant, in the original state of the Soul; complete in peace, power, knowledge, love and bliss. Human Souls, on the other hand, by coming on to the stage of life, forget their identity and believe they are their bodies.

A Soul has everything that it needs within it. Forgetting the awareness of ourselves as a Soul, we look outwards for peace, love, power and knowledge. By connecting with the *paramatma*, we get reintroduced to our origin and our return to that is enabled. To connect we need to take our minds beyond this physical dimension of time and space where our thoughts wander in a world that is never still; it is always changing.

The father of modern-day yoga is Sage Patanjali who systemised yoga in the 4th Century. He is considered to have developed the post-classical period. Many yoga schools link the origins of yoga with Patanjali, when in fact it is far more ancient. The earliest illustration of yoga postures is from the Mohenjo-Daro seals, said to be dated 3300 -1300 BC. These seals show one person standing on their head, and another sitting cross-legged. They are among the remains of an ancient city located in present day Pakistan, part of the Indus Valley civilisation.

Now in the 21st century, by secularising yoga, it has been brought to a status internationally never previously known. However, the ancient wisdom and meaning of yoga has almost been lost. When I first arrived in Cambodia hatha yoga was not well known and when I asked people what yoga is, most said that it was spiritual, a kind of meditation. Within just one or two years, with the arrival of hatha yoga on to the scene, when I would ask what yoga is they would say "exercise". As beneficial as this is, all yogic disciplines, such as the *asana, karma yoga, bhakti yoga, pranayama* and *meditation*, were developed to take one toward *raja yoga*, a union with the *paramatma*.

The ultimate goal of the meditation path is to attain equanimity, a *samadhi* state; achievable whether meditating in total isolation or performing daily activities; a state of being in the world and yet not affected by it. Surrendering to *paramatma*, the Supreme soul beyond, is considered to be the method to attain this state of being.

Relaxation – Meditation – Yoga

"It's not about being good at something. It's about being good to yourself."

Anonymous

The teachings of the BKs focus on two practices. Firstly meditation, which helps an individual understand their own Self and the workings of their mind, intellect and subconscious mind, *'sanskaras'*. Secondly, as mentioned above, *Yoga* means a connection and relationship between *atma*, the Soul, the Self, and *param atma*, the Soul beyond, also translated as Supreme, who is understood to be a living, non-physical energy, 'the Light'.

Many people ask if the Brahma Kumaris are a Hindu organisation. The teachings are actually pre-Hindu. Raja Yoga dates back to the Vedic times, around 1200BC. Hinduism is a synthesis of various Indian cultures and traditions, with diverse roots and no single founder. The word *Hindu* was first used by the Greeks around 4 BC to describe the country and people who lived beyond the Indus River in the north western part of India. By the 13th Century the name *Hindustan* began to be popularly used for those living in this land, and by the end of the 18th Century the name *Hindu* was used to describe the followers of the Dharmic religions, (Hinduism, Jainism, Buddhism and Sikhism), and also the Sanatanis and Aryans, who were not following the Abrahamic religions. None of the Hindu scriptures, such as the Vedas, Upanishads and Puranas, use the name 'Hindu'.

It could be said that meditation is the balance of relaxation and concentration. Generally when we relax we are not focused and concentrated, and when we are concentrated we are not relaxed, but with practise we can keep both happening simultaneously.

There is the belief that if we are relaxed we will not be efficient. I had an interesting experience of this upon returning from a trip to India once. Part of my work at the time involved statistics. Figures are not one of my strengths and my mind was still in India; I kept drifting back there, daydreaming. I wondered what effect this was having on my work as I was not as concentrated as I felt I needed to be. However surprisingly, I was being more accurate. It was a case of less effort, better result!

I often ask people if it's easier to relax or run a kilometre. I guess it depends on the culture. Whilst living in Hong Kong, I learnt not to take relaxation for granted. It was very difficult for people to relax and feel a sense of calmness there. This was evident in the speed at which people walked. At the MTR, underground train stations, the left side of escalators were always made available for people to run up and down, even though the trains ran every 3 minutes – and the timer told you so! Lunches there were often served in restaurants that had no seating, and that was when people had time for lunch!

We know from research done on brain waves that relaxation brings us into an alpha state and produces healthy hormones. The opposite is true for 'high beta', a state of stress and survival. When we need to overcome a situation or state of stress, being able to relax is important, but this is just the beginning of meditation and certainly not the end. Meditation is much more than relaxation.

When teaching people Raja Yoga Meditation, we explain that meditation and *yoga* are two different things. Meditation is connecting with ourselves to understand and realise that the Self is non-physical light energy, *atma*. Yoga is tuning in and being in union with the Supreme. In spite of this, in Australia The Brahma Kumaris are not permitted by the Tax Department to use the word *yoga* when referring to what we teach as it is classified as a sport!

The first recorded mention of meditation is in reference to *yoga* which means, as explained before, to yoke, connect or join. It means having a unified outlook, a serene mind, right action and the ability to stay tuned to *atma*, the Self, **and** to connect to *param atma*, the Soul beyond.

In the Bhagavad Gita, there are various references to yoga, the main four being *Bhakti Yoga* in which one satisfies the longing for an emotional and personal approach, dharma which focuses on seeking the help of the Supreme through bhavana and surrender, *Karma Yoga* which is maintaining connection with the Supreme whilst performing action, helping one to transcend one's ego by not looking for the fruit of action but just doing right action, *Jnana Yoga*, referring to knowledge, which explores the universal spiritual truth through hearing, reading, thinking and meditating, and *Raja Yoga*, the path of self-mastery, through a union with the Supreme.

Experiment: *Practise being relaxed when you are concentrated and concentrated when you are relaxed.*

* * * * *

24

Meditation Practice

Stages of Meditation
"It's all just potatoes!"

Dadi Gulzar

Various stages, or states of being are talked about and explained in Raja Yoga meditation – the 'seed stage', 'soul conscious stage' and 'bodiless stage' to mention a few. Once, when a student began splitting hairs about the differences between the various stages, one of our very senior teachers, Dadi Gulzar, responded "Don't worry, it is all just potatoes!" She explained, "If we eat potatoes every day we need to cook them differently otherwise we will get bored. In the same way with meditation, when we use different words to describe the experiences, they give a different 'flavour' to our meditation."

Basically, there are four stages that we experience when we begin meditation:

The first is what is often referred to as **Initiation**. This is when we feel drawn to a person, place or space and we usually do not know why. It just feels good. We enjoy the atmosphere. Our sense of feeling and intuition begin to awaken from a gross body conscious stage, where we are quite oblivious to atmosphere, vibrations and feelings. We may find ourselves being drawn towards softer, lighter colours, fabrics, music, lights, food and company.

The next is when we start to question, "What is happening?, Why do I feel like this?, What do I want?, What am I living for?, What is the purpose of life?" We are waking up! Concentration begins to develop and we begin to **Contemplate** these questions. Sometimes we may try to suppress them, especially when our friends and relatives chide us, "Come on, don't be so serious." They consciously or unconsciously try to pull us back to 'their world'. As we begin to move away from the status quo they become frightened. Change? Scary! ... "If you start to think deeply, I may also start to think deeply." "Stop it!" "Let's not take this too far." People resist change.

Thirdly, we start reflecting on eternal truths. We **Meditate**, and begin cultivating the soul. We start to see how everything is connected and can have profound experiences of co-incidence and synchronicity. Or rather, we become aware of them! And, we are often amazed as inter-connectedness becomes apparent. The easiest and most enjoyable meditation always arises from interest and not force. We enjoy going within and literally, enjoy our Self! We enjoy our mind as it delves into experiences of peace, love and bliss and we begin to feel alive and interested in everything and everyone around us; energised, light and detached.

Fourthly, we slip effortlessly into the stage of **Realisation**. There is a feeling of becoming free of burdens, ignorance, confusion and the feeling of 'being stuck'. When we have an 'aha!' experience, we feel joyous and liberated. We realise that our sorrow has come due to being under an illusion. We move into the light where we feel free and beyond pain. Things that previously affected us no longer evoke a reaction. In this, we are re-programming ourselves and the old buttons no longer work when pushed. ... "Previously it was easy to manipulate me, but now I am clear and beyond reactions. I am me. I am not a reaction to you." We begin to feel we are in charge.

Experiment: *Explore with the different 'flavours' of meditation: the seed stage, the soul conscious stage, the bodiless stage, etc.*

The Observer

"Only he lives his life who observes it, thinks it, and says it; the rest let life live them."

Nicolás Gómez Dávila

Simon Blow was invited to speak at our Meditation Centre in Sydney, Australia. He had been involved in a head on collision at the age of nineteen, and sustained multiple injuries. For some time he did not feel his body, and felt no pain. When he eventually reconnected with his body and began experiencing pain, he began to wonder where the place where he had been was, where he was not connected to his body, and how he could get back there. In search for an answer he started exploring meditation and qigong. He fully recovered and is now a recognised Qigong Master, teaching Medical Qigong.

Some years ago I realised that although I am in this world and participate in life, I am never fully here. I am the Observer. Many who meditate regularly will find that they too live in this space 'between', even though they may not have realised it earlier. This small margin acts like a buffer between life and our Self, and in that miniscule space we can stop, think and then act, rather than react. We can be CREATIVE rather than REACTIVE. It all depends how we 'c/see' things.

Four words describe the stage of being beyond and being an observer, *Niara* – stand apart, distinct, unique; *Saakshi* – witness, pure awareness; *Drshta* – seer; *Upram* – stay beyond, above. Again, these are simply different 'flavours' of the stage of detachment.

The higher my perspective, the clearer I can see, just like the view from a mountain. Whenever I had overseas visitors in Hong Kong, I would take them to Victoria Peak so they could see the whole of Hong Kong. In Causeway Bay, where our Centre is located, it is very congested and one could get the impression that this was Hong Kong.

However from the Peak, one can see beyond the city to the islands and the national parks and experience the silence and stillness also.

It is like this with people. I have often been surprised when I have met someone who has been described very differently by another person. It is as if it is a completely different person to the impression I had been given of them.

Whether it is a situation, inner turmoil or confusion, or an interaction with another person, if I can fly above with my mind, I get a broader perspective to see a way forward. This is transcendence. It is the way to use meditation to resolve a situation; not by thinking about the situation but by going beyond and becoming the witness. With a pure consciousness and detached, we regain clarity of thought.

Experiment: Think of a situation you are facing. Imagine yourself as a bird, flying high above. Go beyond the atmosphere, the vibrations and the world of thoughts you had created about this issue. Be the witness. Do not think about the situation. Be still, detached. Don't even think of finding a solution. Let go.

When Insights Just Drop In
"Love is not an emotion, it's your very existence."

Rumi

In silence, insights come to us. After a decade of exploring the meaning of love, an insight spontaneously arose within me as I sat in an extended meditation session with a group of others ... "I do not love anyone and no one is to love me." I was surprised by these words and yet the feeling was pure and deep. As I explored the words during the remainder of the meditation session I realised that we can only *be* love, we cannot *give* love. We merely mirror love to another. Love is. The only way to truly love is to be love. The idea of 'giving' love needs to be reworked. As long as we think of 'giving love' we calculate, and this leads to judgement of who is worthy of our love, who we will connect with and invest emotion or feeling in. Then it is no longer love.

For me, this experience answered questions that came up in discussions I was often a part of, about the possibility of loving everyone equally. It would be agreed that to love everyone equally is no doubt the highest state of being, and yet on a personal level it was agreed that it was quite impossible. And here was the answer! ... to be love, not to give love.

Today my attention is on being love and allowing others to experience my state of love according to their own filters. I am not responsible for the way I am perceived. Sometimes our state of love may even bring out a negative reaction in others just as a flower can produce hay fever. The flower is not responsible for that reaction. It is just being itself.

The second part of the phrase that had come to me, 'no one is to love me', went even deeper. It was an experience of loyalty and being faithful in my love for the Supreme. I am 'spoken for' and just as a partner would not flirt and attract the attention of another, the purity of my love was a feeling of complete contentment where I do not need to attract anyone's attention to myself. It was a deep feeling, loving fully and being completely and utterly loved and cared for.

Whenever I remember this experience, I feel complete within myself. The wonderful thing about insights is that they can be re-experienced at will. They are like precious jewels in the heart, and for them not to get locked away in a distant memory we need to keep them emerged in our minds.

Experiment: *Do I really need love? Or am I love? Realise this. It is the shortcut to all effort!*

Churning
"Grind your own ingredients."
Indian saying referring to home-made curry.

On my first visit to the Brahma Kumaris' Centre in India, I churned fresh cream to make butter in a basin that had two-foot-pedals. White, pure, fresh butter. (I am vegan now, and each family usually kept their own loved cows in those days, so hopefully milk was obtained with less violence than it is today.) Just as a cow chews cud in order to extract all nutrients, it is a practice of students of Raja Yoga to mull over philosophical thoughts in order to realise the depths of their meanings. We call it Churning. It nourishes the soul, just as fresh food nourishes the body.

This practice focuses the intellect and diverts it away from wasteful thinking and is key to improving meditation. It could be likened to filling a plane with fuel so that when you are ready to take off, you are all set to go. Otherwise, when we sit to meditate the mind will start going over the events of the day. I once helped a friend at his import-export office in Hong Kong and noticed it used to take me half an hour of my meditation time to empty the thoughts I had accumulated during the day. It caused me to reflect on what business people do when they don't download all of that!

Churning helps us to understand ideas and concepts. By thinking about them deeply, and in various ways, it is as if we experience them instead of only theorising them. Churning also enables us to put words to our experiences so that we can then share with others, helping them with their meditation and spiritual journey. Churning ideas empowers our consciousness because the result is realisation.

Churning also increases gamma waves, which produce those 'aha!' experiences. This increases our capacity for creativity and makes us feel energised and alive. When we have our own insights it empowers our intellect. This perhaps can be a change to the practice of being lazy and not working on our own realisations, being dependent on others to do our thinking for us and being spoon-fed ideas and beliefs, often not doing the work of thinking through the deeper implications of those beliefs.

In Cambodia a small group of us enjoyed reading Mike George's Clear Thinking articles on a weekly basis. He stated some very obvious truths that none of us had thought about. "True or not?!", we would exclaim. Then we would laugh because the points he was making were so obvious and so important yet we had not seen them ourselves.

Experiment: *Churn on this: What is love? Is compassion the same as love? Write or share your experience with others to broaden your understanding. Try asking others what they understand love to be.*

Vibrations and Atmosphere
Atmosphere: The Sphere of the Atma
... just a play on words!

Literally, the word atmosphere comes from the Greek *atmos* meaning vapour, and *sphaira* meaning sphere or ball. Atmosphere is used to describe feelings that are 'in the air' such as the dense feelings created by a heavy vibration, as in "You could have cut the air with a knife" describing walking into a room where there had been an argument. Vibrations cannot be seen with the physical eyes, yet they are almost tangible. When someone tries to pull attention to themselves, we can sense that and generally we feel the urge to move away. The mind is very subtle and affected by everything, including food, atmosphere, cleanliness etc.

Meditating can be easier in some places more than others and this is generally due to the atmosphere. It has been a key focus of mine to maintain meditative atmospheres in all the Meditation Centres I have lived in. When I lived in the Centre in Hong Kong many business people attended and invariably they would end up networking with each other and talking business. I would quickly intercept those conversations and send them packing to the nearby teashop! I would say that 70% of the 'work' of teaching meditation is done through creating the atmosphere. Then, we only have to support it with some simple guidance.

After living in Hong Kong for a few years, I noticed that when I visited my parents in Australia I felt very sleepy even though I was not really doing anything. Although my parents are great people, their habit of sitting and watching TV and making small talk created a very different energy to what I was used to. It was interesting that when I started to cook and clean and engage in conversation, it heightened the energy and they became happier. Similarly, when I worked in the Central district of Hong Kong, I was pulled to spend many of my lunch times at St John's Cathedral. It became my oasis. These days, I find when I go anywhere new, I am like a cat; I sit in one place and then another until I find my spot!

I once attended a funeral for a well-known managing director of an iconic hotel in Hong Kong. It had been my intention to 'spread light' and give support to his wife and family during the service. The church was fully packed with the 'who's who' of Hong Kong and I found that I was overcome by the atmosphere of sorrow - not helped by the priest who focused on this man's 'sins' which created a very heavy atmosphere! I needed the support of more yogis there, or to be able to heighten my spiritual energy so I could affect a change in the atmosphere myself. I only just managed to keep myself from crying, and thankfully was eventually able to be the light I had intended to be and support the family.

After the tanks rolled into Tiananmen Square in Beijing in 1989, killing hundreds, perhaps even thousands of nonviolent protesters, the atmosphere in Hong Kong was of a city numbed with disbelief. Students could not study and teachers could not teach. There were feelings of powerlessness, sadness, fear and defeat. Thousands had demonstrated on the streets, and in Victoria Park opposite our Meditation Centre. We had a clear view from our window. There was a high energy of unity, sacrifice and oneness as they demonstrated in the heat, the rain, and even in a typhoon. I especially chose to be out on the streets after the violence to spread loving, soothing vibrations into the atmosphere and I did not need to make an effort to vibrate these feelings. In this atmosphere, I was naturally drawn into myself, connected with The Light and radiated healing vibrations.

If we are sensitive, we need to make ourselves internally powerful as atmospheres can affect our health. It's important to create an atmosphere around us and not absorb the atmosphere outside of us. We can only give or take at one time ... not both. If we are not emitting energy, like a sponge we will absorb whatever is in the atmosphere.

Experiment: *Become aware of the atmosphere in the places you visit often. Practise changing the atmosphere through your thoughts, words and behaviour.*

Aligning With Our Destiny
"Destiny is the push of our instincts to the pull of our purpose."

T D Jakes

There is no reason why I am not still a Catholic, or why I did not choose to pursue a Buddhist practice or any other spiritual practice, except that it was not my destiny. As much as I appreciate other paths I feel truly in harmony with the teachings of soul consciousness and God consciousness that I have studied for the last four decades. These teachings resonate with my being in a way that no others have, and none of us can do anything but follow our own dharma.

Destiny confuses many people. From many religious perspectives, it is understood that God is doing everything, and this is how many understand destiny or predetermination. However, this is not a concept I subscribe to. I do not see God doing, I understand 'being'.

I do believe our destiny is 'written' so to speak, but we cannot know what lies ahead of us and therefore sit back and not act for our future. If we are thirsty, waiting to see if it is in our destiny for someone to give us a drink will not quench our thirst. It is therefore inappropriate to apply the hidden powers of destiny to our future, but it certainly helps to apply them to our past. When we make a 'mistake', perhaps it's good to reflect on whether it really was a mistake. After 9/11 stories emerged of people who had been booked on one of the flights, who for one reason or another, were just not 'destined' to be on them, for instance.

Denise Lawrence, the first non-Indian woman to take up Raja Yoga Meditation with the Brahma Kumaris, puts it very well in one of her guided meditations. She asks, "Is this a moment where I can choose my destiny? Or is this a moment where life imposes its rigours upon me to deepen the carvings in my soul, to get me in touch with greater truths?"

Knowing that The Law of Karma is woven intricately into the concept of Destiny, those who have some spiritual awareness, instead of choosing victimhood "Oh, my karma!", choose to develop wisdom from the experience. The words, "Wisdom comes to those who serve", spoken by author and speaker Carolyn Myss, remind me of people such as Helen Keller, Christopher Reeve and Nick Vujicic, to name just a few, who have faced major challenges and have inspired many with their wisdom, to move forward in their lives.

I have mentioned earlier that much of what I think happens. Is it because I am tuning in with my destiny and the thoughts are arising from that deeper awareness? Or is it that I am attracting those things to myself through my thoughts? This is one of the areas I am still exploring but I am leaning towards the former. If we are able to align with our destiny then we will be 'on our line' and experience being in the right place at the right time and the magic that comes from that experience.

Intuition and destiny are inextricably linked and the more we trust our intuition, the more we will be moving towards our destiny. This can even be in relationship to very small things. On one of my returns to Australia from India I kept thinking that I wanted to visit a Bowen therapist. I have no idea why, as I had never experienced Bowen therapy before nor known any practitioners. Coincidentally, someone I was working with was visiting a Bowen therapist for treatment, so I accompanied her. We were able to be seen simultaneously; it was just too convenient. And, the therapist also knew the BKs, so offered me the appointment at a very small fee. No particular part of my body needed to be treated, however I trusted that I was meant to have it. I suspect I was treated for something that could have given me trouble but I have no way of knowing if this is right. I trust my intuition.

In his book *Breaking the Habit of Being Yourself*, Joe Dispenza says "We constantly think of people, things and matter." What would we think of if we did not think of these three? There is in fact so much more to think about! Life is an interplay of three distinct energies -

Atma (Soul), *Paramatma* (Soul Beyond), and *Prakrti*, (Matter, the elements). These three energies make up what The Brahma Kumaris term 'The Eternal Drama'; life as a large and continuous play. Their interplay is what makes up destiny.

The energy of matter is what we refer to as gross – it can be seen, measured and weighed. In the realm of matter, we connect and interact with matter, and if our awareness or belief is that we too are matter, that is, we are the body, our thinking and experience will be of a gross energy level known as *beta*.

The energy of the Soul on the other hand is light. If we move our awareness away from our body and inwards to *atma*, the Soul, we can experience an energy that is light. This is known as an *alpha* state.

If we then take our awareness and thoughts beyond, to *Paramatma*, the Soul Beyond, the energy in this place, the place known as *Paramdham* or *Nirvana*, where there is nothing but silence, we can experience a state that is pure, constant and powerful, known as *theta* and *delta states*.

All of these states can be experimented within meditation; we can transcend the physical, to be light enough to go beyond what is gross.

The 'sweet spot' in life can be found when we maintain and experience the balance of these three great energies. We achieve this by making our own efforts to maintain awareness of the real Self, taking support from the Soul Beyond, God, and by remaining stable on the 'Drama', i.e. keeping the awareness that life is like a big play, all Souls are actors playing their own parts, and the parts being played are directed by The Law of Karma – there is a consequence for every action.

When we do not feed the body with the nutrients it is made of, i.e. minerals, vitamins and water, it becomes undernourished and depleted of energy. In the same way, we need to replenish the Soul with the elements of its constitution - peace, love and happiness. We make a lot of effort to research, purchase and consume what is necessary for the body, so it makes sense to make just as much effort to take care of the Soul. It's important to 'stop and smell the roses' from time to time, to absorb presence and peace into our being.

Together with meditating, getting up an hour earlier and spending time in the garden or silently enjoying another peaceful pastime will nourish the Soul with the peace it needs. If feeling the love of, or love towards, other people is proving too challenging, expressing affection to an animal or a plant will help. We need to *live* peace and love. We also need wisdom. Our neurons need a blast from the occasional 'aha!' of new ideas. Crossword puzzles and Sudoku are better than nothing but the energising 'aha' of something new has a greater impact.

Experiment: *Practise being in the 'sweet spot', balanced in your efforts to live a spiritually nourished life, with God's support, and maintaining stability on 'The Drama'.*

The Three Eternal Energies

* * * * *

25

The Soul

Being True To The Self
"This above all: to thine own self be true, And it must follow, as the night the day, Thou canst not then be false to any man."

William Shakespeare

One of the greatest gifts we get from travelling is the exposure to diverse peoples with different backgrounds, beliefs and lifestyles. When I was growing up, Australia was very mono-cultural and my worldview was far too narrow. I was eager to expand my horizons, so at the age of 18 with my first back pay cheque I began travelling.

Over the years I have explored many different paths and learned from many great and enlightened masters. People ask me why I chose to stay with the practice of the Brahma Kumaris for so many years. The philosophy and practice just seems to comfortably 'fit in my intellect'. I do not struggle with any of the teachings. In fact, I feel more enriched as I understand the teachings more deeply.

My practice is enhanced by continuing to explore and compare different philosophies. As much as I enjoy perfection of any art, I also enjoy intelligent sharing and reflection on different ways of viewing the world and learning about practices that work for others. At some point however, I think it is beneficial to choose one particular path in order to experiment and go deeply into its practice.

Some have posed the question "Do we choose our path or do we awaken to it?" I tend more towards the latter, however we need courage to stay on a path - there are always challenges. By skirting around and cherry picking what we would like to follow and what we would rather ignore, we can avoid challenging ourselves and real change will not happen. We can deceive ourselves by avoiding challenges.

After many years of committing to the practise of Raja Yoga, I observed my meditations were often quite Buddhist in expression. "Nothing and no one" was the conclusion of many of my experiences. This caused me to begin thinking that perhaps I really was meant to be a Buddhist after all! My attachment to the path I had chosen was challenged, however I came to realise that at the end of the day, I am what I am. I needed to be honest and clear, and follow the path I felt was true for me in order for me to find my 'content'. As a friend of mine instructed when conducting a workshop on discovering our innate values, "This is detective work - not creative work. It is not a time to use your imagination but a time to be real, to be honest with who you are and to align with that." This has been my commitment throughout all of these years – to align with what is true for me.

Experiment: Am I being true to myself in all ways? Spend some time with yourself letting go of any labels of caste or creed and be 'naked' in your originality.

Soul Consciousness
"The mind is the pilot of the soul."
Socrates

Before taking up the practice of meditation, I had experienced a sense of separation from my body. I felt I was a distinct entity, not physical. It therefore resonated with me when I learned, in the first lesson of Raja Yoga Meditation, that I was a Soul. In Buddhism, I had struggled with the concept of *anatta*, 'no Self'. I could not understand, nor could anyone explain to me, how there is no Self and yet there are the concepts of The Law of Karma and reincarnation. Rinpoches are recognised as reincarnations of previous Buddhist Masters, and in Tenzin Palmo's wonderful book *Cave in the Snow*, although she "felt sick" when she first heard the word Soul, by the end she was determined to come back as a woman in all of her future births to prove that a woman can also attain enlightenment!

In some Buddhist doctrines, it is clarified that it is only the impermanent elements of sentient beings that are not the Self, *anātman*; that there is truly a real, intrinsinc essence, *svabhāva*. In the *Mahaparinirvana Sutra*, the *Tathagata*, is termed the 'true Self' or the 'great Self'. The Buddha tells of how he can see this hidden jewel within each and every being: "Hidden within the kleśas, mental contaminants, of greed, desire, anger, and stupidity, there is seated augustly and unmovingly the Tathagata's wisdom, the Tathagata's vision, and the Tathagata's body ... all beings, though they find themselves with all sorts of kleśas, have a tathagatagarbha that is eternally unsullied, and replete with virtues no different from my own".

I have had many dialogues with Buddhist teachers over the years about these anomalies. In the end they have usually agreed that there is a soul, but that it is better not to talk about it as people become attached to their individual identity. In the early days of the Brahma Kumaris, many experienced trance and it became a desire causing a distraction to practice. At one point it was said that trance no longer exists, just as when a child is hankering after something and it is hidden and we say "its gone." So I do understand the reluctance of the Buddhists, as the Self is so quickly confused with the ego.

Knowing that Pali, the language used by Buddhists, is a derivative of Sanskrit, I compared a Sanskrit and Pali dictionary. In both were details of the soul as having a mind, intellect and sanskaras, as taught in the Raja Yoga of the Brahma Kumaris. Many different philosophies refer to the soul. Islam refers to it as *ruh*; Jains as *jiva*; and the Jewish tradition as *nefesh*. However as seen in Christianity for instance, there are many different interpretations of the soul including whether it is immortal or not. Many Christians believe that it merely sleeps until the resurrection.

Another word for soul is psyche. However it seems that often, instead of researching and encouraging the experience of the soul in its original nature, we have developed sciences that deal with the anomalies of the soul, like psychotherapy and psychiatry.

The basis of the Brahma Kumaris practice is to create a paradigm shift from body consciousness to soul consciousness. Meditation cultivates the soul, so obviously it is very important for this practice. The understanding of the Brahma Kumaris is that the soul is a being of peace, love, wisdom and power. We have forgotten our original nature and allowed ourselves to become influenced to the point we can no longer even recognise our true selves. When someone suffers from amnesia it is very difficult to orient one's self and there is a great deal of confusion. A very trustworthy person is needed to be by their side to help them to remember who they really are. In silence, I learn to trust myself. Silence is the way to access my true self and remember who I am.

The Brahma Kumaris use the greeting "om shanti". *Om* refers to the eternal consciousness and *shanti* means peace, silence. It is more an awareness than a greeting. Dadi Janki, the Spiritual leader of the Brahma Kumaris once said, "If you are confused about your direction, do not ask anyone for help. Follow the signpost of Om Shanti." I have found this to be very wise guidance. When I am silent, I go beyond emotions and bring myself back to soul consciousness. I know my way forward then. Only when I am soul conscious can I connect to the Soul Beyond and in this dimension I am not only clear, but empowered.

In soul conscious awareness, I am aware that I am a soul and that I have a body through which to express myself, to experience this thing called 'life.' The soul is understood to be an infinitesimal point of spiritual light residing inside the forehead of the body. When I am centred in this awareness I am balanced.

The soul is eternal and immortal. It cannot die. It leaves the body when the body can no longer sustain life and enters a womb when the foetus has developed, at around 4-5 months. Unlike other Eastern traditions, the Brahma Kumaris do not believe that the human soul can transmigrate into other species. This becomes clearer when you read the rest of this chapter on the three faculties of the soul. Each animal has a different set of *sanskaras* or traits, and a human's *sanskaras* are unique to the human species.

In soul consciousness I realise that everything I need is within myself. This is an empowering realisation and practice.

Experiment: If we were soul conscious, everything would look different. Shift your paradigm to soul consciousness and go for a reflective walk in this awareness.

Mind: The First Faculty Of The Soul

"If you always think what you always thought, you will always do what you have always done, and you will always get what you have always got."

Anonymous

Anatomy of The Soul - Mind, Intellect & Sanskaras

In the teachings of Raja Yoga, the mind is understood to be one of the three faculties of the Soul. In its most natural state the mind just 'is'; present and still. For many of us it is hard to imagine this because of the incessant chattering going on in our minds. But it is not actually natural for the mind to think. Observe a young baby and how they look at you, staying in their own world, detached. Through the practise of Raja Yoga meditation, this is the state we aim to experience, even for brief moments. When we taste the sweetness of the experience of this quiet mind, we want more. This is why even a very brief experience is so valuable - it reminds us of our essence.

It is a common saying, "Your mind is your own best friend or worst enemy" and it's important that we understand and nourish it. Yet too often we just get fed up with it! Its function is to think, feel, create and imagine. Ideally we want to be using the mind as and when we want and not have it running like a caged mouse on a wheel, going nowhere. Just as we use our arms and legs when needed and then let them rest, we need to be able to use our mind in the same way. We do not continually keep our arms and legs moving, so it is sensible that we don't continually keep our mind moving. On the other hand, if we do not use the mind it will atrophy, just as with our physical organs if they don't get used. Raja Yoga meditation does not advocate that we stop our thoughts when we practice meditation. The mind will naturally become quieter as it lets go of thoughts that are unnecessary. It will come to a state where it enjoys rest, quietly waiting to be used.

Many are so tired of their mind and the incessant thinking that it is not surprising that the most popular meditation sought these days is to stop the mind ... to not think ... to watch the breath. However, it is not natural for the mind to be focused as you may have noticed! This is not its strength. The mind is better to be engaged constructively, to think creatively, deeply and clearly. It is energised by these states.

Every thought creates a chemical. Studies of brainwaves show that the hormones that create states of happiness and calm, like serotonin and melatonin, are created when the mind is engaged in calm, positive and constructive thinking. On the other hand, when we let it run riot it produces cortisol, the unpleasant feeling of agitation. The physical organ that the mind depends on is the brain. There are certain foods that nourish the brain, and also exercises to strengthen the brain. Taking care of the brain will also support the mind.

I think one of the most wonderful aspects of the mind is imagination, but it sadly seems to elude many people today. Whilst some choose not to imagine - they say it is not real, others seem to have just lost the art. I cannot envision a world without it. It is the seed of creativity. Without an image in the mind; a plane, a sewing machine or a sculpture, creations and inventions would not follow. Anything can be created through imagination, even a new world! It would be very sad if the world was taken over by 'the Nothingness' depicted in Wolfgang Petersen's movie *The Never Ending Story*, because people became cynical and no longer looked to the future, imagined and created something better.

Imagination allows us to rise, going beyond ourselves and our circumstances, and dream of something better. The English classic *The Little Princess* by Frances Hodgson Burnett, is an example in point. It tells the story of a young girl who uses her imagination to create a beautiful world for herself and others. Although she had lost all her wealth and become a scullery maid, her imagination enabled her to rise above her circumstances and help others to do the same.

Equally though, our imagination can bring harm if our mind is following a false or negative narrative. The imagination is part of my mind and I need to guide and direct it for my benefit and not just let it run wild.

Experiment: *Reflect on how you are using your imagination. It is a most wonderful tool and can be used for so much good. Practise creating an experience through your imagination.*

Intellect: The Second Faculty Of The Soul

"We need an intellect filled with wisdom, a still mind, a clear conscience, free of outside influences, a heart filled with good clean feelings, an attitude of benevolence, and to clean the memory tract."

Sister Jayanti, European Director, Brahma Kumaris

The Intellect is the second faculty of the Soul and in contrast to the mind, it functions well when focused. The practice of Raja Yoga Meditation is to firstly focus the intellect on a subject or theme. Anchoring the mind to that focus, the second step is to allow it to expand into thinking, feeling and imagining while it remains anchored. Concentration creates a high energy field. It's empowering.

When we harness our mind in this way, encouraging deep and broad thoughts, feelings and imaginations on one focus, it will take us away from all other distractions and bring us into an experience. As we get immersed in the experience there are no more thoughts. For example, I may choose the subject of peace for my focus. I anchor the intellect on the theme of peace and the mind can then visualise, and use memory and imagery to create feelings of peace. As we think, so we feel. As we begin to experience peace, our thoughts become quiet, there is no need to create thought, we rest in the experience, savour the experience, and fill ourselves with the experience. We are peace. This is what we refer to as the Seed Stage. I am that. I remember peace as my true and original state of being and I experience myself as that. Om shanti. I the eternal being am peace.

By remembering any colour, food, person or place, we will get a different feeling. The longer we dwell on something, the stronger the feelings that emerge. We experience this when we dwell on a painful memory. In meditation, we use the same process to create a positive experience.

Sister Jayanti of the Brahma Kumaris further elaborates, "The intellect is the vessel of spiritual understanding. Everything in human life depends on what is going on within the intellect. When we need to take a decision, we need to let the mind become quiet, keep spiritual wisdom in the intellect and stay connected with the Divine to receive power and clarity. When the intellect is without spiritual wisdom the conscience becomes dysfunctional."

Experiment: Choose an interesting aspect on which to contemplate. The more interest you have in gaining an insight or experience the easier it will be to concentrate.

Conscience and Intuition

"The conscience will dictate your life, whether you want it to or not."

Mike George

More subtle aspects of the Intellect are Conscience and Intuition. Conscience has been described as the inner voice guiding us to our own truth. It is however often hard to hear that small voice as it is mixed with the voices of our parents, teachers, religious leaders, peers and society. We get lost in these voices of influence and can struggle sometimes with what is right or wrong, good or bad, true or false.

It can be easy to adopt the mindset that nothing is right and nothing is wrong, as today it seems 'anything goes!'. In the larger picture, according to destiny, it could be said that this is correct. However karmically, we receive the fruit of whatever thoughts or actions we sow, and so whilst everything is accurate, there is actually always a price to pay and there is a 'right' after all!

The more we are able to see things clearly, as they are, we can be honest and 'know' what is right and wrong. A friend once said to me, "I know it is not right to eat animals because it causes them suffering, but I am not yet able to stop eating meat." I really appreciated his clarity and honesty. To have an understanding about violence is at least at the root of knowing right from wrong and good from bad.

When people do our courses in Raja Yoga Meditation, they are taught about spiritual principles. According to yogic tradition, to achieve mastery over the mind we need to adopt a plant based diet. It is also recommended to get up in the early morning. This time, between 2.00 - 5.00am, is known as *amrit vela*, the early hours of nectar, and is most conducive to meditating. Also, celibacy is suggested as a means to be able to capture and direct our internal energies, and not be 'pulled' by the senses.

It can be rather overwhelming for people to contemplate making changes in their life. I always suggest to students that they listen to their own conscience; it will guide them at their own pace. Adopting a new set of rules and not really knowing what best aligns with our own inner truth will not serve us. Also, if we are not ready for change, we may stop and start with a new lifestyle and then find we are living in guilt. A young man once shared with Dadi Janki that he understood all of the principles he should live by at a young age, but he felt it was unfair that he came to know them at that time! "I have lived with guilt all these years." Dadi responded, "At least you felt guilty. Many do not feel anything!"

The conscience is like the heart of the intellect and it has a clear connection with the mind. When we follow our conscience we feel at rest within. The mind is peaceful and clear. But the more we suppress and try to kill our conscience, the foggier our mind becomes as we choose not to see (or feel) our truth. If we are not following our *swadharma*, our own righteous way of being, we cannot feel at ease with ourselves. Actually, I would say that most stress is caused because we go against our conscience, not by the external environments of our homes or workplaces, and the greatest antidote to stress is to 'live' our values.

With the help of meditation, our intellect, *nous*, or *buddhi*, will become divine, subtle, broad and deep, and our mind will become pure and clear. We can then attune to our intuition and discern on a more subtle level - not based on rationale, but rather on 'a hunch', a gut feeling, or an instinct. The fact that we use the word 'instinct' indicates there is an innate knowing that is aligned with our truth. It is not learned nor acquired, but is always there.

This inner knowing has been referred to as *the Akashic records*. *Akasha* is a Sanskrit word meaning aether or space. The akashic records are considered to be a record of all knowledge of all time. References to these records are found throughout Asia as well as in Egyptian, Greek, Chinese, Christian, Persian and Mayan texts. In Islam they are referred to as *al-lawhl al-mafouz*, the Preserved Tablets. They have been used to explain how Edgar Cayce, the sleeping prophet, and others, have been able to predict the future. They are also used to explain the phenomena of astral travel, where people can see details of places they will soon be visiting, and other types of powers like clairvoyance and deja vu.

I wonder, does the past, present and future exist simultaneously? Or, is it just that the needle of the record is on the moment we are witnessing now?

Experiment: *Why am I reluctant to do what I know is right? (Become vegetarian? Share my wealth?) What is my conscience telling me to do? How do I know it is my conscience and not the voices of others?*

Sub-Conscious Mind: The Third Faculty Of The Soul

"The closer you come to knowing that you alone create the world of your experience, the more vital it becomes for you to discover just who is doing the creating."

Eric Micha'el Leventhal

Where do all of our thoughts come from?

The *Sanskaras*, the third faculty of the soul, could be said to be a combination of personality traits, memories, habits, and what is often referred to as the sub-conscious mind. It is from here that thoughts arise into the mind, and it is therefore the faculty that needs to be sorted and cleared. Within the *sanskaras* is the *chit*, often translated as the memory tract. It is the chit, in particular, that needs to be cleaned.

Meditation is a way to access our subconscious mind so that we can see the memories, habits and beliefs that are no longer useful to us, and clean them out. In neuroscience, this is called disassociating one thing from another. For example, disassociating a dog from feelings of fear;

fear that was created when I was hurt by a dog in the past. I use my Intellect to rationalise, "Not all dogs create hurt. Many are loving and friendly." Meditation helps us to notice inappropriate and unreasonable responses to people, things and events in life, and with the guidance of the Intellect, our reasoning faculty, we can re-wire our habitual responses.

When we are in the experience of any one of the original states of the soul – peace, joy, love, knowledge, power, purity and bliss – we are in our natural and eternal state of being – in our original Sanskaras. The process of transforming our Sanskaras includes focusing our Intellect on one of our original Sanskaras, love for instance, and then using our mind to imagine or remember experiences of pure love, or what we have learnt about love, such as compassion, spontaneous expressions of giving, and the secure feeling of being loved. We may think about how love is felt and expressed differently in various relationships in our life. We can practise opening our heart to love, especially the pure and unconditional love of The Divine. When we focus on that love, and immerse ourselves in it, it will fill our being so much that we will feel both loved and loveable. By dwelling in the experience, we can go deeper into it until the pure feeling of love replaces our thoughts about it. We may then realise and experience, "I am love, I do not need love. Love is my essence." When we experience love, we know love. It is not just affirmation or positive thinking, it is real. This creates new neural pathways, and transformation, especially if repeated often.

There is a difference between Sanskaras and *swabhava*, nature. Nature is more superficial. We can do a personality course and change our nature, but it is much more difficult to change our deep-rooted Sanskaras. We can be attracted by someone's nature and not be alert to his or her Sanskaras. A person may speak roughly, and yet their inner essence is like gold. We could say that the nature of a lion is to roar and yet its Sanskara is courage; a goat may have a gentle nature, however its Sanskara is fear. Narcissists often develop the very disarming nature of being pleasant, courteous, gentle and charming, however they have the Sanskaras of manipulating and controlling.

Experiment: Make a note of any reactions you have observed in yourself recently and spend time alone contemplating why these emerged. What is the seed of the Sanskara? Is it a memory of an experience from the past? Is it a deep-seated belief?

* * * * *

26

The Source

Getting Comfortable With The 'G' Word

"Men occasionally stumble over the truth, but most of them pick themselves up and hurry off as if nothing had happened."

Winston Churchill

It took me a long time to feel comfortable using the word *God*, so I am sensitive here to your reaction to it. There is probably no other word in any language that evokes so much reaction. In my childhood, I conjured up a picture of a being who was superior and unapproachable. An image of an old man with a beard sitting up in the clouds and waiting to punish us for our sins was altogether too much for me! I was taught I could only know God when I died, and that when I died I would be punished for my sins ... so, I wasn't particularly looking forward to getting to know Him!

In the 1980s I remember reading the results of a survey which showed Americans had the highest belief in God and Japanese had the lowest. I had just recently visited America and felt scared for my life while in New York as I had been warned many times about the dangers in the city and how best to protect myself. When I read the survey I happened to be in Japan where we did not even lock the door - deliveries were even made into the kitchen! I stayed at a hotel for a few nights as our visiting senior teacher preferred the simplicity of the Centre and so I was nominated to enjoy her room. On enquiring if it was safe to walk alone through the alleys at night I was assured that it was perfectly safe! I was perplexed ... What does believing in God actually mean?

I have discovered there is very little understanding of God in most religions actually. Once, I was with a group of Roman Catholics in the Philippines, and I asked them what God looked like. Although their religious training had been similar, each had a different idea about God. One said she believed God was an old man with a beard, another envisioned Jesus Christ, another saw God as light and the other said that "God is everywhere and in everything and has no form." When I asked them what they had been taught about God's appearance, they admitted, after some consideration, that so many aspects about God had never been clarified for them. If you ask most Christians if Jesus Christ is God or not, you will find that some believe he is God, and others will say that he is the Son of God!

Richard Rohr, a Catholic priest and author of over thirty books, is very clear about his thoughts on this topic. He says, "The surname of Jesus was not Christ!" He believes that God and Jesus are two separate beings. He speaks of Christ as the Holy Spirit, and Jesus as the one who struggled to be 'God' in the flesh. He instructs that if we see them as one, we miss the message, the necessity to struggle, to fall, and all that a seeker goes through on their journey.

Similarly, I have found this lack of clarity amongst people of the Jewish and Hindu faiths also. I was once on a panel with a rabbi at an interfaith gathering. The topic for discussion was *Love for God*. The rabbi told us that we couldn't know about God, death or anything about the after world until we went there. My conversation with him went something like this ...

"Do you love God?" I asked.

"Yes." He replied.

"How can you love God if you cannot know God?" (Me)

"It is a Jewish law to love God." (Him)

"Is this a common belief and attitude in the Judaic tradition, or your own thoughts?" (Me)

"Most rabbis would say the same." (Me)

One of the unique aspects in the study and practice of Raja Yoga is the aim is to be 'like' God, that is, equal to God in terms of developing the same virtues. This is what differentiates worship from study. After all, what is the benefit in worshipping God and not becoming like Him? Would we worship a professor or aim to become equal? We cannot bring benefit to the world by merely praising. Greatness in any field needs to be passed on. Some would call it a sin or blasphemy to consider that we can be equal to God, but is that not what God would want? Most parents want their children to be greater than them – it's only natural!

The aim in Raja Yoga is to experience God for ourselves through meditation and yoga so that He is no longer a 'belief' but someone we are in relationship with; there is a 'knowing', and an intimacy between us. I have often felt it strange when people ask, "Do you believe in God?" I know my parents. I have experienced a relationship with them. I do not believe in them!

Experiment: *Try talking to God directly. Ask, "Do you want me to worship you or to be like you?" Write your experience of your dialogue with God.*

What Is In A Name?
"God said to Moses, "I AM WHO I AM.
This is what you are to say to the Israelites: 'I AM has sent me to you."

Exodus 3:14, New International Version

What is in a name? When the name is God, a lot! One of the biggest problems in creating an awareness of God, is the name. The word *God* is now used in a general way to include all gods, not just the Supreme. There seems to be no clear idea of the origins of the word and it doesn't seem to have been used in many religious scriptures. Some say it is an acronym for Generator, Operator and Destroyer. Although clever, I am not sure if that is in fact its origin! Others say it comes from 'good', which is probably an acceptable substitute if you are struggling. Some friends of the Brahma Kumaris, who would describe themselves as 'non believers', opt for this and simply replace the word good for God in conversation.

Globally, it may do us well to create a new word or name for God so that we all know we are talking about the same One. It would be good to be able to talk about God on neutral grounds. I have put this suggestion to singers, thinking that one of them could popularise a new name, but no one as yet seems to have come up with one ... It is a big ask I know!

The Brahma Kumaris use the word *Shiva*, which means benefactor, the seed, and the point.

Another issue is, in English there is no neutral gender, so God is generally referred to as 'He'. Due to language we therefore greatly limit our understanding and experience of God, and most understand Him/Her in a very narrow way. As British author and commentator, Karen Armstrong states, "We often learn about God as children, at the same time we learn about Santa Claus. Our ideas about God can get stuck in an infantile mode and become incredible."

One of my favourite writers, Barbara Bossert -Ramsay, wrote the following beautiful poem. It captures the need to connect to just One, whoever we call Him, or Her.

You call me God .. Jehovah .. Allah .. Shiva
You have built churches, temples, mosques and statues to Me
You have waged wars in my name and made sacrifices to Me
You say that I am in nature, or in the sky
You say that I am everywhere
When you suffer you call out to Me for help
When you are happy, you forget Me
You have worshipped Me in human form and yet you do not know Me

Prophets and Teachers have tried to point the way to Me, but no one has found Me.
I am your Mother and I am your Father
I am the one with whom you can have all relationships
I am not born, and like you, I never die
I am light
My form is a tiny invisible point of light
My world is the world of silence and peace
You used to dwell with Me there, in that golden silence
Then you were born into a body and began to create your story
You forgot your Home and Me
I have come again to remind you of who you are
I have come again to reveal to you the secrets of time
I have come again to fill you with all the love and power and peace that you have missed for so long.
I have come again.
Remember.

In Raja Yoga, we use the word 'remember', as in "Remember God." Not 'pray', not 'worship' ... 'remember'. God has no language. 'Remember God' ... be with God in silent communication and wisdom emerges from within. We remember who we are eternally and originally, whom we belong to ... where we come from ... where we are going. This is ultimately what yoga is all about, the ultimate union with the Supreme re-connects us to ourselves.

In crisis we become entangled with thoughts, draining our much-needed energy and leading to confusion in the mind. In Raja Yoga, *manmanabhav*, be Mine with your mind, is the way out of this confusion. The mind becomes still and the path forward becomes clear. This is the daily practice of Raja Yoga, and the path of the mystic.

There seems to be more agreement on the form of God; another example of how much easier it is to connect beyond words! Light radiates an oval aura. Light, and its form of an aura, appears to be a commonly shared image for God. For many Christians, "God is Light". Some

Japanese Buddhists meditate on *Chinkonseki*, a small oval stone. When taking a solemn oath, Jews take an oval shaped stone in their hands. Muslims refer to *Noor*, spiritual light. Prophet Mohammed destroyed and removed all idols leaving only the oval stone image, *Kaba* in Mecca. Sikhs open their scripture prayer with *"Ek Omkar"*, One Creator, light. And, in their *dreaming*, the Australian aboriginal people see *min min*, an unexplained light phenomena. When the Dalai Lama visited the headquarters of the Brahma Kumaris in Mount Abu we were surprised to hear him say "God is light" - we had not expected him to talk of God, but I have spoken to practising Buddhists who have shared experiences of Light in their meditation.

Experiment: *I am the light connecting to the Light. Imagine God as infinite non-physical light and yourself an infinite non-physical light also.*

Omnipresence

*"The challenge with running from God
is that you will always run into Him."*

Kingsley Opuwari Manuel

Some say that God is beyond name and form and believe He is omnipresent. However there are just as many different perspectives on that concept as there are on all other spiritual concepts. In an article on his blog, Lecturer and Author, Domenic Marbaniang points out "Omnipresence doesn't mean divine occupation of all space, nor divine distribution over all space, nor indwelling of every entity, nor that God cannot move in space; but that God is fully present everywhere, and that God can do different things at different places at the same time."

According to quantum physics, so can we. Many scientists such as Rupert Sheldrake, David Bohm and Ervin Laszlo to name a few, share the belief that consciousness is not a product of the brain. It has been termed 'non-local'. And, most are familiar with what are now called OBEs, out of body experiences, with much documented evidence about people who are clinically dead being able to, from a distance, observe their bodies and what was happening in the room after they had 'died'.

In meditation I experience something akin to omnipresence. When I first went to Mahduban, the headquarters of the Brahma Kumaris, I felt that the walls were vibrating with God. When my heart was full of God's love, it really did feel like I could see God in everything and everyone. However, this is where we need to use our nous and discern the reality of this concept.

In a close relationship, like a marriage, we can be enamoured with words like "We are one". In reality though, this is a dangerous and painful belief to have. If one partner dies or leaves, we are then left feeling that we are half a person. We were never half; we are always complete and whole. I experience being at one with God, however I know that it is an *experience* of God and not that we have somehow merged into one entity. I certainly do not feel that we are one when I am judgemental or small-minded. If I remember God, if I take the company of God, I can sometimes bring myself back up to His/Her level, but the first step in this is to be soul conscious. It is only then that I can be God conscious.

The concept of omnipresence does not work for me at all in terms of my relationship with God. If I am God, then with whom can I have a relationship? I enjoy being *with* God. It fulfils my need for companionship and I enjoy being able to have the experience of various relationships with Him as well. If God is in everything and is everywhere God becomes so abstract... just a mental concept!

When I was young I remember watching some fish in our aquarium. I asked my father, "Do Catholics believe that God is in everything?" "Yes," he replied. "Is He in that fish?" I asked. "Oh, I am not sure about that!" he said. Likewise, would God be in the mosquito we are so annoyed with and may carry malaria or dengue fever, to name just a couple of the diseases they carry?!

Also, I have read in many scriptures that say that God is omnipresent, that He is to come. How can we speak of God coming if He is already in everything? I cannot make sense of this.

We all want perfect relationships. We look for a perfect partner, a perfect teacher or friend, but I have not met anyone who is perfect! One of the most powerful aspects of having all relationships with God is that it can heal a relationship where we have a 'block' or where there is pain. For example, if there has been a painful relationship with a father, or if the father has not been present or has passed away, I have seen on many occasions that if the person experiences a child-father relationship with God, the void gets filled.

Experiment: Using your nous in its entirety - intuitively, with reason, with a sense of higher wisdom ... see what you make of this: "Omnipresence is roughly described as the ability to be present everywhere at the same time, referring to an unbounded or universal presence."

The Link of Love
"Where there is love, there is no effort."
Bapdada

Experienced meditators are sometimes surprised by the seeming lack of discipline in the meditation practised by the Brahma Kumaris. As the teachings moved out of Asia, it became common to sit on chairs to meditate rather than cross legged on the floor. Raja Yoga Meditation as taught by the Brahma Kumaris is now in over 130 countries, in many cultures that do not have the practice of sitting on the floor. Our aging senior teachers are also no longer able to achieve the lotus or cross-legged posture that they once could. There is however, still the practice of keeping the back straight as it helps with circulation and staying alert in meditation. Many students also like to listen to songs or music whilst meditating.

Brahma Kumari students meditate daily at 4am, even whilst holding down full time jobs, running a business or a marathon, or raising a family. They also spend time in spiritual study every morning. They are at the very least, vegetarian. Many are vegan. They try to only eat food that has been cooked 'in yoga' and avoid eating at restaurants for this reason. They attempt to remain in a state of soul and God consciousness as much as they can during the day. And besides all of this, they have a drive to spiritually serve others wherever possible.

I would argue therefore that Brahma Kumari students do not lack discipline at all. Yoga is the link of love with the Supreme and attention is placed on maintaining this link rather than on sitting in postures and silence. I personally think that silence and sitting in a disciplined way is important, however in India particularly, they love listening to songs that create feelings of love and connectedness.

In many of our Centres instrumental music is often played as a 'white sound' to divert attention away from any noise that may be affecting the meditation room. I find that the aim of most instrumental music is to relax, which is vastly different to meditation. Relaxation is a good beginning, so starting meditation with a song or five to ten minutes of music can be helpful. To delve into the depths of our consciousness, improve concentration and experience other dimensions is best facilitated by silence.

I once picked up a book at a friend's house. I did not have time to read it but the title struck me, *How Big is your God?* by Richard Rohr. When I began practising Raja Yoga Meditation I was happy to make Him very small. It helped me to create intimacy and took away the 'old man in the sky ready to punish me when I die' image that I had picked up in my childhood. I wanted to feel close and equal, and experience being a friend, even a lover, of God. In my conversations with Him, I delight in the very accessible and easy way He 'talks' to me. I find He/She has a very subtle humour that is sweet and light.

I am also conscious of keeping God 'big', in the way of not feeling judged for my mistakes, nor being not good enough. God is too big for these petty types of thoughts. On one occasion a student did something that I did not think was appropriate. I asked him, 'What would God say?' He thought for a moment and cheekily responded, 'He said that he loves me very very much.' Touché! A big God is one who is available to all people, no matter their belief or persuasion. I do not need to be possessive or defensive. He/She just IS.

At other times I am aware of GOD ... the unlimited, eternal, all-powerful constant being that I can draw power from, that I can plug into and be recharged. In electronics, there is Ohm's Law, which states that available power is the source divided by resistance. The spiritual Law, 'Om's Law' is the same, the Source divided by our Resistance equals the available Power!

No one can prove to another that God exists, however we can use our *nous* to understand and perceive God. My 'proof' is that I lived in Hong Kong from the age of 25 to 47. Tom, my husband, had meanwhile established the Brahma Kumaris Centre in Malaysia with his brother, Robert. He was busy there and I was busy in Hong Kong. We would meet in Malaysia, Australia and India from time to time but we were both living very full and independent lives by this stage. In Hong Kong I did not have 'friends' as such, and we do not get to choose who comes to our Centres nor who we will spend our time with on a daily basis, even to the extent of who we live with in our Centres. Yet I have never felt lonely nor in need of human company and support. I have felt a deep companionship, love, support and joy in my relationship with God.

After sixteen years in Hong Kong (when I had only signed up for three months!), I felt it was time to leave. The pollution was getting worse by the day as across the border, China had become fully industrialised. The 'hand over' in 1997 was to take place on July 1st (my birthday - it is now celebrated as a public holiday in Hong Kong). There was a feeling among some of the students at the Centre that they would prefer not to have '*guilos*', (literally translated as 'foreign devils'!) running the Centre, and after so many years of colonisation I understood this. To me, British rule was not so obvious unless I entered a government office. You would find mostly white people sitting in the offices; the staff doing the other jobs were Chinese.

I put forward my request to leave Hong Kong whilst on a visit to Australia but was asked to stay on. I dreaded the thought of returning and shed a few tears on the plane. In my early morning meditation I decided that if I was going to stay in Hong Kong I had to be happy, and I pondered how I would do this.

Our morning classes always start with thirty minutes of meditation, and on that day it was as if my whole head was completely re-arranged in those thirty minutes. I emerged actually quite happy to be back in Hong Kong. Someone asked how long I would be staying and I very happily stated, I'd probably die there! My only explanation for my feeling like this is that it had come as a result of my connection with God. How else could I have changed in such a short time without any effort?

Unlike in established religions, where a 'middle man' has been put between us and God, yoga is a direct connection. For a very long time, preachers have been telling us what God wants from us and how he wants us to behave; what we must wear, eat, think, do, say etc. The unique and beautiful thing about Raja Yoga is that we learn that we can have a direct and personal link with God, develop any relationship we want with Him and thereby come to our own understanding of what He wants from us. It has been the experience of many students of Raja Yoga that healing takes place in their relationships with parents, siblings, work colleagues and partners after they start connecting in this way with the One who is perfect. They are able to then let go of any expectations they have had in other relationships. After all, how can we expect perfection in a human relationship when we are not even perfect ourselves?!

Experiment: *Ask yourself the question, 'How big is my God?'*

* * * * *

27

Smrti, Vrtti, Drshti, Srshti, Prakrti, Krti

Consciousness *Smrti*, The Seed

"Our world is in crisis because of the absence of consciousness."

Terence McKenna

On several occasions I have experienced what I can only describe as super-consciousness where I felt I knew everything in the universe. Upon seeing others, I observed each one was operating in their 'own world', and interconnectedness between everything was absolutely clear. I would have expected that I would have experienced this type of awareness during or after an intense meditation session, but the experiences came to me when I was doing very ordinary things like driving the car, and another time, standing at the lights after shopping at a supermarket during my lunch break.

The 'highest' stage we can attain in Raja Yoga Meditation is the Seed Stage. It is an experience of fullness. It is not *Samadhi*, emptiness. I experienced the Seed Stage very early on in my practice and understood why it had that name. It is an experience of being completely full of peace, love, power, and bliss, like a seed brimming with life, ready to sprout; powerful and complete. It was only after I had had this experience that I could even describe it. In that state there is no thought, only awareness ... I am ... 'thus-ness', and afterwards I questioned how could I be anything but this. I felt it was truly who and what I am; everything else seemed to be some kind of illusion. I was flawless and brilliant, like a multi-faceted diamond. I was not at all conscious of time and I do not know if the experience lasted for seconds or minutes!

Consciousness or awareness of the real Self is the seed, or beginning, of all transformation. It is easy to change things on the periphery, but if my consciousness does not change, then like a seed, whatever is in it can grow again. If my consciousness changes so does my worldview. Everything I see, then looks different.

When we experience the Seed Stage, we draw into ourselves exactly what we are in need of, just like the seed of a capsicum will fill itself with Vitamin C and the seed of a carrot with Vitamin A, even though they are planted in the same soil.

Our aim in Raja Yoga Meditation is to attain this stage as much as we can. It is helpful, actually necessary, in order for me to make the changes in myself that I need to in an effortless way. I grow myself from that Seed.

Experiment: *Practise seeing through all the illusions that surround you. Have the courage to look at everything with the eyes of Truth – from your true consciousness.*

Attitude Vrtti, Nourishment
"If you say only one prayer in a day, make it 'thank you'."

Rumi

No matter what we are going through in life, our faith would be reflected in what Rumi refers to as a prayer ... "Thank you." An attitude of gratitude makes life easier for everyone, both the one who has feelings of gratitude, and those who come into contact with them, (not to mention the larger cosmos).

I remember a friend complaining once about how busy she was. When I asked her what she had to do, she told me she had to go to the hairdresser, meet a friend, buy a gift for her daughter, etc, etc. It sounded like 'good' busy to me!

When we are realistic about things, it is easy for us to have an attitude of acceptance. In his book *Power versus Force*, Dr David Hawkins says that on the scale of energy, feelings of acceptance are amongst the highest. He says, "At this level of awareness a major transformation takes place with the understanding that one is oneself, the source and creator of the experience of one's life ... Acceptance is not to be confused with passivity, which is a symptom of apathy ... Acceptance is emotional calm, and perception is widened without distortion or misinterpretation."

Similarly, Elizabeth Kubler-Ross places acceptance at the final stage in her 'Stages of Grief'. This is when one accepts the reality of a situation, like a physical condition that threatens our mortality, or the absence of a loved one. With courage we adjust ourselves to what will now become the new norm.

Our attitudes have a lot to do with how we evaluate people, places and things, and it is these that we work with in order to bring a change in our awareness. There are many ways that we can do this. For instance, we can create positive experiences in purposeful ways by having the intention of creating more positive attitudes about things. Often, we have created our attitudes towards people of other nations or religions just through hearsay. We need to be particularly wary of the media and opinions of others and come to our own conclusions by creating opportunities through our own experiences. It is possible to ease our attitude towards others simply with exposure; in this regard attitudes are not very difficult to change.

My attitude is a direct result of the consciousness I have and colours everything I see. If I am jealous of someone, everything they do, or not do, will disturb me. In reality it is not that there is anything wrong with them. It is my attitude. Conversely of course, if I have an attitude of benevolence, I would not 'see' 'the wrong' with anyone or anything, and would be able to maintain good wishes and pure feelings.

Stories of inspiration told by others who have changed their attitude, help *us* to build resilience for life's unforeseen circumstances. During a retreat in the Blue Mountains in Australia, I heard of a Book Club presentation which was to happen the next morning and decided to stay on to meet Peace Prize nominee Izzeldin Abuelaish, MD, MPH, author of *I Shall Not Hate: A Gaza Doctor's Journey on the Road to Peace and Human Dignity*. After his daughters were killed by Israeli soldiers in 2009 he called for the people in the region to start talking to each other rather than seeking revenge or sinking into hatred.

Experiment: What change of attitude would make the greatest difference in my relationship with myself? With others?

Outlook *Drshti*, Environment

"I can see why a number of saints spoke of prayer itself as simply receiving the ever-benevolent gaze of God, returning it in kind, mutually gazing, and finally recognising that it is one single gaze received and bounced back. The Hindus called this exciting mutual beholding darshan."

Richard Rohr

From the Brahma Kumaris, I have learned to connect with others through the eyes. When I was younger I rode horses in a riding school. I always chose the horse I would ride by looking into their eyes because I could discern whether they could be trusted to not throw me off, if they were flighty, agitated, sluggish or angry.

When I lived in Hong Kong, it was generally too noisy to hear another speak in the street - no one really had time to stop and chat anyway, and eye contact was the way we 'met' each other. Through thirty seconds of deep eye connection, I could communicate my happiness on seeing them, together with my love and best wishes.

The Hindi word *Drishti*, means vision or outlook. In Raja Yoga, the method of communicating through the eyes makes words superfluous. Whenever I conduct silence retreats, I often use an exercise where participants form a circle and spend a little time looking into the eyes of each other. Initially confronting, when people relax into it they are very moved. They feel seen, deeply seen, because it's as if the other person is looking into their soul.

It is a well-known saying, "The eyes are the windows of the soul." We can see many things through the eyes, including the motivation or agenda of another. When there is the clear aim not to give sorrow to someone, the eyes reflect this; they are soft and are a safe place for others to rest. At a drug rehabilitation centre in Argentina, I once opened a meeting with the greeting *"Namaste"*, meaning "I bow to the light in you." Respect was exchanged through our eyes. It brought us close and opened our trust for each other.

Greeting through the eyes, with or without holding the palms closed in front of the chest, seems infinitely more simple and hygienic than a kiss on the cheeks, a hug or a handshake. When I met the President of India, Shri Moraji Desai, with a group of fellow Brahma Kumaris on the lawns of the presidential palace, others started to shake hands with him. I noted that as soon as the opportunity arose, he joined his palms together and met the rest of us through eye contact, finishing all formality with a simple rotation of his head - a very royal and expedient gesture, yet filled with respect.

When someone shouts at us, do we look at them with our 'third eye', our inner eye of knowing and understanding and see what is really going on? Do we contemplate what the need in this person might be? Or, do we immediately perceive them as aggressive, and react? The third eye, also known as the eye of wisdom, can 'look' behind what is happening on the surface. Author, Karla M. Nashar explains very simply, "I have three eyes, two to look, one to see."

The form of meditation that the Brahma Kumaris teaches is practised with the eyes open. One of the benefits is that it deters us from falling asleep. If we do, at least we know we have! Another, is that we can meditate anywhere and at any time - on the bus, chopping vegetables, walking, and in our other usual daily routine activities. A study was recently done on meditators from different traditions and it revealed that the brain readings of those who practised meditation with the Brahma Kumaris, were the same whether meditating or performing an activity.

If you attend a group meditation at a Brahma Kumaris Centre, you may find an experienced meditator sitting at the front 'leading' the meditation. They will have their eyes open and their gaze will move slowly around the room and rest on each one's third eye for a short time. The meditators are not looking at the other person or reading what they are thinking; whilst staying concentrated and 'beyond', they are helping the others in the group do the same. Many will share that this is a subtle, yet very powerful form of meditation.

I experienced once, how a young man in Hong Kong who had a drug addiction slowly opened up to accept *drishti* and witnessed the journey of trust that this involved. Of all the people in the world, I find Australians to be the most open to *drishti*. It is humbling as it requires trust to allow someone to look into our eyes.

Similarly, *Darshan* implies being seen or beheld, perhaps by a holy person, in a way that we receive a transmission of energy through their eyes and are transformed by it. It often refers to the way we may look at a holy person or object, such as a sacred image; we see it in a way that makes us feel uplifted. This is a practice I like to use, of seeing others as God would see them. But of course we have to see ourselves like this first!

The energy transmitted through the eyes is powerful. A woman attending one of our retreats near Sydney was living with cancer. Not wanting to compromise her health by taking painkillers, she was in a lot of pain. She informed me that she was thinking of leaving the retreat, but I invited her to stay on as our Senior, Didi Nirmala, a very experienced yogi, was visiting in the afternoon to lead meditation with *drishti*. Thankfully she accepted my invitation, and the experience took her completely away from her body and the pain disappeared for the rest of the retreat.

Experiment: *Practise seeing the third eyes of others - looking at them in the centre of the forehead, not being distracted by their appearance, the colour of their skin, their clothes, etc.*

World *Srshti*, Tree

"I wasn't looking for religion; I was looking for a world view."

John Eldredge

The word 'worldview' was borrowed from the German word *weltanschauung*; *welt* meaning world and *anschauung* meaning view or outlook. It is a comprehensive view of the world, including one's philosophy of life and perceptions, which would naturally change over time.

In Sanskrit it is said *"yatha drishti, thatha sristhi"*, meaning as is your vision so is your world. Our consciousness, attitude and vision directly impact the way we view our world. For instance, are we those who see the glass half full or half empty? Whilst each of us lives in our own 'little worlds' it's important that we choose perspectives that embrace a bigger view. Instead of asking why something is happening to us, our 'broad mindedness' can give us a clarity and understanding that will enable us to learn and move on from the situation. Understanding that the world we create for ourselves is created from the consciousness, attitude and vision that we create and sustain, teaches us to take responsibility for our awareness.

I had developed a rather negative vision towards the world when I was younger. From the Buddhist perspective I saw the world as one of suffering, so naturally my aim was to get out! If you were to explain what spring was like to someone who was in the middle of winter and had totally forgotten everything about spring, it may sound like a fairy tale. After I had been introduced by the Brahma Kumaris, to the concept of time being cyclic rather than linear, I began to liken suffering to time spent in a deep, dark, cold winter. It would pass. Seasons change after all. I began to acknowledge and appreciate the beauty of the physical world and could see incredible harmony and balance. Reassessing my relationship with the world, my worldview changed.

I've noticed that I come across two very distinct groups of people who I would broadly describe as conservative and innovative. Conservatives are cautious and think of the risks involved in innovation. They struggle with change and are concerned about every possible aspect. They generally come from a space of love and care, wanting to protect either individuals or a group of people, an organisation, at large. Innovators on the other hand, are open to experimenting, trying things out, and taking risks. Neither tend to understand the other and so naturally there is often a clash of these two perspectives.

Society no doubt does best with both, however the challenge is finding the compromise. How can we move forward yet maintain just enough caution? With patience, maturity and understanding, the people who tend to be more innovative can improve their communication skills and demonstrate that they are not putting the individual, group or organisation at risk. Trust must be gained through dialogue. On the other hand, those who tend to be risk averse, need to stretch their trust quotient, slowly stretching the parameters in which they can allow innovation to happen.

Personally, I have always jumped into opportunities and remember only a few occasions where a more conservative approach may have helped me avoid danger or loss. Fortunately, I have landed on my feet most of the time ... sometimes to my surprise!

Experiment: *Reflect on whether any fears are inhibiting me from achieving my dreams. In their final hour, most people regret what they didn't do rather than what they did!*

Actions *Krti*, Fruit

"All work is done through the three gunas, but in ignorance people think they are doing. ... You have ability, privilege and right over doing your duty but not over the result."

Bhagavad Gita

There are many influences that affect our actions including past actions or past karmas, our sub-conscious, omens, destiny, the atmosphere and the influence of others. *Guna* is the energy and power of our nature, qualities and state of being. The *guna* that a living being identifies most closely with will determine their experiences in life, both good and bad.

The first *guna* is *Sattvas* meaning truth. This energy informs our not wanting any return from charitable acts; we do things just because they are right. It can often take courage to do what is right; there can be a cost and we can foresee the backlash. However in these instances, short-term loss will be followed by long-term gain.

I have tested this theory and have been delighted by the results. When I first arrived to manage one of our Retreat Centres in Australia, I was given a small, old car. If I drove it over 90 kilometres per hour it would shake, but it worked. One day we were offered a better car, however I was aware that our other Retreat Centre desperately needed a truck and suggested the car be sold so a truck could be purchased for them. I trusted that when we really needed a car it would come to us. A year or so passed by and the little old car got to the stage where it would not have passed the required tests to be re-registered. Within days of having the thought "We need a new car", a truck was donated to us! One of our friends, a first class mechanic, accompanied us to the nearest car sales showroom. We tried just one car and it was perfect! We got a good trade and were back up the hill within an hour. It was that easy! This is what *sattvas* looks like.

The second guna is *Rajas*, meaning passion, active, and doing actions whilst being mindful of the returns that they will bring. It is clear that our world today operates in this mode, from relationships, to studies and basically anything where something is given to another. This mindset can only end in some type of suffering though and often this is due to unmet expectations. We judge that what we have received in return for what we have done has been too little, too much, or too different.

Tamas is the third guna; the lowest of the three. It is a state of ignorance, heaviness, caring only for survival - the more 'base' instincts. It includes the 'don't care' attitude paralysing our world at present. Actions in this element only create more and more delusion. Once in its cycle it's hard to get out; it is as if the Soul is dead and many in need of help find it so difficult because of the prevailing 'don't care' attitude. Over the last couple of years many of us have been horrified to learn of children, who separated from their parents, were imprisoned on the Mexican-US border. What concerned me more than the government policy was that staff were willing to comply with them. Similar scenarios were played out during the holocausts in Germany and Cambodia. Self-preservation makes people compliant; survival takes over the sense of one's humanity.

So, how does someone go beyond all the gunas and what does it look like? Perhaps the answer lies in the Bhagavad Gita ..."One who acts equally when suffering and joy are present, who is equally disposed to a lump of earth, a lump of stone, and a lump of gold. One who is equally disposed to the desirable and undesirable, and equally steady when one's soul is being praised or defamed by others. Equal in honour and dishonour, equal to groups of friends and enemies, renouncing all efforts, that one is said to be risen above the gunas."

We need action, and of actions, the Gita speaks of *Karma Yoga*, performing action whilst in remembrance of the Supreme. "Knowledge is better than ritual, meditation better than knowledge and being detached from action, a karma yogi, better than meditation. No one attains perfection by merely giving up work. In Karma-yoga no effort is ever lost, and there is no harm. Calmness of mind is the fruit of selfless action, karma yoga, free from vice and virtue. ... The wise see action in inaction, and inaction in action. Be content and dependent only on God - such a one does nothing at all and incurs no karma."

Experiment: *Reflect on an experience where you feel that you did what you considered to be the 'right' thing. What was the outcome in the long-term? Do you really believe that doing the right thing produces a better outcome.*

Material *Prakrti*, Expansion
"In your sadhana, spiritual pursuit,
do not become dependent on sadhan, things."

Bapdada

Prakrti means nature, primal matter, the potency that brings about evolution and change. As destiny would have it, through our collective consciousness and individual actions, we have destroyed natures balance. We see our natural world struggling to cope with population growth, unsustainable lifestyles and what we are literally throwing at her (think plastic!). Many are starting to feel it is too late to re-dress the balance. Sea mammals are being driven crazy and even out of the oceans because of noise levels, bees are being poisoned by pesticides, deforestation is destroying habitat at an alarming rate and pollution levels are literally killing people. It is inevitable that there will be even more tumultuous natural calamities; we are already witnessing these on an almost daily basis. Our cleverness in manipulating matter has resulted in extremely efficient weaponry!

There are very few people living in this world who are living in comfort and in a position to choose what they will do, eat, wear, think and say. If you are reading this book, you are probably within the small percentage who have choices in your life – you can read, have freedom of thought, you are not working 16 hours a day for very little, and you probably have electricity and a little extra cash to buy a book to read. In fact, if you think about it, you are probably one the most fortunate 5% in the world today.

I consider myself one of the few fortunate, and yet it is still a struggle to maintain happiness as I face daily challenges of personalities (including my own!), weather, travel, body pain, bureaucracy etc. Some of us 'haves' may not want to contemplate a massive transformation, happy in our air-conditioned homes and offices, driving in air-conditioned cars to go to the supermarket and fill our trolleys with all we need, and more. Yet according to the World Bank, 3.4 billion people struggle to meet the most basic needs. Most people in the world have to count their pennies for basic survival. Some do not even have pennies.

Our relationship with matter is as vital to understand as our relationship with our Self and others. With every interaction we are creating an account of karma and will experience the fruit of that. We are horrified by the devastation in the world, yet are we innocent in this play of events? Most of us must admit to being selfish when it comes to the resources we use, giving little or no consideration to the replenishment of them.

I accept that a cataclysmic change is inevitable, and necessary for renewal, even though I admit I am still not yet prepared to face what this actually means! Transformation of the World to such an extent will give back a fair playing field.

Experiment: *Reflect on my relationship with matter and the resources I could be sharing if I were more conscious. This would include water, material possessions, etc. Am I ready to simplify my life? Soon I may not have a choice.*

* * * * *

28

Where to From Here?

The Doomsday Clock
"Business has become, in this last half-century, the most powerful institution on the planet; it is critical that the dominant institution in any society take responsibility for the whole, as the Church did in the days of the Holy Roman Empire. But business has not had such a tradition."

Willis Harman

Cranes. They were everywhere as I was coming into my teenage years... and they gave me a sinking feeling. In 1950 the population of the world was only 2.5 billion. Just over half a century later we are nearing 8 billion. Something has to give; the planet and its resources are what they are. People are optimistic that we can still save the planet. However, for whom? I love the words of Warren Buffett, "If you're in the luckiest one per cent of humanity, you owe it to the rest of humanity to think about the other 99 per cent."

In India it is said that we are nearing the end of *Kaliyuga*, the Age of Death. This correlates with the time shown on the Doomsday Clock. I first heard of the Doomsday Clock from Willis Harman when he was visiting the Brahma Kumaris in Mount Abu. As President of the Institute of Noetic Sciences, he had his ear to the ground with regards to the state of the world. The initial setting of the clock, in 1947, was seven minutes to midnight. Since 2018 it has remained at two minutes to midnight due to the threats of both nuclear war and climate change. As we will soon witness, Mother Nature does not negotiate. Her task is to maintain balance and she is very stretched to achieve this. Something will give.

Many cultures talk about both the cyclic nature of events and an apocalypse in some way or another. In the Mahabharata, dated around 400 BCE, it is written "Gurkha, flying a swift and powerful vimana (aircraft) hurled a single projectile charged with the power of the Universe. An incandescent column of smoke and flame, as bright as ten thousand suns, rose with all its splendour. It was an unknown weapon, an iron thunderbolt, a gigantic messenger of death, which reduced to ashes the entire race of the Vrishnis and the Andhakas. The corpses were so burned as to be unrecognisable. Hair and nails fell out; pottery broke without apparent cause, and the birds turned white ... After a few hours all foodstuffs were infected ..."

In the Buddhist Pali Canon *Aṅguttara-Nikāya, VII, 6.2*, it is written in the *Sermon of the Seven Suns* "A third sun will dry the mighty Ganges and other great rivers. A fourth will cause the great lakes to evaporate, and a fifth will dry the oceans. Finally: again after a vast period of time a sixth sun will appear, and it will bake the Earth even as a pot is baked by a potter. All the mountains will reek and send up clouds of smoke. After another great interval a seventh sun will appear and the Earth will blaze with fire until it becomes one mass of flame. The mountains will be consumed; a spark will be carried on the wind and go to the worlds of God.... Thus, monks, all things will burn, perish and exist no more except those who have seen the path." This is said to precede the coming of *Maitreya* who will rule over an earthly paradise.

Norse mythology speaks of the end days, "People will flee their homes as the sun blackens and the earth sinks into the sea. The stars will vanish, steam will rise, and flames will touch the heavens. This conflict will result in the deaths of most of the major Gods and forces of

Chaos... After the cataclysm the world will resurface new and fertile, and the surviving Gods will meet. Baldr, also a son of Odin will be reborn in the new world, according to Voluspa. The two human survivors, Lif and Lifprasir, will then repopulate this new earth."

And the Gospel of Luke describes widespread calamity and war 'Nation will rise against nation, and kingdom against kingdom. There will be great earthquakes, and in various places famines and pestilences. And there will be terrors and great signs from heaven."

The threat of extinction in our generation is serious enough to have attracted top scientists, including the late Stephen Hawkings, to the Centre for the Study of Existential Risk at Cambridge University. The CSER was founded in 2012 by Professor Lord Martin Rees, the Astronomer Royal and one of Cambridge's most distinguished scientists, Jaan Tallinn, co-founder of Skype, and Huw Price, the Bertrand Russell Professor of Philosophy. Their aim - to ensure the human species has a long-term future. Professor Rees stated "Our century is special, because for the first time in 45 million centuries, one species holds the future of the planet in its hands – us."

Only 4% of all animals in the world are wild. With the devastating fires in Australia in 2019-2020, that has no doubt been reduced. Human beings have caused the annihilation of 83% of all wild animals and 50% of all plants. 70% of all birds in the world are chickens and other farmed birds. There is so little left already and we still are not taking things very seriously!

There are over 4 million preppers in the USA. A prepper is someone who takes steps to mitigate long lasting effects of a severe impact on their world. Perhaps the Brahma Kumaris are 'preppers' as we have been storing food and emergency equipment in readiness for crisis for many years. It is becoming more and more important to prepare for any unforeseen situation.

Seven key risks are outlined in the Honey Colony website:

1. Climate Change
2. Species extinction
3. Food crisis - purity, supply and allocation
4. Overpopulation where we are looking at increasing up to 9 billion by 2050.
5. Epidemics due to the overuse and inappropriate use of antibiotics.
6. Super intelligent Technology including artificial intelligence, biotechnology and nanotechnology. There is an increasing risk of technological terrorism.
7. Dwindling fresh water supply. WHO estimates 1.1 billion people globally have no access to clean drinking water and that 3.4 million people, mostly children, die of contaminated water annually. Fracking poison is also affecting developed countries at an alarming rate.

Political violence increased in 2018 by 11%, 124 million people face a food crisis, and 68 million are displaced every year with 85% hosted by developing countries. Some people still believe we are in heaven, but I would say "Look around!"

We need to prepare ourselves for what inevitably lies ahead of us, on many levels – physically, emotionally, and most importantly, spiritually. If there was ever a time that the Soul Beyond, was needed to intervene down here, it is now! The Supreme, a point of light, cannot 'do' much, nor does the Sun actually 'do' anything, and yet without the Sun there would be no life. The Sun simply exists and it is up to us to harness its extraordinary power. In the same way, the Supreme Soul just 'is', and we can get great works done through our connection with this extraordinary Power Source.

The Big Questions

"If you want the answer—ask the question."

Lori Myers

Why do we exist? Where did we come from? What are we doing here? Where are we going? Will we ever know these answers?

The actors on the stage have no idea who the director is, and do not know what they are meant to be doing. Talk about a leadership crisis! Many do not ask. Others do not want to know. Still others do not believe we are meant to know. I, on the other hand, am curious and actually enjoy being so. Curiosity engages me with life and I feel alive. Is it natural? Well children ask a million questions. There must be something to that. I hope that it makes me more intelligent.

If God were to appear, what would you be curious to ask? .... Or, would it be best to be completely still and let that energy, which many refer to as God, awaken the innate wisdom within the self? Allowing our selves to be in the 'presence' of the Supreme, connected, allowing inner knowing to emerge from within, with clarity, will certainly help guide us in these challenging times.

In the Brahma Kumaris, an older man who had the experience of life came to be known as Brahma, a channel of deep wisdom. He emptied himself of everything in his life, especially in his mind, attuned to the Divine, surrendered completely and became simple and light, a mystic. The mystics learnt how to be very close to the essence of God, communing and perceiving through God's mind. This is what is called *manmanabhav*, be Mine with your mind, surrender your mind to Me. Each of us can connect in this way and sit next to God's mind ... and know.

This ancient wisdom of Raja Yoga has resonated with me to the extent that I have dedicated my life its teachings and practice, and I continue to understand and delight in its subtlety more and more with each passing year. It changes slowly from faith to experience over time, and then to words to describe my understanding.

But wait, is it The End? Is there ever an end?

Linear or Cyclic Time?

"And everything worthwhile came to their hand, as the grain-growing earth bore fruit without tilling, plenty of good food crops unbegrudged; so they lived at their pleasure, peacefully minding their own business, amid numerous good things. Wealthy in flocks were they and beloved of the blessed immortals. After this whole first gold generation was finally buried, even today they are called pure spirits inhabiting earth and noble protectors of mankind, warding off evils from mortals, givers of wealth, which royal prerogative still is their business."

Hesiod

The sun rises and sets, the seasons rotate, everything is born and dies, is created and destroyed. Even fashions go around in cycles. All of our most common time measurement systems in daily life are cyclic. Even now, the lives of many people are governed by the endlessly repeating seasons. For at least 95% of humankind's existence, time has been cyclical and circadian. If time were linear, all the prophecies quoted above may be frightening, however each one speaks equally about renewal, a second coming of the Mesiah, and a time of peace on earth, another Buddha incarnation.

Cyclic time implies that God neither creates matter nor souls. He is the Creator in the sense that like a Master Sculptor, He holds a vision in front of us, his children. As students of the Master, by aligning with this vision, we then sculpt away what we learn is not us. This drama of life is an interplay between souls, matter and the Divine. In a cycle, it is a closed system, so the concept of eternal recurrence is logical.

Well aware of the dangers of going against mainstream scientific beliefs, Jules Boles took over forty years to thoroughly research his hypothesis on the cycle of time before publishing his book *Flashtime: The Discovery and Meaning of Cyclic Time*. History tells us of the reactions to Nicolaus Copernicus when he proposed the earth was round. Even Isaac Newton and Einstein were accused of being heretics, atheists or communists. A scientific mind is not as open as one would hope for.

The ancient wisdom of India, long before the term *Hindu* was coined, speaks of a cycle of time with four ages: *Satyug*, the Age of Truth; everything in the world was natural and there was nothing artificial, including human beings. The second age is referred to as *Tretayug*, literally Three Quarters Age, where there is just a slight degree of ordinariness creeping in. In these two ages the world was perfect. There were no concepts of duality like victory and defeat, heat and cold, love and hate. The third age is *Dwapuryug*, the Age of Duality; balance has gone and the extremes begin to appear. The fourth age is referred to as *Kaliyug*, the Age of Death, where everyone lives in fear of death and there is so much 'untimely' death.

The Brahma Kumaris speak of a fifth age *Sangamyug*, the confluence, the meeting point between the Age of Death and Age of Truth. The focus that the Brahma Kumaris have, is on this most critical time. Standing at the confluence we can observe the worst time in human history as well as a great movement back to nature, to truth. The mystic is poised here.

The Greek poet, Hesiod referred to the ages as Gold, Silver, Copper and Iron Ages. He too speaks of a fifth age, the Age of Heroes which describes our present time, where to stand for truth is a hero's journey and requires great courage. Yes, the mystic is poised ready!

Chuang Tzu refers to the people of that time, "They were honest and righteous without realising that they were doing their duty. They deceived no one, yet did not know that they were men to be trusted. They lived freely together, giving and taking and did not know that they were generous."

Many others, including the more recent Aztecs and Mayas also saw history as a cycle. In an introductory article written for Mexicolore in the UK, Dr. Jonathan Reyman, Curator of Anthropology at Illinois State Museum Research and Collections Centre, wrote about cyclical views of time among three native American cultures. Dr Reyman stated that like many cultures, the Hopi "have a cyclical view of time in which a defined period of time ends and a new one begins." He went on to say "The Maya did note the end of a time cycle (*pik* or *bak'tun*) on our calendar date of 21 December 2012, but it was to be followed by the start of another 5,000-year cycle, not the end of time itself and the world." …. "Aztec cosmology had a cyclical view of time that structured their daily lives over longer periods of time. Using the stone calendar wheel, probably the best-known Aztec artifact, contains a 52-year cycle called *Xiuhmolpilli*, The Binding of the Years. The end of this cycle was celebrated at the New Fire ceremony, a ritual held every 52 years to prevent the end of the world. It last occurred in 1507."

The Swastika was High Jacked!
"In its origin it is a Hindu symbol for light, and well worth rescuing."
Christopher Hitchens

The *swastika* is symbolic of the four ages. It is translated as 'well-being', however as with all ancient symbols, the meaning runs much deeper. The oldest images are found in a seal in Mohenjo-Daro and in the Ukraine. In Christian catacombs in Rome it is found with the words *zotiko zotiko*, meaning 'Life of Life'. It has been found in ancient emblems all over the world including in China, Greece, Iran, Germany and France.

In Buddhism the swastika is considered to symbolise the auspicious footprints of the Buddha and the *dharma* wheel. In Chinese, Japanese, and Korean it is also a homonym of the number 10,000 and is commonly used to represent the whole of creation, e.g. "the myriad things" in the Tao Te Ching. In Vietnamese it is written as *van*, meaning eternity.

The fascination of the German people with Aryanism arose when Heinrich Schliemann found artefacts with swastikas on them near the Trojan city of Troy. The Nazi party was looking for a symbol that would catch the attention of all of Germany and the *swastika* had that potential. It became a symbol to unify the German people, a conjecture about their ancestors, the Aryan identity, and nationalistic pride.

It is said that Vishnu spins the swastika cutting of the heads of the devils. He is referred to as *Swadarshanchakradari*, *swa*, self; *darshan*, to view; *chakra*, cycle; *dari*, hold. It is one of the longest words I know! The nonviolent explanation is, when we see the cycle of the Self (the soul) in relationship to time, we cut away illusion.

Festivals
"The darkest hour is just before the dawn."
Common idiom

I have started to avoid festivals. I really enjoy the dancing and coming together, however I cringe at all the waste, including Christmas wrapping and bonbons, the *Ganesh* festival in India where colourful idols are thrown into the rivers and *Shivratri* festivals where gallons of ghee and other foodstuffs are sacrificed into a fire.

Shivratri is one particular festival that has fascinated me as there are so many forms of Shiva ... Shankar the destroyer, Nataraj the dancer, the Jyoti Lingam and the Shivalingam, representing an incorporeal point of light. Shivratri is observed through chanting, prayer, fasting and staying awake throughout the moonless night; known as the 'night of Shiva' rather than the 'birthday of Shiva'. The Shivalingam is one of the most misunderstood images and yet the most ancient. It is especially worshipped during the last month of the Indian calendar, symbolising the end of a cycle. *Shiva*, the World Benefactor, the Seed, The Point; *lingum*, from *li* or *laya*, meaning destruction; and *gam* from *agaman*, recreation - the Entity that destroys and recreates. It is wrongly understand to be a phallic symbol. If it were so, it seems strange that parents would give their children names like *Mahalingum* and *Lingaraj*.

In Greece this image is also worshipped and has the name *Phallos*, a derivative of the Sanskrit word *Phalesh*, the 'Giver of Boons'. Perhaps it was from here that the misunderstanding occurred. I was fascinated to discover that the Shivalingam is a form that has been worshipped by people in the Sumerian Valley, Java, Sumatra, Rome, Germany, Egypt, France, Syria, America, Brazil, the Hawaii Islands and also the Australian Aborigines. In Kaba, Mecca, a black oval shaped stone is kept. The people wear white and circle the stone just as Hindus wear a white *dhoti* and circle the Shivalingam. God is represented in all religions either as a form of light, the sun or an oval shaped image, symbolic of the incorporeal form. Perhaps if we studied the undercurrents that unite us, we would see the intra-religious links.

Festivals remind us of significant times in history, of heroes and gods, spring and creation. Great leaders have worked hard to create a better world, and people reading this may also be included in them. However without the willingness to share resources with a vastly increasing population, we do not seem to be making much headway. Many experts are concluding that it may be too late. Is it possible that enough people will bring the changes required to make the monumental shift now needed to stop the decline?

If not, then ... ????

Who Were The gods?

"The immortals who dwell high up on the top of Olympus fashioned the firstborn race of articulate men, which was golden,
Godlike, they lived like gods, and their hearts were entirely carefree, distant strangers to labor and suffering; neither did wretched age overtake them; instead, their members intact and unchanged, they took much pleasure in banquets and parties, apart from all evils till they died as if sleep overcame them."

Hesiod

Deities are worshipped in Egypt, Sumeria, India, Greece, China and many other lands. Myths and legends, passed down, share many similarities. Not only is there a great deal of reference to a Golden Age from very diverse cultures, there is also reference to the gods and goddesses of that period. Many have now put those gods and goddesses in the sky, as they cannot conceive humans being so divine. The Cycle shares the human story of how we have fallen from our state of truth, purity and innocence to our present one. The Brahma Kumaris give just one reason for this – we forgot who we were. We *were* the gods and goddesses. We were them, you and I. We have forgotten ourselves and need to connect again to truth in order to return to our origin. The meaning of religion comes from the Latin *relegere*, meaning to re-examine carefully, gather, and connect.

There are many references to the Golden Age, beginning with the ancient Chinese who refer to *The Age of Perfect Virtue* where, in ancient philosopher Lao Tzu's words "The whole creation enjoyed a state of happiness ... all things grew without labour; and a universal fertility prevailed." Much later, philosopher Chuang Tzu wrote, "the men of old, while the chaotic condition was yet undeveloped, shared the placid tranquillity which belonged to the whole world. At that time the Yin and Yang were harmonious and still; their resting and movement proceeded without any disturbance; the four seasons had their definite times; not a single thing received any injury, and no living being came to a premature end. Men might be possessed of knowledge, but they had no occasion for its use. This was what is called the state of Perfect Unity."

From the Sumerian priests who referenced "The days of old when the gods gave man abundance, when vegetation flourished", to the Hopi Indians, "They knew nothing of sickness or conflict, and all things were provided by Mother Earth without any requirement of labour", all the way 'down under' to the Aborigines of Australia, people reflected on a time where they "... enjoyed a Golden Age, a Paradise of abundant game and without conflict of any kind." This also resonates with Herman Baumann stories from Africa where "Everything that happened in the primal age was different from today. People understood the language of animals and lived at peace with them; they knew no labour and had food in plenitude". Also, the Caribs of Surinam who speak of "A time long past, so long past that even the grandmothers of our grandmothers were not yet born, the world was quite other than what it is today: the trees were forever in fruit; the animals lived in perfect harmony, and the little agouti played fearlessly with the beard of the jaguar."

Conclusion

In the movie of 2006, *The Chronicles of Narnia: The Lion, The Witch and The Wardrobe*, when the children are told of the heroic parts destined for them, they are incredulous and try to convince the people of Narnia that they are just kids from up the road, not heroes and heroines. This, I fear is our greatest obstacle in being able to step-up, as we all need to do. There are many myths and tales about Heroes and Heroines, and just as there is a need for the presence of the Supreme at this time, there is a need for each one of us to step up and make a difference. We will soon find ourselves either on the side of desperation, or on the other side – the ones helping those in desperation. I have chosen the side I will be on. What about you?

Yes, we are in for a very rough ride as war, natural calamities, pandemics, civil unrest and the ever-increasing refugee crisis continue. We have no choice but to stretch our comfort zones as all comforts will turn out to be very temporary supports from now on. There is no turning the clocks back, but it is time to fasten our belts and move forward. For me, knowing that time and life is cyclic certainly helps. Otherwise, I would be rather distraught. Now, I am fixing my aim on getting through this transformation whilst preparing myself to spiritually uphold the coming world of truth.

END

Bibliography

Books

A Case for God: What Religion Really Means, Karen Armstrong (Vintage Publishing 2010)

A Different Drum, Community Making and Peace, M. Scott Peck (Touchstone 1998)

Across Asia on the Cheap, Terry and Maureen Wheeler, self-published 1973

BEING Your Self: Seeing and Knowing What's in the Way is the Way, Mike George (Gavisus Media 2014)

Boundaries: When to Say Yes, When to Say No – to Take Control of Your Life,

Henry Cloud and John Townsend (Perseus Books 2017)

Breaking the Habit of Being Yourself: How to Lose Your Mind and Create a New One, Joe Dispenza (Hay House Press 2012)

Calm: No Matter What (Pan Macmillan Australia, 2014)

Choosing Happiness, Stephanie Dowrick (Allen & Unwin, 2005)

Creating We: Change I-Thinking to We-Thinking and Build a Healthy, Thriving Organization,

Judith E Glaser (Adams Media Corp 2005)

Entering the Castle: An Inner Path to God and Your Soul, Caroline (Free Press 2007)

Falling Upwards: A Spirituality for the Two Halves of Life, Richard Rorh (John Wiley and Sons Ltd 2011)

Flashtime: The Discovery and Meaning of Cyclic Time, Jules Boles (Self Published 2018)

Flourishing Enterprises: The New Spirit of Business, Chris Laszlo and Judy Sorum Brown

(Stanford Business Books 2014)

Healing Words: The Power of Prayer and the Practice of Medicine, Larry Dossey (Harper Collins 1993)

How Big is Your God, The Freedom to Experience the Divine, Paul Coutinho, SJ (Loyola Press 1984)

In Love with the World: What a Buddhist Monk Can Teach You About Living and Nearly Dying,
Yongey Mingyur Rinpoche (Pan Macmillan UK 2019)

In Praise of Slowness: Challenging the Cult of Speed, Carl Honore (HarperOne 2005)

Inner Space, Anthea Church Brahma Kumaris Information Services Publications 1997)

The Prophet, Khalil Gibran (Alfred A Knopf 1923)

Life Before Life, Helen Wambach (Bantam Books 1979)

Living Values Activities for Children Ages 8-14, Diane Tillman (HCI 2001)

Mysteries of the Dream-time: The Spiritual Life of Australian Aborigines, James Cowan (Prism Press 1992)

Nonviolent Communication: A Language of Compassion, Marshall Rosenberg (Puddledancer 1999)

Power and Innocence, A Search for the Source of Violence, Rolland May (W.W. Norton & Company 1998)

Power and Love: A Theory and Practise of Social Change, Adam Kahane (Berrett-Koehler Publishers 2009)

Power vs. Force: The Hidden Determinants of Human Power, David Hawkins (Hay House Inc.)

The 7 Habits of Highly Effective People: Powerful Lessons in Personal Change, Stephen R. Covey (Free Press 2004)

The 7 Myths of Love ... Actually! The Journey from Your Head to the Heart of Your Soul, Mike George (O Books 2010)

The Carousel of Time: An Alternative Explanation of Our Existence, Ken O'Donnel (Release Your Wings 2016)

The Celestine Prophecy: An Adventure, James Redfield (Second Edition Warner Books 1997)

The Conscious Activist: Where Activism Meets Mysticism, James O'Dea (Watkins Publishing 2014)

The Little Princess, Frances Hodgson-Burnett, (Published 2002 by Penguin Books, first published 1890)

The Message from Water Children's Version, Masaru Emoto (www.WaterPeaceProject.org)

The Power of the Other: The startling effect other people have on you, from the boardroom to the bedroom and beyond – and what to do about it, Henry Cloud, (Harper Business 2016)

The Road Less Travelled: A New Psychology of Love, Traditional Values and Spiritual Growth, M. Scott Peck (Touchstone 1998)

The Tao of Leadership: Lao Tzu's Tao Te Ching Adapted for a New Age, John Heder (Green Dragon Books 2005)

The Way of the Wizard: 20 Lessons for Living a Magical Life, Deepak Chopra (Ebury Publishing 2000)

Three Cups of Tea: One Man's Mission to Promote Peace ... One School at a Time,
Greg Mortenson and David Oliver Relin, (Penguin in 2007)

Today I Will: 100 ways to make your life calm and creative by Carmen Warrington (Hatchette Australia 2001)

Why Women Believe in God, Liz Hodgkinson in conversation with BK Jayanti (John Hunt Publishing 2012)

Women Who Love too Much, Robin Norwood (First Edition 1985, Pocket Books)

Films
The NeverEnding Story, Michael Ende (Directed by Wolfgang Peterson 1984)
Kanyini, Bob Randall (Directed by Michelle Hogan)

Poems
You Call me God..., Barbara Bossert-Ramsay
Our Deepest Fear, Marianne Williamson (From her book, A Return to Love, HarperOne 1996)

Other

Mexicolore (https://www.mexicolore.co.uk/aztecs/calendar/cyclical-views-of-time)

Omnipresence (http://domenicmarb.blogspot.com/2016/03/omnipresence.html)

About The Brahma Kumaris

The Brahma Kumaris is a network of organisations in over 100 countries with its spiritual headquarters in Mt Abu, India. The University works at all levels of society for positive change. Acknowledging the intrinsic worth and goodness of the inner Self, the University teaches a practical method of meditation that helps people to cultivate their inner strengths and values.

The University also offers courses and seminars in such topics as positive thinking, overcoming anger, stress relief and self-esteem, encouraging spirituality in daily life. This spiritual approach is also brought into healthcare, social work, education, prisons and other community settings.

All courses and activities are offered free of charge. For more information visit www.brahmakumaris.org.

SPIRITUAL HEADQUARTERS
 PO BOX No 2, Mount Abu 307501, Rajasthan, India
 Tel: (+91) 2974-238261 to 68
 Fax: (+91) 2974-238883
 E-mail: abu@bkivv.org

INTERNATIONAL COORDINATING & REGIONAL OFFICE
FOR EUROPE AND THE MIDDLE EAST
 Global Cooperation House, 65-69 Pound Lane,
 London, NW10 2HH, UK
 Tel: (+44) 20-8727-3350
 Fax: (+44) 20-8727-3351
 E-mail: london@brahmakumaris.org

AFRICA REGIONAL OFFICE
  Global Museum for a Better World,
  Maua Close, off Parklands Road, Westland,
  PO Box 123, Sarit Centre, Nairobi, Kenya
  Tel: (254) 20-374-3572
  Fax: (+254) 20-374-3885
  E-mail: nairobi@brahmakumaris.org

THE AMERICAS AND THE CARIBBEAN REGIONAL OFFICE
  Global Harmony House, 46 S. Middle Neck Road,
  Great Neck, NY 11021, USA
  Tel: (+1) 516-773-0971
  Fax: (+1) 516-773-0976
  E-mail: newyork@brahmakumaris.org

AUSTRALIA AND SOUTH EAST ASIA REGIONAL OFFICE
  181 First Ave, Five Dock, Sydney, NSW 2046, Australia
  Tel: (+61) 29716-7006
  E-mail: fivedock@au.brahmakumaris.org

RUSSIA, CIS AND THE BALTIC COUNTRIES REGIONAL OFFICE
  2, Lobachika, Bldg. No. 2, Moscow – 107140, Russia
  Tel: (+7) 499 2646276
  Fax: (+7) 495-261-3224
  E-mail: moscow@brahmakumaris.org

Other Resources

Websites
www.brahmakumaris.org
www.learnmeditationonline.org
www.centreforoptimism.com
www.livingvalues.net
www.ivoh.org
www.nonviolentcommunication.org

Apps
Happidote
Bee.Zone

www.ingramcontent.com/pod-product-compliance
Lightning Source LLC
Chambersburg PA
CBHW020315010526
44107CB00054B/1855